Cuba's Foreign Relations in a Post-Soviet World

CONTEMPORARY
CUBA

Florida A&M University, Tallahassee
Florida Atlantic University, Boca Raton
Florida Gulf Coast University, Ft. Myers
Florida International University, Miami
Florida State University, Tallahassee
University of Central Florida, Orlando
University of Florida, Gainesville
University of North Florida, Jacksonville
University of South Florida, Tampa
University of West Florida, Pensacola

CONTEMPORARY CUBA
Edited by John M. Kirk

A multidisciplinary series focusing on balanced, current, and provocative aspects of Cuban history, culture, society, and politics. Of special interest are works that examine the dramatic changes in Cuba since 1959, such as the role of the military, the nature of economic reforms, and the impact of foreign investments, human rights treaties, and tourism on the island.

Afro-Cuban Voices: On Race and Identity in Contemporary Cuba, by Pedro Pérez-Sarduy and Jean Stubbs (2000)

Cuba, the United States, and the Helms-Burton Doctrine: International Reactions, by Joaquín Roy (2000)

Cuba Today and Tomorrow: Reinventing Socialism, by Max Azicri (2000)

Cuba's Foreign Relations in a Post-Soviet World, by H. Michael Erisman (2000)

Cuba's Foreign Relations in a Post-Soviet World

H. Michael Erisman

University Press of Florida

GAINESVILLE · TALLAHASSEE · TAMPA · BOCA RATON
PENSACOLA · ORLANDO · MIAMI · JACKSONVILLE · FT. MYERS

Copyright 2000 by the Board of Regents of the State of Florida
Printed in the United States of America on acid-free paper
All rights reserved

First cloth printing, 2000
First paperback printing, 2002

07 06 05 04 03 02 6 5 4 3 2 1

Library of Congress Cataloging-in-Publication Data
Erisman, H. Michael
Cuba's foreign relations in a post-Soviet world / H. Michael Erisman.
p. cm. — (Contemporary Cuba)
Includes bibliographical references and index.
ISBN 0-8130-2587-7 (alk. paper)
1. Cuba—Foreign relations—1959–. I. Title. II. Series.
F1787.5.E75 2000 00-027176
327.7291—dc21

The University Press of Florida is the scholarly publishing agency for the
State University System of Florida, comprising Florida A&M University,
Florida Atlantic University, Florida Gulf Coast University, Florida
International University, Florida State University, University of
Central Florida, University of Florida, University of North Florida,
University of South Florida, and University of West Florida.

University Press of Florida
15 Northwest 15th Street
Gainesville, FL 32611–2079
http://www.upf.com

Contents

List of Tables   vi

Foreword by John M. Kirk, series editor   vii

Preface   xi

Map   xiv

1. Prelude: Setting the Cuban Stage   1

2. Cuban Foreign Policy and Counterdependency Politics   22

3. In the Shadows of the Superpowers, 1959–1972   49

4. Beyond the Superpowers: The Halcyon Days of Cuban Globalism, 1972–1985   79

5. Engulfed by the Maelstrom: Cuba and the Passing of the Cold War, 1985–1992   105

6. Cuba Confronts the Post–Cold War Order, 1992 Onward   142

7. Conclusion: The End of a Road Less Traveled?   206

Notes   227

Index   261

Tables

1.1 Estimated income distribution, Cuba, 1953 and 1978 7

1.2 Cuban basic needs performance data 8

3.1 Cuban trade with the USSR, 1959–68 69

3.2 Cuban trade with the USSR, 1969–78 77

4.1 Estimated numbers of Cuban troops in Ethiopia 97

4.2 Cuban developmental aid personnel in sub-Saharan Africa 101

5.1 Cuban trade with the USSR/CMEA 108

5.2 Cuban trade with the USSR/Eastern Europe, 1980–85 109

5.3 Cuban exports and their destinations and imports and their sources 112

5.4 Basic Cuban economic indicators, 1989 and 1993 113

5.5 Composition of Cuban trade 117

5.6 Cuban export profile, 1985–92 118

5.7 Cuban exports and their destinations, 1985–92 119

5.8 Cuban import profile, 1985–92 121

5.9 Cuban imports and their sources, 1985–92 121

5.10 Cuban–Central American trade profiles 126

5.11 Canada-Cuba trade 135

5.12 Cuban trade with Japan and China 140

6.1 Cuban export-import performance 149

6.2 Cuban export profile, 1992–97 150

6.3 Cuban exports and their destinations, 1992–97 151

6.4 Cuban import profile, 1992–97 153

6.5 Cuban imports and their sources, 1992–97 154

6.6 Cuban exports and their destinations and imports and their sources 156

6.7 Total Cuban trade with CARICOM, selected years 161

6.8 Cuba and Cuban policies: U.S. public opinion polls 189

Foreword

The changes that have taken place in Cuba since the demise of the Soviet Union are extraordinary. The ensuing "special period" has led to the Cuban government introducing major innovations in economic matters. As a result, the Cuba of today is vastly different from what it was just six or seven years ago.

While these changes have been commented upon (and are the focus of Max Azicri's book in this Contemporary Cuba series), little has been said about the significant changes in Cuba's foreign policy during the same time. Many people still have not come to appreciate how radical these developments have been since the days when Washington considered Cuba a mere "Soviet satellite." This work by H. Michael Erisman seeks to fill the gap and does so admirably.

The visit of Pope John Paul II in January 1998 captured international media attention, of course, but few would have imagined that in the same year a dozen heads of state would also visit Havana, together with the foreign ministers of twenty-five countries. While the United States may still perceive Cuba as an international pariah, this is not the case for anyone else. Put simply, Cuba has changed—and so has the perception of it held by the rest of the world, notwithstanding Washington's views.

Michael Erisman's essential goal is to chronicle how this change has come about and why. He shows clearly that Washington's policy of isolating Cuba, begun some four decades ago, has failed—as can be seen from the annual vote at the UN General Assembly condemning the U.S. embargo against Cuba. In the seven years since this motion was first debated, the number of countries supporting Cuba has gone from 52 (in 1992) to 157 (1998). On the most recent occasion, of all UN members, only Israel supported Washington's position.

In short, Cuba's foreign policy has undergone a radical overhaul in the past seven years. This change can be seen also in the changing commercial relations developed by Havana. Whereas a decade ago tourism was insignificant, it now drives the economy, with some 1.7 million tourists in 1999 alone (mainly from Canada and Europe). Similarly important are the 365 joint ventures with foreign companies and the 600 foreign firms that have offices in Havana. Finally, trade patterns, which used to depend upon commerce with the Soviet bloc, have now been significantly changed too: almost half of Cuban trade—47 percent—is now with European countries (EEC members have seen their share increase from 7 percent in 1990 to 30 percent in 1998), and 37 percent is with the Americas. None of this would have been conceivable before the special period.

Cuba—which was rudely turfed out of the Organization of American States in 1962—now has diplomatic relations with virtually all countries of the hemisphere. At international summits Cuba's president, Fidel Castro, remains one of the most popular political figures. And Cuba is widely respected in international fora, so much so that it has been asked to intervene in political disputes in Latin America and Africa, signaling the shift from international outcast to honest broker.

Cuba's support for revolutionary groups in the early 1980s has now been overtaken by international development assistance missions around the globe, putting to shame the efforts of developed nations. Following the devastation caused by Hurricane Mitch in Central America in 1998, Cuba responded by sending 1,200 health care professionals (including 900 doctors) to the region, where they provided free health care. To alleviate a shortage of doctors in Latin America, the Cuban government has also provided scholarships to nearly 1,000 students from Latin America and expects to train (for free) some 6,000 medical students at Havana's Latin American School of Medical Sciences. Cuba has also offered to send up to 1,000 doctors to help refugees in Kosovo and at present has 1,500 doctors providing humanitarian assistance to thirty-six countries—an astounding record. Finally, Cuba has treated (again for free) some 15,000 children from Russia and the Ukraine who have been affected by the nuclear reactor accident at Chernobyl.

Cuba's humanitarian assistance (which understandably has won Cubans many friends abroad), the changing patterns of international relations developed by Havana in the past decade, and the shift in commercial ties are all significant developments. Erisman provides the basic elements required to analyze the shifting paradigm of Cuba's foreign policy and the reasons behind its evolution. He begins by examining the various perspectives on Havana's approach to international relations. Then he traces the evolution of this policy, focusing on key periods (1959–72, 1972–85, 1985–92, and 1992 to the present).

For the past four decades this small nation (population 11 million) has been striding the international stage with a confidence befitting a superpower. At one time it was shunned by many nations, chief among them the United States. Now there has been a significant reversal in its international fortunes. Erisman's overview is well argued and clearly focused—and it is also timely. Despite continuing concerns held by many countries about the human rights record in Cuba, all nations apart from the United States have realized that a policy of isolation has simply not worked. This study in engagement over those four decades—both by Havana and by the international community—reveals the need for pragmatism over ideology in foreign policy. It is a lesson from which we could all learn.

John M. Kirk, series editor

Preface

Probably quite a few people would have been willing in the early 1990s to make a substantial bet that a book such as this would never be written, for the conventional wisdom at the time held that the days of the Cuban Revolution were numbered and that its run as an actor on the global stage was quickly coming to an end. Such sentiments were based on the assumption that Fidelista Havana, much like the socialist regimes of Eastern Europe, would not be able to survive the political and economic challenges confronting it as the Soviet bloc disintegrated and what has become popularly known as the post–Cold War world emerged. According to this logic, future studies of revolutionary Cuba would become the bailiwick of historians rather than specialists in the dynamics of contemporary international relations.

Certainly it is not unfair to say that such obituaries were in many instances just one more example of a phenomenon common to Cuban affairs, in which wishful ideological thinking has often overshadowed serious objective analysis. On the other hand, it must likewise be recognized that the Revolution was confronting a situation that even its most ardent supporters often characterized as perhaps the most serious threat to its survival since such counterparts of the early 1960s as the Bay of Pigs invasion, the assassination plots, and the nuclear missile crisis. Ultimately Cuba's success in meeting this challenge may come to be seen as one of the Western Hemisphere's most extraordinary twentieth-century epics.

The primary thrust of this volume is to explore the international dimension of Cuba's response to the cataclysmic developments of the early 1990s as well as the dynamics of its foreign relations in the ensuing years, as both the Revolution and the global community approached the dawning of a new millennium. In so doing, however, a serious effort has been made to place Cuba's evolving foreign relations in a larger, longer-term context in order to assure that the continuities involved are not totally eclipsed by the more dramatic recent changes to Havana's status in world affairs.

Obviously, as indicated, the unique role that Havana had played abroad did not escape the transformation affecting the global landscape in the early 1990s. No longer could Havana pursue its ambitious agenda of the 1970s and early 1980s, which led Jorge Domínguez to characterize Cuba as one of the few cases in which a small country was indeed operating like a great power in world affairs. But Havana's contemporary international personality also includes some important continuities that should not be ignored, counterdependency concerns being pinpointed here as a foreign policy constant that merits special attention.

Like that of other countries, then, revolutionary Cuba's foreign policy can be seen as involving both certain strategic ends, which tend to persist over time, and various tactical means to achieve them, which may at some points have to be modified to accommodate changes in the larger international environment. This dualist scenario has been incorporated into the analysis in this volume via emphasis on weaving together two threads:

- Counterdependency politics, which are presented as a central theme that has run through and heavily influenced the Revolution's foreign policies throughout its history.

The key proposition here is that Cuba, given its historical experiences going back to the era of Spanish colonialism and the Platt Amendment, has always been highly sensitive to the danger of being absorbed into some external power's sphere of influence, and hence the Fidelistas' foreign policies have always entailed a strong counterdependency dimension. I examine Havana's implementation of such strategies in both the Cold War period and its aftermath.

- The process of restructuring Havana's political and especially its economic relations, an endeavor that in some respects had been going on for some time and that assumed special urgency in the 1990s.

The end of the Cold War meant that Cuba, along with other developing nations, could no longer rely on superpower assistance to help it solve its problems. Revolutionary Havana, however, represents a special case because it has steadfastly resisted Washington's demands that it abandon its commitment to radical, Cuban-style socialism. Consequently the island has continued to be the target of a concerted U.S. effort to destabilize its economy and destroy its government.

Under such conditions, restructuring its international relations has become imperative for the Revolution to survive and to begin to regain some of the prosperity that it once enjoyed. This work is heavily focused on that effort, with special attention being devoted to the dynamics of contemporary U.S.-Cuban affairs and the prospects for some normalization of what has long been a tempestuous relationship.

Whether one admires or despises Castro's Cuba, it is difficult to avoid the conclusion that the profile emerging from such an exercise represents one of the most remarkable political sagas to be found in the modern Latin American experience.

Few authors can claim sole credit for their work, and this book is no exception. Thus my heartfelt thanks for their invaluable contributions to this endeavor go to the following groups and individuals.

To my Cuban colleagues in Havana at the Centro de Estudios Sobre Estados Unidos (CESEU—the Center for U.S. Studies) and at the Instituto Superior de Relaciones Internacionales (ISRI—the Primary Institute of International Relations), who graciously handled the local logistics for my various research visits as well as sharing their expertise and data with me.

To the University Research Committee of Indiana State University, which awarded a grant that helped to defray the expenses incurred in connection with the field research (in both Cuba and the United States) that was absolutely crucial to this book.

To the American Council of Learned Societies (ACLS) and the Social Sciences Research Council (SSRC), which also provided a grant under their Faculty Exchange Program. This facilitated collaboration with Cuban academics (involving, among other things, reciprocal research visits) that helped significantly in accumulating information and ideas subsequently incorporated into the manuscript.

To the editors and reviewers of the University Press of Florida whose excellent guidance helped to transform the project from a concept to a reality. The UPF staff in Gainesville was especially supportive, graciously extending their submission deadline several times in order to allow the material to be fine-tuned and repeatedly updated.

Ultimately, my daughter, Tamara, and my wife, Marge, deserve the greatest accolades, for they had to deal almost daily with the disruptions and inconveniences that such a project brings to family life. Indeed, vacations and birthday and anniversary celebrations sometimes had to be rescheduled because they conflicted with research trips. Probably most disconcerting was living with someone whose attention was often far from the major concerns of the home. They handled these burdens with grace and dignity; they are truly coproducers of this book.

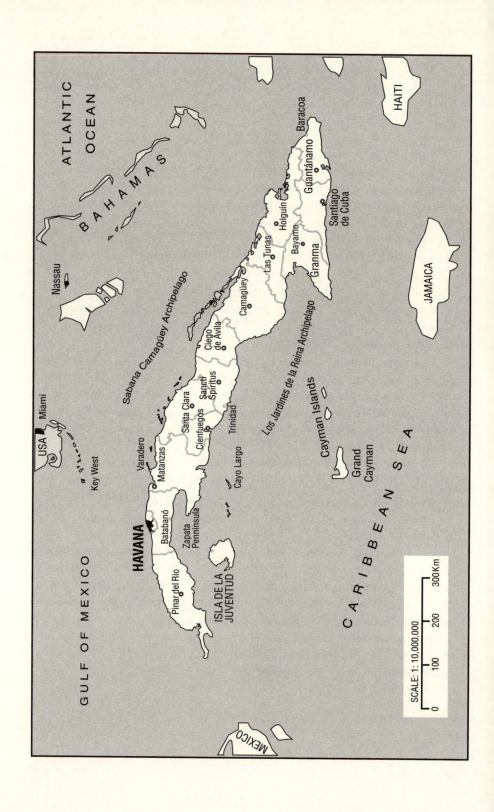

Prelude: Setting the Cuban Stage

Two roads diverged in a wood and I—
I took the one less traveled by,
And that has made all the difference.

Robert Frost, "The Road Not Taken"

The words of the North American poet Robert Frost seem to convey a dual message: a feeling of exhilaration associated with the pursuit of a unique identity and a sense of the trepidation that comes with excursions into the unknown. Although Frost was speaking in terms of a personal quest, his observations can be applied to countries and governments that choose to be trailblazers rather than followers. Certainly revolutionary Cuba would seem to fit Frost's vanguard profile, for it has been engaged from its inception in an odyssey that has taken it down paths unexplored by any other modern Latin American nation.

A special aura has always seemed to surround Cuba. The Spanish, for instance, called the island the Pearl of the Antilles in recognition of its status as the crown jewel of their Caribbean empire. Later, writers such as Graham Greene and Ernest Hemingway would add to its exotic luster by using it as the locale for some of their most famous works. Most recently, of course, it has been Fidel Castro and the Revolution he unleashed that have thrust the country into the international limelight.

Practically any social upheaval, whether in Cuba or elsewhere, unfolds within a vortex of decidedly mixed feelings, with passions often running high as supporters/admirers and opponents/critics line up to confront one another. Yet the Cuban Revolution emerges as unusual even by these standards. Almost, it seems, from the moment that the Fidelistas marched triumphantly into Havana, they unleashed a firestorm of emotions and controversy that has displayed exceptional staying power. Such turmoil has been especially intense in the realm of relations with Washington. Indeed the dawning of a new millennium reveals that *nine* U.S. administrations have been frustrated in their attempts to tame the Fidelistas.

A major factor contributing to the mystique that has grown up around the Cuban Revolution has been the country's ability to exert an impact within the global arena far out of proportion to its modest size and rather meager natural resources. The normal assumption is, of course, that small states such as Cuba simply do not have the capacity or, in most cases, the inclination to play a significant role in world affairs over an extended period. Rather, they tend to be seen as bit players, who at most might experience a fleeting moment of international notoriety. Revolutionary Cuba, however, has refused to fade meekly into the background. Instead it has emerged as one of the few developing countries that has routinely pursued a high-visibility agenda on a truly global scale: participating in the Cold War's only venture to the brink of the nuclear abyss (the Cuban Missile Crisis); playing a major role in winning two wars in Africa (in Angola and Ethiopia); providing inspiration to revolutionary movements in various parts of the world and leadership to the larger nonaligned community; and doggedly defending its sovereignty and its ideological principles in the face of unrelenting hostility from the Colossus of the North. Revolutionary Cuba has, in short, traveled its own road into history, carving out in the process a niche for itself in the pantheon of modern nations.

In this book I seek to explore and explain that drama, devoting special attention to the foreign policy survival strategies that the Revolution has employed in the attempt to make a successful transition to the new international order of the post–Cold War world and, within that context, to its continuing tumultuous relationship with the United States.

Cuban Geography

Situated at the entrance to the Gulf of Mexico, Cuba is the largest island in the Caribbean.[1] It is 780 miles (1,250 km) long, 44,218 sq. miles (114,524 sq. km) in area, and only 90 miles (145 km) south of Florida. The island commands the two entrances to the Gulf of Mexico—the Straits of Florida and the Yucatan Channel. To the east, it is separated from the island of Hispaniola by the Windward Passage, a shipping route between the North Atlantic Ocean and the Caribbean Sea. The United States maintains a naval base at Guantanamo Bay in southeastern Cuba.

As of 1999, the population of Cuba was slightly more than 11 million. About 70 percent live in urban areas, including the capital, Havana (2 million), Camaguey, Santiago de Cuba, Holguin, and Guantanamo. Cuban people are of Caribbean, African, and Spanish descent. Estimates of racial distribution vary. About half of Cuba's population is reportedly black or of interracial descent.

About one-fourth of the country's surface is mountainous or hilly, the remainder consisting of flat or rolling terrain. The mountainous areas are scattered throughout the island and do not stem from a central mass. The principal ranges are the Sierra de los Organos in the west, the Sierra de Trinidad in the central part of the island, and the Sierra Maestra in the southeast. The first two ranges are under 914 m (3,000 ft) in height; the Sierra Maestra, which includes the Sierra del Cobre and Macaca ranges, is the greatest in mass, extent, and altitude, its Pico Turquino being the highest point in Cuba at 2,000 m (6,561 ft). Most of the soil is relatively fertile.

The climate is semitropical, the mean annual temperature being 25°C (77°F). Extremes of heat and relative humidity, which average 27.2°C (81°F) and 80 percent, respectively, during the summer season, are tempered by the prevailing northeast trade winds. Annual rainfall averages about 1,320 mm (about 52 inches). More than 60 percent of the rain falls during the wet season, which extends from May to October. The island lies in a region occasionally traversed by violent tropical hurricanes during August, September, and October.

The land and climate favor agriculture, and the country also has significant mineral reserves. Nickel, chrome, copper, iron, and manganese deposits are the most important. Sulfur, cobalt, pyrites, gypsum, asbestos, petroleum, salt, sand, clay, and limestone reserves are also exploited. All subsurface deposits are the property of the government.

Economy and Social Development

For many years Cuba enjoyed special and highly beneficial economic arrangements with the USSR and the socialist countries of Eastern Europe.[2] These ties, combined with the determined efforts of the Revolution's leadership to transform the island into a showcase of radical Third World socialism characterized by prosperity, egalitarianism, and social justice, created a standard of living among the highest in the developing countries of the world. Indeed the Revolution's efforts in some high-priority areas such as health care and education produced dramatic results comparable to those of the most highly modernized nations, leading some observers to conclude that Cuba represented the best possible blueprint for Third World development.

What must be kept constantly in mind, however, is the fact that the Revolution constitutes an *ongoing process* rather than a finished product. As such, except for some general long-term goals that are common to many contemporary Third World nations and some basic strategic principles entailing certain socialist mechanisms of development, there is not in the final sense of the term any "Cuban model" for other countries to emulate. Instead, what exists is a Cuban "experience" or "experiment" that can be seen as a dialectic, the dynamics of which have yet to be fully or even mostly played out.

Within this somewhat crude Hegelian framework, one must be careful not to focus too heavily upon the extremes involved (that is, what are perceived to be the thesis and antithesis occupying opposite ends of the spectrum). Otherwise there is a tendency to see the Cuban Revolution in highly polarized terms—for example, as a paradigm to be either totally embraced or totally repudiated; as an exercise in either the highest social principles or the lowest human degradation; as either a complete success or an abject failure. Rather, primary concern should be directed at the syntheses the process has produced at any particular point in time, examining their adequacy both as responses to the current environment and as vehicles for making progress toward the Revolution's long-term goals.

The basic developmental challenge confronting Cuba or any other society is essentially binary, demanding increases in both productivity and the establishment of structural safeguards to assure a roughly equitable distribution of the material benefits created. Any serious modernization program must, therefore, concern itself not only with mastering the highly technical complexities of generating new wealth but must also come to grips with the often explosive political issue of distributive justice.

During the 1970s the Cuban economy, despite a shaky start attributable in part to the disruption caused by an unsuccessful campaign to bring in an unprecedented 10 million-ton sugar harvest in 1970, functioned quite well from a macroperspective. Although the specific figures for overall growth rates vary somewhat from one source to another, there is nevertheless general agreement that the trends were solidly upward throughout the decade. The most vigorous expansion, which was driven primarily by the high sugar prices being paid at the time on international markets, occurred during the 1970–75 period. The productivity rates contracted a bit in subsequent years but still remained healthy for the rest of the seventies.[3]

In the 1980s, however, the situation for most developing countries became much more difficult. In the Western Hemisphere, chaos reigned from the Rio Grande to Patagonia as the Latin economies reeled under a series of blows. These included dramatically reduced prices for many of their commodity exports, escalating costs for their petroleum and other imports, reduced markets for their goods due to recession in many developed Western countries, high levels of inflation, and increasing unemployment. According to figures released by the Economic Commission for Latin America (ECLA), such factors combined to produce an overall GNP growth rate of *minus* 2.8 percent for the period 1981–83.[4]

Initially it appeared that Havana, given its privileged relationship with the Soviet bloc, would be able to weather the storm. A striking example of the peculiar advantages the island acquired from its Moscow connection can be found in the dynamics of the sugar/oil trade. The USSR had for years been purchasing Cuban sugar at prices often markedly above the prevailing international rate. The rubles that the Fidelistas earned could then be used to finance imports from the Soviet Union and Eastern Europe. Among their purchases was Russian petroleum. A new wrinkle added to these transactions in the early 1980s involved an agreement on Moscow's part that Havana could reexport whatever Soviet oil it did not use. Thus, with no reserves of any significance, Cuba nevertheless became an exporter, earning $1.9 billion in precious hard currency from 1981 to 1985.[5] Such bonanzas along with a solid performance by many other sectors of the Cuban economy produced a respectable average growth rate of approximately 8 percent a year from 1980 to 1984.[6] But by the mid-1980s it was becoming apparent that not only was it unreasonable to expect such a pace to be sustained, but the specter of an economic tailspin was also increasingly looming over the island. This possibility became reality as the rest of the decade unfolded, with foreign trade, debt, and unemployment emerging as three special areas exemplifying the Revolution's productivity problems.

International trade has always been a key element affecting Cuba's economic health. During the 1980s, however, its contribution was by and large not very positive. For example, between 1980 and 1985, Havana ran up a negative trade balance of almost $16 billion with the Soviet bloc and a little over $2 billion with Western countries.[7] Conditions improved somewhat in the late eighties, with Cuba demonstrating the capability to transform a 1986 deficit of $199 million in convertible currency to a 1987 surplus of $22.5 million. But as often happens, there was a price to be paid—in this case, the reversal was accomplished by drastically limiting imports rather than by significantly expanding exports, which meant greater austerity for both the domestic economy and the general populace.[8]

Such negative trade balances were an important (although certainly not the only) component of the difficulties Cuba confronted in trying to satisfy its Western creditors. Havana had, of course, also run up large debts with the Soviet Union and various Eastern European countries, but it did not in practice have to worry about these obligations since it was standard practice to reschedule the payments whenever necessary. Similar accommodations were not forthcoming from Western banks and governments, where the total amount owed by the Cubans increased from $2.853 billion in 1981 to approximately $6.77 billion in 1989. As the island's deteriorating economic situation made it more difficult to service these debts, Havana made repeated efforts to renegotiate the terms of repayment. A series of such agreements were concluded during the 1982–86 period that did relieve some of the immediate pressure. The debts were not forgiven, however, and it was therefore necessary to take some steps in preparation for their eventual repayment. Consequently various measures were instituted, involving among other things increased austerity for the Cuban public, some diversion of resources that could otherwise have been applied to broadening and strengthening the economy's productive capabilities, and reduced employment opportunities.

Communist Cuba, like other socialist states, has always prided itself on its commitment to assuring everyone a full-time job, and the data indicate that it has indeed gone far toward achieving this target. Its unemployment rates have consistently been far below those of the prerevolutionary period in particular and of the Latin American/Third World experience in general (a few illustrative percentages: 13.6 in 1953, 11.8 in 1960, 1.3 in 1970, and 4.1 in 1980).[9] The ranks of the island's unemployed did expand in the late 1980s, the official statistics indicating a rather high rate (for revolutionary Cuba) of 5–6 percent. Estimates for the 1990s were even higher, standing at 8 percent in 1996 and then dropping slightly to 6.9 percent in 1997. Moreover, there were increasing complaints, often voiced most vehemently by Castro himself, that too many Cubans who had jobs were not working hard at them. Such criticisms suggested that the Revolution's traditionally low unemployment could not necessarily be seen as a factor conducive to higher economic growth rates (i.e., more people at

Table 1.1. Estimated income distribution, Cuba, 1953 and 1978 (in percentages)

Population deciles	1953	1978
Lowest, 0–20	2.1	7.8
Lower middle, 21–40	4.4	12.4
Middle, 41–60	11.1	19.7
Upper middle, 61–80	24.5	26.7
Highest, 81–100	57.9	33.4
Gini coefficient[a]	0.55	0.27

Source: Claes Brundenius, *Revolutionary Cuba: The Challenge of Economic Growth with Equity* (Boulder, Colo.: Westview Press, 1984), 113, 116.
a. The Gini coefficient is a measure of the degree of inequality. In the case of perfect equality, the coefficient is zero, and in the opposite case, that of perfect inequality, the coefficient is 1.0.

work translating into greater output of goods and services). Instead, these analyses implied that upgrading worker efficiency was the key to greater productivity.

Productivity obviously provides a means to measure a society's economic muscle. But to fathom its *heart* one must focus on its commitment to distributive justice. Ideally, maximum productivity will be combined with perfect distributive equity. Yet too often concern with the latter is sacrificed to pursuit of the former, one popular rationale being that to do otherwise would simply mean equal poverty for all. The Fidelistas, while perhaps recognizing that there is some truth to this proposition, have long insisted that they have achieved an acceptable balance, pointing with particular pride to the advances they have made in promoting greater socioeconomic justice on the island.

Redistributing wealth has always been a major theme of the Cuban Revolution; Fidel embraced it early in his guerrilla career, and for many it has represented a key litmus test of the Revolution's success. As table 1.1 indicates, Castro's government made remarkable progress during its first two decades in establishing more equitable income patterns. There could of course be those who would contend that the changes indicated in the table are not particularly dramatic, especially when one considers how far the lowest-paid decile still remained from its 20 percent share in 1978 after twenty years of Fidelista social engineering. According to Claes Brundenius, however, the critical statistic is the Gini coefficient. Based on what it indicates, he concludes that there has indeed "been a radical redistribution of income in Cuba since the revolution with the major transfer of

8 | Cuba's Foreign Relations in a Post-Soviet World

Table 1.2. Cuban basic needs performance data

			Most recent
Level of social security coverage in relation to total workers (%)	53.0 (1958)	100.0 (1984)	100.0 (1999)
Illiteracy rate (%)	23.6 (1953)	1.9 (1981)	4.3 (1997)
Life expectancy at birth	61.8 (1955–60 average)	73.0 (1984)	75.6 (1998)
Infant mortality rate	32.5 (1958)	15.0 (1984)	7.2 (1997)
Inhabitants per doctor	1,067.0 (1958)	500.0 (1984)	203.0 (1994)
Per capita expenditures on public health (in pesos)	3.5 (1958)	72.6 (1984)	
Total housing (percentages)			
In poor condition		47.0 (1953)	31.0 (1980)
In average condition		40.0 (1953)	47.0 (1980)
In good condition		13.0 (1953)	22.0 (1980)

Sources: José Luis Rodríguez, "Cubanology and the Provision of Basic Needs in the Cuban Revolution," in Andrew Zimbalist (ed.), *Cuban Political Economy* (Boulder, Colo.: Westview Press, 1988), 91–94; *Revista Bimestre Cubana,* vol. 79 (January–June 1996), 172; and U.S. Central Intelligence Agency, *World Factbook 1998* (on the Internet at www.odci.gov/cia/publications/factbook).

income going to the bottom quintiles during the first years after 1959 and more moderate transfers during the latter part of the 1960s and the 1970s."[10] At least in his opinion, Cuba has therefore definitely met the challenge of economic growth with equity.

In addition to their regular pay, practically all Cubans receive a hidden income in the form of various programs operated and wholly financed by the state and designed to satisfy their basic needs. Indeed, it is in these human services areas, especially education and health care, that the Revolution has made its greatest strides, as illustrated by the pre- and postrevolutionary comparisons presented in table 1.2.

Moving beyond these internal comparisons, Cuba's equity/basic needs performance in relation to Latin America in particular and the Third World as a whole can measured by utilizing the Physical Quality of Life Index (PQLI). Admittedly the PQLI, which is computed on the basis of life expectancy, infant mortality, and literacy rates, has been criticized as being too simplistic, and probably rightly so.[11] Nevertheless, it does represent one of the few mechanisms whereby social development can be measured on a broad cross-national scale. In 1984 Cuba had a PQLI score of 98 (out of a possible 100 points), which was the highest index for any Latin American country and in fact was equal to that of the United States.[12]

Recognizing the danger of oversimplification, what conclusions might now be reached regarding how well Cuba fared during the 1980s in confronting the two key developmental issues for less developed countries—increasing overall productivity and wealth and assuring distributive justice? Certainly the macroindicators suggest that Havana's attempts to expand its economic base suffered a series of setbacks during the decade; overall growth rates were down, the foreign debt was up, and considerable work remained to be done in moving beyond the island's traditional sugar monoculture. But these trends were hardly unique to the island, for almost every other country in Latin America had similar experiences. Counterbalancing these productivity problems was Cuba's ability to maintain a level of achievement on the equity front unmatched by practically any other developing nation. Distributive justice rather than sheer economic muscle has, of course, always been the Revolution's strong point, and this did not change significantly during the 1980s.

Whatever economic difficulties the Revolution might have faced in its first thirty years paled into insignificance as the 1990s dawned and upheaval swept through the socialist camp, which had heretofore served as the anchor for Cuba's tradition of relative developmental stability and prosperity. Communist governments with which the Fidelistas had cultivated a complex web of beneficial relations, the epicenter of this network being the USSR, were driven from power and replaced by regimes that displayed little sympathy for the Revolution and even less interest in helping it. The Council for Mutual Economic Assistance (CMEA, also known as COMECON), the Soviet bloc's rough counterpart of the European Economic Community, had been a lucrative source of developmental aid for the Cubans as well as having provided them with privileged access to Eastern European markets, but it gradually unraveled and finally was disbanded in June 1991.

Battered by these convulsions, which were further complicated when Washington took advantage of the situation to intensify its long-standing campaign to destabilize the island's economy, Cuba rapidly sank into a deep and unprecedented recession.[13] Some sense of the extent of the catastrophe emerges from data released by the Cuban government in 1995 showing a 35 percent decline in gross domestic product (GDP, a general measure of a country's economic health and productivity) during the 1989–93 period. The decline in GDP apparently was halted in 1994, with government officials claiming that it increased by 2.5 percent in 1995.

Export earnings rose by 20 percent in 1995 to $1.6 billion, largely on the strength of higher world prices for key commodities and increased production of nickel through joint ventures with a Canadian firm. Higher export revenues and new credits from European firms and Mexico enabled Havana to increase its imports for the first time in six years. Imports rose 21 percent to almost $2.4 billion, or 30 percent of the 1989 level. Statistics from subsequent years would show similar evidence of slow but steady recovery. But even if it can be assumed that such successes will continue, it will still be some time before the island's economy rebounds to its former levels (and some skeptics insist that anything even vaguely resembling such a resuscitation is impossible).

Despite the terrible shocks that the economy has had to absorb, Havana has managed to preserve many of the social benefits that have long been the pride of the Revolution. The vanguard areas that have drawn special attention are education and medical services. Some recent performance statistics in these two areas (which, as noted, are comparable to services in the most developed nations) are: infant mortality rate (1997), 7.2 deaths/1,000 live births; life expectancy at birth (1998 estimate), total population = 75.64 years, females = 78.13 years, males = 73.29 years; literacy rate (age fifteen + who can read and write, 1995 estimate), total population = 95.7 percent, females = 95.3 percent, males = 96.2 percent.

Taking a broad look at the island's economic profile reveals a 1995 per capita GDP (a measure that is often used as a rough indicator of a society's overall standard of living) of approximately $1,300. Since this figure is not particularly high by Caribbean or Latin American standards, critics frequently cite it as evidence that the Revolution has failed to deliver a quality of life comparable to that of many other countries in the hemisphere.[14] Such claims must be viewed with considerable skepticism, however, since they fail to take into consideration the fact that Cuban society provides *all* its people many benefits (e.g., free education and medical services, subsidized food and housing, free social security programs, and so on) that either simply do not exist in other Latin American countries or are available only to a narrow minority with the money or the political influence necessary to procure them. In other words, the Revolution's egalitarian ethos translates into a more finely woven social safety net than is characteristic of general living standards elsewhere in the hemisphere.

The main sectors of the Cuban economy break down roughly into agriculture, 7 percent, industry, 30 percent, and services, 63 percent. Among the leading industries in terms of overall foreign revenue generated are sugar and its by-products, tourism, tobacco, and minerals (particularly nickel). The government has in recent years launched major programs to develop new export lines in the area of pharmaceuticals in general and biotechnological medical products in particular.

Although the state retains a primary role in the economy and controls practically all foreign trade, various reforms designed to raise labor incentives and to increase the availability of food, consumer goods, and services have been instituted in recent years. The liberalized agricultural markets introduced in October 1994, where state and private farms are authorized to sell any above-quota production at unrestricted prices, have broadened legal consumption alternatives. The number of self-employed workers licensed by the government to operate small private enterprises (in such areas as minor repair services and home restaurants, for example) increased slowly from 160,000 in December 1994 to about 210,000 in January 1996. Discussions continue within the leadership concerning the problem posed by the relative affluence of many self-employed workers and the resultant growing inequality of income in what has historically been a strictly egalitarian society, with one unique remedial measure (at least for revolutionary Cuba) under consideration: the implementation of an income tax system.

History

Christopher Columbus landed in Cuba on October 28, 1492, during his initial westward voyage.[15] The indigenous inhabitants he encountered there were the Ciboney, a friendly people related to the larger Arawak nation that at one time controlled many Caribbean islands. Colonization began in 1511, with the Spanish transforming Cuba into a supply base for their expeditions to Mexico and Florida. As a result of savage treatment and exploitation, by the middle of the sixteenth century the Ciboney were nearly extinct, forcing the colonists to depend on imported black slaves for operation of the island's mines and sugar plantations.

Despite frequent raids by buccaneers and naval units of rival powers, the island prospered throughout the sixteenth and seventeenth centuries. Following the conclusion in 1763 of the Seven Years' War (during which the English captured Havana), the Spanish government liberalized its previously restrictive colonial policies, especially concerning trade with non-Spanish partners. Consequently Spanish immigration to the island increased markedly, agricultural development occurred, and foreign commerce expanded. Between 1774 and 1817 the population increased from about 161,000 to more than 550,000.

During the third decade of the nineteenth century, however, Spanish rule became increasingly repressive. This situation generated among the colonists widespread sentiment for independence, which played itself out in a series of revolts and conspiracies against the Spanish regime that dominated Cuban political life throughout the remainder of the century. One of the most serious of these outbreaks occurred in 1868 when revolutionaries under the leadership of Carlos Manuel de Céspedes (1819–74) proclaimed independence. The ensuing Ten Years' War (1868–78)—a bitter and costly struggle for both sides and one characterized by widespread government brutality—ended inconclusively in a truce that, while granting some concessions to the Cubans, left the island still under Spanish control. Despite the promised reforms, the colonial power structure soon reverted to many of its oppressive practices.

On February 23, 1895, mounting discontent culminated in a resumption of the Cuban revolution under the leadership of the writer and patriot José Martí and General Máximo Gómez (1826–1905). The U.S. government intervened on behalf of the insurgents in April 1898, precipitating the Spanish-American War. Many nationalistic Cubans were not particularly enthused by this development, for there was considerable suspicion that Washington's involvement was motivated primarily by its own long-standing hegemonic designs (the United States had for years expressed an interest in buying or annexing the island) rather than by an idealistic commitment to Cuban independence. These fears would in many respects prove to be valid once the war was over.

José Martí (1853–1895)

José Julian Martí y Perez, who would ultimately come to be revered as the "Apostle" of Cuban nationhood and independence, was born in Havana on January 28, 1853.[16] Martí devoted his life to ending colonial rule in Cuba and to preventing the island from falling under the control of any country (including the United States) whose political ideologies were inimical to the principles he held.

As a teenager he became involved with a revolutionary group and was sentenced to six months at hard labor. At age eighteen he was exiled to Spain, where he finished his schooling at the University of Saragossa in 1874. He then fled to Mexico by way of France. After a brief visit to Cuba in 1877, he settled in Guatemala as a teacher. In 1878 he returned to Cuba under a general amnesty, but he conspired against the Spanish authorities and again was banished. He went back into exile in Spain, then came to the United States. After a year in New

York he left for Venezuela, where he hoped to settle, but yet another dictatorship forced him to depart. Martí then went back to New York, where he lived from 1881 to 1895.

In 1892 he became head of the Cuban Revolutionary party and began planning an invasion of the island. He and other revolutionaries arrived in Cuba on April 11, 1895. He was killed by the Spaniards on May 19, 1895, in a skirmish during a battle at Dos Rios.

The conflict ended on December 10, 1898, with Spain relinquishing sovereignty over Cuba (as well as such other major colonies as Puerto Rico and the Philippines). An American military government ruled the island until May 20, 1902, when an independent Cuban republic was formally instituted. However, the new country's sovereignty was from the beginning severely undermined by the Platt Amendment, a piece of U.S. legislation that in effect demanded a blank check for future American intervention into Cuba's affairs.

The Platt Amendment was the price the Cuban rebels had to pay to get a withdrawal of U.S. troops and to achieve formal independence. Grafted into the Cuban constitution of 1902, it guaranteed Washington the unilateral right to intervene in Cuban affairs (by armed force or other means) anytime it wished to do so to protect U.S. interests on the island. During the next thirty-two years Washington repeatedly exercised this option; its military occupied the island on several occasions, and it routinely conspired to assure that governments acceptable to the United States were installed or maintained in power.

Certain improvements, notably the eradication of yellow fever, had been accomplished during the U.S. occupation. Simultaneously, U.S. corporate interests invested heavily in the Cuban economy, acquiring control of many of its resources, especially the sugar-growing industry. Popular dissatisfaction with this state of affairs was aggravated by recurring instances of fraud and corruption in Cuban politics.

The first of several insurrections (which Washington perceived as threatening to U.S. political influence and/or economic interests) occurred in August 1906. In September, Washington promptly dispatched troops to the island, which remained under U.S. control until 1909. Another uprising took place in 1912 in Oriente Province, resulting again in Yankee military intervention.

Mounting economic difficulties, caused by complete U.S. domination of Cuban finance, agriculture, and industry, marked the period following World War I. In an atmosphere of crisis, Gerardo Machado campaigned on a reform platform and was elected president in November 1924. Contrary to his promises that things would improve, economic conditions deteriorated rapidly during his administration. Before the end of his second term he succeeded in acquiring dictatorial control of the government, and all opposition was brutally suppressed.

Increasingly, however, popular discontent caused by the depression and disaffection within the military combined to undermine Machado's position. In August 1933 the crisis reached a breaking point. Major uprisings along with pressure from U.S. Ambassador Sumner Welles led to Machado's resignation and the establishment of a U.S.-backed regime under Carlos Manuel de Céspedes. But the de Céspedes administration quickly fell victim to the continuing violence and unrest that Machado's overthrow had unleashed. With its departure, the short-lived 1933 revolution began.

The radical nationalist Ramón Grau San Martín took over the government in September 1933, supported by organized labor, the influential Student Directorate of Havana University, and a powerful army faction headed by former Sergeant Fulgencio Batista. Grau San Martín promised the people a true social revolution, and indeed he did begin to institute some reforms, primarily benefiting urban labor groups. But in reality, his programs were more rhetorical than substantive: The regime pledged a lot but delivered little.

Faced with stiff U.S. opposition and mounting domestic restiveness generated by the Communists, Grau San Martín was unable to restrain the armed forces. Led by Batista, who had become chief of the army, the military deposed Grau San Martín in January 1934. Although the 1933 experience boasted few concrete achievements, it did create a mystique that was to permeate Cuban politics for years. San Martín had, in other words, opened a Pandora's Box of great expectations, and for the next twenty-five years the Cuban people would be engrossed in a search to retrieve their "Lost Revolution" of 1933.

From 1934 to 1940 Cuba's presidency changed hands six times. The real power behind the throne, however, was Fulgencio Batista, who controlled the government through a series of puppet regimes. He first gained prominence in September 1933 when, as a sergeant in the Cuban Army, he helped to mount the uprising against the Céspedes government that drew support from both the military and student revolutionaries. Batista, a mulatto of modest background, would oversee and manipulate Cuban politics for the next twenty-six years.

Batista maintained an iron grip on the army and used it as the base from which he cast an ever longer shadow over the island's political landscape. No president could remain in office unless he followed Batista's bidding. For the former sergeant, a president was merely another underling to be ordered about.

In the period 1934–36, Batista pursued a Machado-like course. He mercilessly ground his political opposition into impotence; he moved quickly to crush several general strikes in 1935, thereby setting the tone for his dealings with Cuban labor; and he reestablished friendly relations with the United States and with American business interests.[17] In short, he resurrected the pre-1933 status quo.

In 1937, however, Batista—for some unexplained reason—abruptly reversed directions and began to shift to the liberal side of the political spectrum, wielding his influence in a manner that seemed to be much more responsive to the needs and interests of the general public. Such reforms as the nation's first comprehensive labor legislation, increased rural education, and mobile health programs became the order of the day. Plans for broad-based economic development were promulgated. However, Batista's crowning glory during this populist phase was his 1940 Constitution, an extremely progressive document containing provisions to protect workers' interests and promising agrarian reform.

Capitalizing on the popularity of the 1940 Constitution, Batista that same year resigned from the army and easily won the presidential election. For the next four years he ran a respectable but uneventful government, devoting his attention primarily to wartime matters. In 1944 Grau San Martín's Auténtico Party, which had spent the previous ten years building a formidable political machine, unexpectedly and decisively defeated Batista's hand-picked successor for the presidency. To everyone's surprise, Batista accepted the defeat and retired to Florida.

Grau San Martín's ascension to the presidency in 1944 reignited hopes that the 1933 revolution would finally become a reality. However, it was to remain, as before, a chimera to be pursued but not captured.

The Auténticos held power for eight solid years, with Grau San Martín being succeeded in the presidency by Carlos Prio Socarrás in 1948. On the whole, their performance proved to be disappointing at best and miserable in the eyes of many people. While instituting some reforms, they never came close to achieving the targets set forth in the 1933 revolution. To some extent this failure can be attributed to internal party dissension and the debilitating influence exerted by the Cuban multiparty system, but the primary reason was that the Auténticos lost their progressive zeal. They had the ability and the opportunity to attain their 1933 goals; what they lacked was the will to do so. Rather than dedication and idealism, the Auténtico governments were characterized by graft, corruption, and gross inefficiency. Within this context, political gangsterism became increasingly prominent as various factions armed themselves and fought to control pieces of political turf (including the University of Havana, where Fidel Castro emerged as a student leader).

Disgusted with this performance, some younger Auténticos broke away in 1946 to form the Ortodoxo Party. The Ortodoxos claimed to be the true heirs to the 1933 revolution, and from their ranks would come a young man who was to alter modern Cuban political history irrevocably—the same Fidel Castro.

Fidel Castro Ruz (1926–)

Fidel Castro was born on August 13, 1926 (some sources say 1927) on a farm in Oriente Province.[18] Years later, of course, he would make the province world-famous when he established the headquarters for his guerrilla movement in its Sierra Maestra mountains. His family was relatively wealthy, his father being a major provincial landowner. Speaking generally, it could be said that he came from a somewhat marginal upper-class background.

Fidel attended good Catholic schools in Santiago de Cuba and Havana, where he did well as both a student and an athlete, baseball being his specialty and his passion. At one point he was seriously considered a potential pitching recruit by the Brooklyn Dodger organization in the United States, but the Dodgers decided to pass him by (much to the later chagrin of various U.S. administrations).

In 1945 he enrolled at the University of Havana, graduating in 1950 with a law degree. He married Mirta Diaz-Balart in 1948, but they were divorced in 1954. Their son, Fidel Castro Diaz-Balart, born in 1949, has served as head of Cuba's atomic energy commission.

A member of the social-democratic Ortodoxo Party in the late 1940s and early 1950s, Castro was an early and vocal opponent of the dictatorship of Fulgencio Batista. In 1953 Castro led an attack on an army barracks—an attack that failed but nevertheless launched the revolutionary process that would bring him to power in 1959.

Presidential elections were scheduled in 1952 with the Ortodoxos expected to make a strong showing, but balloting never took place. Instead, the ever opportunistic Fulgencio Batista seized on the deterioration of civil society under Prio Socarrás to justify a coup that took place on March 10, 1952. Batista suspended the constitution, dissolved the congress, and instituted a provisional government, pledging elections the following year.

Such promises did not mollify those elements of Cuban society that were becoming increasingly infuriated by his high-handedness. In particular, Batista's reemergence as Cuba's strongman shattered practically all hope of many Ortodoxos (including Fidel Castro) that they could ever achieve power legally and peacefully.

Any expectations the Cuban people harbored that Batista might resume his populist course of 1937–40 were quickly demolished when the new president proceeded to impose a vicious Machado-like dictatorship on the island. Although certain special interest groups profited from Batista's rule, the masses received few if any benefits; instead they were subjected to the institutionalized violence and corruption that became the regime's hallmark. On July 26, 1953, the opening shot in the anti-Batista struggle was fired by Castro when he led a suicidal attack on the Moncada Barracks, a major military base in the eastern province of Oriente. His poorly armed students were cut to pieces by Batista's soldiers, and those rebels who were not killed were soon rounded up.

Captured and placed on trial, Castro electrified the country with the patriotism and charisma he displayed as he conducted his own defense, assuming in the process the mantle of the 1933 revolution. The capstone of this extraordinary performance was his closing statement, a brilliant exercise whereby he turned the tables on his accusers, in effect putting on trial the Batista regime (and its incestuous ties with Washington). He closed with the famous remark "Condemn me, it does not matter. History will absolve me."

Castro was, of course, found guilty and sentenced to fifteen years in prison. Nevertheless, the Moncada assault and his "History Will Absolve Me" speech established him (and the 26th of July Movement that he later organized, in November 1956) as a key rallying point for anti-Batista sentiment as well as Cuban revolutionary and nationalistic fervor.

After crushing the Moncada uprising, the Batista government felt secure enough to announce that elections would be held in the fall of 1954. But Batista's opponent, Grau San Martín, withdrew from the campaign just before the election, charging that his supporters had been terrorized. Batista was thus reelected without opposition. On inauguration day (February 24, 1955), partly in response to domestic appeals for reconciliation and also in what was widely construed as an attempt to improve his deteriorating image in the United States, he granted amnesty to political prisoners, including Castro. Fidel then went into exile in the United States and later in Mexico, where he concentrated on building his 26th of July Movement and preparing to unleash a guerrilla war in Cuba.

He returned to Cuba in December 1956, landing on the Oriente coast with eighty-six men. Batista's troops soon learned about the invasion and decimated the landing force. Only Castro and about a dozen companions (including a young doctor from Argentina named Ernesto "Che" Guevara, who would ultimately become legendary throughout Latin America as a symbol of revolutionary audacity and ideological idealism) managed to make it to the Sierra Maestra mountains. Once in the Sierra, Fidel began the fight that would culminate in Batista's downfall. Gradually Castro built a mass revolutionary movement that drew support from all sectors and classes in Cuban society.

Although history has glorified Fidel's rural guerrillas, other groups also made important contributions to the struggle. For example, in March 1957 the student-based Revolutionary Directorate in Havana launched an attack on the Presidential Palace, which almost brought the assassination of Batista. Then in September 1957, a naval revolt erupted at Cienfuegos, with military personnel and their Castroite allies taking over the city. The regime managed to crush the rebels and retake the city, but military morale and discipline were badly shaken by the incident. Finally, the Civic Resistance was indispensable in the war against Batista. Operating in the urban areas, it collected money and supplies for the rural guerrillas, carried out terrorist raids, collected intelligence, and conducted extensive sabotage activities. The Civic Resistance tied down thousands of troops who could otherwise have been deployed against Fidel's irregulars and ultimately suffered more casualties than any other revolutionary group.

By 1958 Cuba was embroiled in a full-fledged civil war. Castro suffered a serious setback when his call for a general strike in April 1958 was generally ignored, especially by the complacent Communist-led Havana workers. Attempting to administer the coup de grâce, Batista unleashed a total offensive against Fidel's Sierra Maestra fortress during May–July of 1958. Castro not only managed to withstand the assault but miraculously inflicted heavy casualties on the government and finally drove Batista's demoralized troops completely out of the Sierra. Sensing victory, Fidel mobilized all his forces for the final push. His guerrilla army (which at the time numbered only about 600 men) came down from the Sierra to fight, fanning out across Cuba in six columns. The Civic Resistance increased its activities, sending its members into the streets to harass Batista's troops and destroy supply lines. The decisive battle came on December 29, 1958, when Che Guevara's guerrilla column took the city of Santa Clara. Realizing he could not win, Batista fled Cuba two days later.

Prelude: Setting the Cuban Stage | 19

> ### Ernesto "Che" Guevara (1928–1967)
>
> Ernesto Guevara was born in 1928 in Buenos Aires, Argentina.[19] Although his parents, especially his mother, were anti-Peronist activists, he took no part in revolutionary student movements and showed little interest in politics at Buenos Aires University, where he studied medicine.
>
> Having passed the exams necessary to qualify as a doctor (specializing in dermatology), he settled in Guatemala during the socialist Arbenz presidency. After a CIA plot succeeded in driving Arbenz from power, Guevara, by now a committed Marxist, went to Mexico City in September 1954, where he met Fidel Castro. When Castro's band invaded Cuba in 1956, Che went with them. Initially serving as a doctor, he soon became a frontline *commandante* of the army.
>
> After the insurgents' victory, Guevara held a series of key posts in the revolutionary government, but he was not particularly happy in these roles, preferring to be in the field with the guerrillas carrying out the armed revolutionary struggle. Consequently he left Cuba in 1965, and after a brief sojourn with African rebels in Zaire, he launched a guerrilla campaign in Bolivia; he was captured and murdered in 1967 by the Bolivian Army and its American advisors.
>
> Because of his dashing style, his contempt for mere reformism, and his dedication to violent, flamboyant action, Che became an icon of the Latin American revolutionary tradition.

Fidel, who now in effect controlled Cuba from his Oriente stronghold, ordered all his forces to converge on the capital. After a seven-day victory march across the entire breadth of the island, marked by almost delirious public adulation, Castro and his guerrillas triumphantly entered Havana. In the months, years, and decades ahead, the Revolution and its Fidelista ethos would take Cuba on a tumultuous political odyssey over roads untraveled by any other modern Latin American nation.

Key Issues and Themes

Any attempt to provide a panoramic analytical survey of a country's behavior on the international stage represents a daunting undertaking due to the potentially large number of variables that can enter into the equation. Even a cursory examination of an introductory international relations textbook reveals the following partial list of considerations that must be taken into account when trying to explain the motivations behind a

20 | Cuba's Foreign Relations in a Post-Soviet World

government's foreign policy actions in any specific instance: the evolving distribution of power among the various actors involved; the availability of military force and the ability to use it to influence the case at hand; the impact of economic factors, both international and domestic; the interplay of governmental and private lobbying groups in the policy-making process; the role of perceptions and other psychological considerations (such as the norms and values engendered by ideological beliefs) in the formulation of a state's hierarchy of vital national interests; and the personalities and capabilities of key leaders. Further complicating matters is the fact that the relative significance of these variables is not constant. In other words, their importance in terms of affecting policy changes not only with time but also from one situation to another within the same rough time frame. Thus, for example, historical factors (e.g., a tradition of suspicion and hostility) may loom large in a government's current dealings with country A and be essentially irrelevant to its relations with country B.

This complexity inherent in the study of international relations cannot and should not be underemphasized, for to do so would be an egregious disservice to those seeking to expand their knowledge of foreign affairs. On the other hand, however, common sense with regard to this broad examination of Cuba's role on the world stage demands that some means be employed to bring an element of continuity and order into what might otherwise prove a rather chaotic exercise. Hence the material here revolves around (but is not limited to) the following three broad and interrelated themes:

- Counterdependency as the central pillar of the Revolution's foreign policy.

  This keystone concept can be seen as rooted in and flowing from the strong nationalistic tradition (established by Céspedes, Martí, and other Cuban patriots) that has long been a key ingredient of the island's political culture.

  Counterdependency concerns are presented here as the leitmotif underlying many of Havana's actions on the global stage, including those related to the remaining themes on this list. It is, in other words, suggested as the single most important analytical concept for understanding the dynamics of the Revolution's foreign policy.

- The distinctive role that Fidelista Cuba has played in world affairs, particularly during the heyday of the Cold War.

  Basically there are two key dimensions to this issue: the inspiration and support that Havana has provided for revolutionary movements and their armed struggles, especially in the Western Hemisphere during the 1960s and to a somewhat lesser degree in the 1970s; and the island's rise to leadership status within the ranks of the nonaligned and developing nations, the main impetus coming in the 1970s with some carryover into the 1980s.

Both of these phenomena, as we shall see, were significantly influenced by the interplay between counterdependency politics and Havana's evolving relationship with the Soviet Union.

- The United States as Cuba's main counterdependency protagonist. As already indicated, Cuba's problems with Washington began long before Fidel Castro's rise to power. The United States, at least as perceived by Cuban nationalists, had long behaved in an imperial manner toward the island: southern interests wanted to acquire it as a new slave state prior to the Civil War; U.S. intervention in 1898 in Cuba's war for independence was seen as unnecessary and unwanted, resulting in the imposition under the barrels of Yankee occupation rifles of the hated Platt Amendment to the 1902 Cuban constitution; and throughout the first half of the twentieth century, the United States dominated both the country's economy and its political life, in the latter instance sometimes intervening (with military force or by other means) to assure governments that were acceptable to Washington. Given such a high degree of foreign influence and control over their affairs, many Cubans felt that the island had become little more than an informal U.S. colony.[20]

This tradition of suspicion and antagonism would intensify in the Castro period, fueled by ideological hostilities and the confrontational psychology of the Cold War. In short, resistance to perceived U.S. hegemonic pretensions can be seen as the dominating theme of the Fidelistas' counterdependency scenario and thus as exerting a major impact on their foreign policy decisions.

Pursuing these themes, a broad overview of revolutionary Cuba's evolving role on the world stage is presented. Primary attention is devoted to the post–Cold War era and to the extraordinary challenges that the island has had to confront during this period in its efforts to adjust to the often harsh realities of a new world order. Within this context, the main topic is the political and economic survival strategies that Havana has employed in its foreign relations to counteract intensified U.S. efforts to isolate and destroy the Revolution. Before moving on to these endeavors, however, the counterdependency concept that stands at their analytical core needs to be explored and developed more fully.

2

Cuban Foreign Policy and Counterdependency Politics

The status and behavior of a state in the global arena can be influenced by such diverse variables as changes in the balance of power in the international system, perceived security threats, historical conditioning, the state's natural attributes, its choice of developmental models, the ideological orientation of its government, its decision-making mechanisms, and its leaders' personalities.[1] Within the array of theories and conceptual frameworks applicable, it is probably fair to say—though admittedly this is to simplify matters somewhat—that the "conventional wisdom" has generally approached revolutionary Cuba's role in world affairs from one of four basic macroperspectives: realist pragmatism, revolutionary messianics, Fidelista *personalismo,* or the surrogate/superclient theses. Although these scenarios are not necessarily mutually exclusive, each has a particular emphasis on which variables are perceived as the basic motivating factors behind Cuban foreign policy and how they are ranked in terms of their significance.[2] In other words, what each viewpoint seeks to provide is a somewhat distinctive explanation of *why* Havana behaves as it does on the international stage. Also, certain normative guidelines can flow from such analyses (usually implicitly rather than explicitly), which may affect how one evaluates Havana's actions—are they seen as being noble or sordid, understandable or irrational, justifiable or illegitimate?

Anyone wishing to delve seriously into the nuances of Cuban foreign policy needs to develop some familiarity with these points of view. Brief overviews of each perspective are presented, followed by a more detailed exposition of the analytical framework to be used here—the counterdependency paradigm.

Traditional Perspectives on Cuban Foreign Policy Behavior

The Realist Scenario

The Realist school (or, as it is also known, the power politics school) revolves around the notion that the essence of foreign affairs is the constant struggle among states for the power they need in order to be able to pursue and protect their vital national interests, the foremost being security. Hence the international arena comes to be looked upon as being akin to a Hobbesian state of nature, in which relationships are almost invariably competitive, the potential for serious violence is high, and preponderant strength is the only reliable guarantor of survival.[3] Employing the basic principles of the power politics perspective, Realists claim (among other things) to be able, with respect to a particular country, to (a) forecast the basic role that it will play in international affairs, and (b) provide a set of policy guidelines that, if implemented, will maximize its performance effectiveness in foreign affairs while likewise allowing observers to understand the motives and rationales underlying its activities.

Realists are usually rather disparaging in their projections concerning the overall station of smaller states such as Cuba on the global stage, for their approach to foreign affairs generally exhibits a great power bias, operating on the assumption that the interests of the weak will routinely be sacrificed to the preferences of the strong in a world where might is considered the only unit of political currency that really matters. Consequently, given this propensity toward Social Darwinism, most Realists feel that the likelihood that a small country will be able to control its destiny and exert any significant autonomous influence in the global arena is minimal. Instead, small actors tend to be seen as the inevitable victims of the global hierarchy of nations created by power differentials, their most common experience being incorporation into a sphere of great power influence. From the Realists' viewpoint, it is immaterial whether the immediate impetus for this process of subordination comes from a government involved in some form of empire building or from a small nation seeking a protective patron, for in either instance the outcome can ultimately be attributed to the harsh and inexorable exigencies of power politics.

Employing this framework over a broad historical time line leads Realists to conceptualize Cuba's foreign affairs as basically a series of client relationships—first as a Spanish colony, second as a subordinate resident in Washington's "Caribbean backyard," and third as a protectorate or vassal of the Soviet Union (see the section on the Surrogate Thesis later in this chapter for a more detailed presentation of this perspective on

Havana's ties with Moscow). Although this model does not readily apply to the post–Cold War Cuba of the 1990s, this can be seen as only a temporary condition while the island goes through a period of transition that will ultimately find it once again ensconced in the shadow of a great power, the most likely candidate being the United States once Fidel Castro passes from the political scene.

Despite the widespread popularity of the Realist school among academics and especially international affairs professionals, many observers are not persuaded that its "sphere of influence" concept has any serious utility as a tool for understanding the essential nature and thrust of revolutionary Cuba's foreign policies. They contend that this perspective grossly underestimates the impact of the strong nationalist sentiments that have always permeated the island's political culture and have led most Cubans to be extremely wary of any external power that might represent a threat to their country's sovereignty and independence. Admittedly, not all Cuban leaders have displayed these traits. Batista, for example, is widely considered to have been little more than a Yankee puppet, especially in the 1950s when his grip on power was heavily dependent on Washington's support. The Fidelistas, however, are strongly connected to this heritage, as exemplified by the fact that while there has been extensive debate as to exactly when Castro became a communist, there has never been any serious doubt about his nationalist credentials. Indeed, despite his strong ideological commitments, many analysts feel that he is first and foremost a Cuban nationalist and that his policies (both domestic and foreign) are deeply rooted in this powerful tradition. These nationalistic considerations are tightly interwoven with the counterdependency theme around which this book revolves.

Turning to the policy guidelines set forth by the Realists, they can, for simplicity's sake, be condensed into the following admonition—be totally *pragmatic* in expanding and using your power to safeguard your vital national security interests. Cuba, like many other small developing states, has tended to adopt a two-pronged conceptualization of its security needs. The military side of this equation demands that Havana take the measures necessary to protect itself from armed attack, either direct or indirect. Equally important, however, are economic concerns, for less developed countries are often highly susceptible to trade warfare and other similar forms of externally induced destabilization that can represent as serious a threat to their sovereignty as can a military invasion. Accordingly, Havana's long-term quest for economic development and its more recent attempts to diversify its trading partners can be seen as having a significant security dimension.

Observers have often overlooked or seriously underestimated the pragmatic security dimension of revolutionary Cuba's foreign policies, with devotees of the messianic and personalismo schools (discussed later) being especially prone to this oversight in their zeal to demonstrate that it is either Marxist ideology or Castro's ego that is the driving force behind Havana's international behavior. Certainly such considerations cannot be entirely discounted. For example, the Cubans have always insisted—and perhaps more important, have confirmed through their actions—that there is a core of socialist principles that cannot be ignored in formulating domestic and foreign policies because they define the very nature and soul of the Revolution. The commitment to and the importance of these ideals is encapsulated in the Fidelista slogan "Socialismo o Muerte" (Socialism or death), with the reference to death indicating both the high stakes involved (the very survival of the Revolution) and lengths to which the island's people must be willing to go in defending their ideals. Likewise, the impact on the country's internal and external affairs of Castro's personality, which combines immense intelligence and talent with one of the rarest leadership commodities—genuine political charisma—must be acknowledged. Realists, however, would contend that digging more deeply into these phenomena will reveal a much greater element of security pragmatism than appears at first glance.

Take, for instance, the controversial question of Cuba's support for the armed struggles of various revolutionary movements, especially in the Western Hemisphere during the 1960s. The messianic school has employed an ideological interpretation to explain these policies, contending that Havana was simply putting into practice the Marxist exhortation to spread communism throughout the world. Others have proposed that such behavior could be better understood in terms of its security implications, especially with regard to the threat posed by Washington's hostility to the very survival of the Cuban Revolution. The basic argument here is that shortly after coming to power, Castro seemed to have developed some serious doubts about Moscow's willingness to take any substantial risks to help defend the island against a possible American attack. The key development, it is suggested, was the Kremlin's actions during the 1962 Missile Crisis, when it ignored Havana's pleas to wring concessions from Washington by remaining steadfast and chose instead to negotiate a separate peace with the Kennedy Administration. The atmosphere was further poisoned by the ideological disputes that were straining the Soviet-Cuban relationship throughout much of the 1960s.[4] Under such conditions, support for armed struggles could be seen as contributing to the island's security by helping to produce a situation whereby the United States could not focus all of its counterrevolutionary attention on Cuba because it was facing simultaneous challenges to its influence on a number of different fronts. This strategy was encapsulated in Che Guevara's exhortation to create "two, three, many Vietnams" throughout the Western Hemisphere. The best-case scenario would see Havana gaining new allies and new international options if its ideological brethren succeeded in their armed struggles.

Realist analyses such as these are predicated on the assumption that security is the central strategic premise shaping Cuban international relations and that any specific moves Havana in general or Fidel Castro in particular might make on the world stage should be seen as constituting the pragmatic tactical means to achieve that end. Others might prefer a more hybrid approach, such as Nelson Valdés's portrayal of Cuba's external affairs as an exercise in principled pragmatism (or principled opportunism), in which certain ideological tenets form an untouchable core of policy guidelines and goals that the Fidelistas then feel free to pursue by the most effective means available.[5] In any case, Cuban foreign policy is seen as having a strong pragmatic component that must be afforded serious consideration by anyone hoping to develop a deep understanding of the complex dynamics of the Revolution's dealings with the larger international community.

Cuban Foreign Policy as a Revolutionary Crusade

The great revolutions often acquire a messianic aura in the sense that their proponents tend to see them as representing not only a new but, more important, a superior social order, the relevance of which goes far beyond the boundaries of the countries that originally spawned them. Accordingly, like the religions to which these secular philosophies are sometimes compared, an assumption of "universality" can become associated with the norms and values underlying these revolutions, which in essence means that the particular ideology involved is presumed to be preferable to any other alternative and therefore should be embraced by all states and peoples. Such was the case, for example, with the U.S., French, and Russian/Bolshevik revolutions. The most fervent adherents of this viewpoint are often willing and indeed anxious to play a missionary role in enlarging the scope of the new order.[6] In many instances this expansionist ambience is reinforced by defenders of the status quo in other countries, who—alarmed about the possibility of a contagion effect—view any revolution as something akin to a highly infectious social disease that must be stamped out in order to protect the health of the larger international community.

Cuba is somewhat different since this messianic quality normally has not, at least in the twentieth century, been associated with revolutions in smaller countries. Indeed, the modern history of Latin America is littered with social upheavals, some of which were genuine revolutions, while others merely appropriated the term as a convenient catch-all label for any extralegal change of government, and most of these upheavals never seriously impacted the consciousness of the international community. An excellent example of this phenomenon is the Mexican Revolution. Its phase of armed struggle, which roughly covered the period 1910–20, unleashed a wave of violence unprecedented in the Western Hemisphere. It is estimated that over a million people were killed in the fighting, a figure that far exceeds the death toll in any other hemispheric conflict (including the revolutionary and civil wars in the United States), and in its aftermath the country's economy, political system, and social structure were in many respects radically transformed. But aside from some short-lived and generally ineffectual intervention into the conflict on Washington's part, the Mexican Revolution did not capture the public imagination in Latin America or beyond, as would its Cuban counterpart fifty years later. Instead, it was seen as a Mexican affair with little relevance to the surrounding world.

Why the Cuban Revolution did not also fade into obscurity, but instead came to be seen as a prominent member of the vanguard supporting socialist struggles for radical change throughout the world, can be explained in part on the following grounds:

- It occurred within the hothouse atmosphere of the Cold War and in a nation the United States had long seen as having some strategic value because of its proximity to key naval passages linking the Atlantic with the Caribbean Sea and the Gulf of Mexico. This geopolitical significance contributed to Cuba's emergence as a theater of superpower competition that was part of its larger struggle to enhance its position and influence within the global balance of power. So the Revolution acquired unusual visibility on the international stage.

28 | Cuba's Foreign Relations in a Post-Soviet World

- The exceptional charisma of such leaders as Fidel and Che Guevara helped to impart a quasi-mythological quality to the Revolution, leading it to be seen as a powerful symbol (especially among young people) for the discontent with the "Establishment" that characterized the turbulent 1960s in Latin and North America as well as in Western Europe. Cuba, in short, became an icon for radicals throughout the Western world who were seeking a new model to inspire and energize their political dreams.

- Particularly during the first decade of the Revolution, Havana often interjected a strong messianic element into its foreign policies in terms of both rhetoric and action. These initiatives revolved around the Fidelistas' commitment to the concept of "proletarian internationalism," which was defined as the duty to help one's ideological brethren in other countries to seize power and/or consolidate their regimes. In reality, for both practical and theoretical reasons, Havana's moral support was always greater than any material aid that was extended.[7] So, irrespective of the specific form that the assistance may have taken, these initiatives did help to bolster the Revolution's reputation for pursuing foreign policies that exhibited a significant crusading dimension.

But whatever the reasons for the messianics that came to be associated with Havana, the opinions flowing from this particular analysis of the essential nature of Cuba's foreign policy tended to be diametrically opposed.

Opponents of the Revolution, obviously influenced by the proposition advocated by hard-line Cold War warriors that the messianic element in Marxism leads inevitably to a lust for conquest, perceived Castro's government as simply another typical communist state committed to subversion and aggression. As such, it represented a threat that had to be at least contained and preferably eliminated entirely. Operating on these assumptions, opponents gave little if any serious consideration to the possibility that there might be less diabolical explanations of Cuba's behavior based on such considerations as security concerns or nationalistic sentiments. Meanwhile, those who were sympathetic toward Fidelismo frequently took a similar bent, portraying Havana as an anti-imperialistic white knight whose every move on the world stage was rooted in commitment to social justice and proletarian internationalism. In short, revolutionary altruism was seen as reigning supreme within the inner circles of the island's leadership, while the more pragmatic aspects of their international initia-

Cuban Foreign Policy and Counterdependency Politics | 29

tives, which in the best realist tradition were often based on cold calculations of their country's vital national interests, tended to be overlooked.

Admittedly there has always been an ideological element within Cuban foreign policy, manifested most dramatically in the mutually reinforcing notions of proletarian internationalism and anti-imperialism, both of which have had a major impact on the Fidelistas' view of their role in world affairs and both of which have certain messianic implications. Proletarian internationalism by definition engages the Revolution in the political affairs of other countries and regions. Moreover, the concept in its most pristine form does not present such activity as a matter of mere policy choice but rather as an obligation that successful revolutionaries must recognize and accept in order to create the united front necessary to overcome the wide-ranging opposition mounted by defenders of the status quo. Specifically, at least as far as the Cubans have been concerned, such solidarity implies a commitment to resisting U.S. imperialism, since they are convinced that Washington's eagerness to impose a Pax Americana wherever it can is one of the main obstacles not only to necessary revolutionary change but also to the aspirations of progressive countries to control their own economic and political destinies.

A case can therefore be made in certain instances for the validity of looking at Cuban foreign policy as a revolutionary crusade. Such an interpretation could be adopted, for example, with regard to its promotion of Fidelista-style guerrilla wars in the Western Hemisphere during the 1960s and (perhaps somewhat less persuasively) to its Central American policies in the late 1970s and early 1980s. In general, however, it would appear that depicting Havana's international behavior in this light has little analytical utility. The Cubans have, of course, always insisted that in principle they have a right to pursue a policy of proletarian internationalism (and they continue to do so). But in reality this claim has not been transformed into concrete policy for some time. By the early 1970s Havana was putting much more emphasis on normalizing its relations with most governments rather than on helping revolutionaries to overthrow them. This pattern has become even more pronounced in the post–Cold War era, now that the global rivalry between East and West that helped fuel ideological confrontations is gone and the exigencies of maintaining cordial state-to-state ties in order to maximize trade and other related economic benefits are paramount. Havana continues to be highly concerned about the issue of U.S. imperialism, but it has been some time since such apprehension has triggered a *messianic* response seeking to promote revolution as a remedy. Instead, Havana has for a long while been more prone to see cooperation among potentially threatened governments as the best response. Ultimately, then, considering all of these factors, the perspective that sees Cuban foreign policy essentially as an ideological crusade does not seem to have much contemporary applicability.

Fidel and the Personalization of Foreign Policy

Greatness is too often an attribute conferred upon people with an excess of partisan baggage; those whose ideas or actions meet with one's approval tend to be lionized while others are likely to be snubbed. More preferable is a dispassionate approach recognizing that such individuals are those who, for better or for worse, have had a significant impact upon some aspect of their societies, their professions, or the world at large. By this latter standard, irrespective of whether one admires or detests him, Fidel Castro must be acknowledged as one of the truly great political figures of the twentieth century. In addition to his impressive intellect and almost inexhaustible energy, he possesses one of the most elusive and desirable of all leadership qualities—charisma, the ability to relate to both individuals and the masses in a direct, emotional manner that generates intense loyalty and serves as a vehicle for mobilizing people behind a particular cause.

Given these qualities, it is tempting and indeed easy to look at the Cuban Revolution (with regard to both domestic and foreign affairs) as essentially an exercise in projecting Castro's ideas and personal preferences into the island's political arena. Illustrative of this tendency is the common practice of using the terms *Fidelistas* and *Fidelismo* as shorthand labels to describe the supporters of and, more important, the essential nature of the Revolution. To some extent, of course, it is legitimate to do this, for Castro has undeniably cast a large shadow across Cuban affairs and the course of modern Latin American history. In some instances, however, observers have tended to highlight this influence to the point where it is perceived in terms of almost total control over events. The tendency here has been to see the Revolution essentially as the externalization of Castro's personality. Basically this approach to analyzing and understanding the Revolution's dynamics falls under the rubric of the classical "Great Man" (or Woman) theory of politics. Its key elements are:

- It is taken as a given that individuals sometimes emerge who are uniquely capable of dominating the political process with respect to making decisions and having them carried out.

  The crucial concept here is *domination*. Any leader can influence policy making; indeed, such a capability is integral to the very concept of leadership. But on rare occasions, it is argued, there emerges a person whose control over and impact upon events is so far-reaching that the mantle of "greatness" is conferred. Whether they wield their exceptional powers for good ends (Abraham Lincoln) or evil (Adolf Hitler), such individuals inevitably become the focus of inordinate attention and analysis.

- In explaining the political behavior of such leaders, the Great Man theory tends to focus upon and heavily emphasize such highly idiosyncratic factors as personality traits, physical and especially mental health, levels of ego and ambition, personal history and unique experiences, and the nature of the person's perceptions (as influenced by such considerations as religious beliefs, ideological values, and moral/ethical codes).[8]

A popular but often controversial application of this approach is to treat the analysis of political behavior as an exercise in (amateur) psychoanalysis. Carlos Montaner, for example, adopts this technique in his highly critical, often vitriolic *Fidel Castro and the Cuban Revolution.*[9] Utilizing a demonic version of the Great Man theory, Montaner refuses to see the Revolution as a complex sociopolitical phenomenon, preferring to portray it as an externalization of what he considers to be Castro's psychotic personality. Thus domestic and foreign policies are presented not as outcomes of a multidimensional decision-making process but rather as the pathetic products of Fidel's alleged "neurotic needs," his "paranoia," and his "sickly vocation for power and glory."

There is some elemental validity to this Great Man theory in the sense that governments, states, and countries are not living entities that act on their own. Rather, it is human beings who formulate and implement political policies. And, understandably, it is the most visible of these people who get the most attention, especially in the popular press and the mass media. As such, it becomes common practice to look at politics from a highly personalistic, leader-oriented perspective (especially when dealing with more authoritarian systems, where there are fewer structural restraints on the exercise of power).

Generally, however, most experts are highly skeptical about the Great Man approach to political analysis. Among the main criticisms raised are:

- Despite the attention showered on some prominent participants, the making and the implementation of policies, both domestic and foreign, are invariably collective (i.e., group) endeavors involving multiple lines of input and influence. Hence these processes can be understood more accurately in terms of group dynamics rather than through individualistic Great Man theories.

- Leaders, even in authoritarian contexts, simply do not have the freedom of action suggested by the Great Man school. Instead, they must invariably operate within boundaries imposed by a series of variables. One is the power of entrenched governmental bureaucracies, some examples in the foreign policy area being the armed forces, the diplomatic corps, and those offices involved in the promotion and regulation of international trade. Other relevant variables include the need to respond to the desires of interest groups, both internal and external; resource inadequacies inhibiting the leader's capability to deal effectively with a particular domestic or overseas issue; and limitations rooted in formal (constitutional) and/or informal (cultural) norms defining the leader's role in society.

A well-known story illustrating pervasiveness of such constraints involves President Harry Truman's observation that incoming President Dwight Eisenhower, who as a general was accustomed to having his orders obeyed without question, was in for a rude awakening once he entered the Oval Office and had to deal with the obstructionism of Congress and the federal bureaucracy. "Poor Ike," Truman is reported to have said, "he will sit here and tell people what to do and NOTHING WILL HAPPEN!"

All of the considerations listed apply, to some degree or other, to Castro's situation. Fidel has, of course, been the foremost figure in the historical development of the Cuban Revolution and remains the preeminent influence in the island's contemporary politics. But "foremost" and "preeminent" are not synonymous with absolute power or total control. Rather Castro, like all politicians, must operate within an environment where there are constraints upon what he can do.

Moreover, Fidel certainly wants to guarantee that the Revolution that has been his life's work survives his departure from the political scene. It will not do so if it exists simply as an extension of his personality, popularity, and power. Rather, to assure its long-term viability, the Revolution must be inextricably "institutionalized" into the fabric of Cuban society. This process, which by definition entails the creation of and the delegation of power to multiple centers of legally constituted authority, has not only already been initiated by Castro but indeed is rather well developed.[10] For example, political and bureaucratic influence has been vested in entities like the Cuban Communist Party and the National Assembly of People's Power (the Cuban equivalent of a national legislature) as well as in

Cuban Foreign Policy and Counterdependency Politics | 33

such important mass organizations as the National Federation of Cuban Women, the Confederation of Cuban Workers, and the Organs of Popular Power.[11] Also, a new generation of leaders is being groomed who will have the training and the experience necessary to assume control when the time arrives. Currently the most prominent among this group are Ricardo Alarcón, former foreign minister and currently president of the National Assembly, and Carlos Lage, a vice-president with primary responsibility for economic reforms and policy. Lage is considered by some, such as Harvard University's Jorge Domínguez, to be Cuba's de facto prime minister. Although Fidel's brother Raúl, who heads the Cuban armed forces, is widely thought to be his most likely immediate political heir, increased attention is being paid to the long-term leadership potential of such younger prospects as those mentioned.

Taking all these factors into account leads to the conclusion that Cuban reality with regard to the power and influence of its leadership, whether dealing with foreign or domestic affairs, is more complicated and nuanced than the rather simplistic authoritarian picture set forth by purists of the Great Man school of politics. Castro's impact should not be underestimated or excessively devalued, but it would likewise be a serious mistake to look at the country's foreign policy as something essentially akin to his personal fiefdom. Such an approach can produce fascinating political theater, but too often serious analysis is the admission price that must be paid.

The Surrogate/Superclient Theses

These two views of Cuba's behavior on the world stage, both of which revolve around the nature of its Soviet connection, were very much creatures of the Cold War.[12] The key difference between them is that the Superclient analysis saw Havana as having some control over the dynamics of its Moscow ties, whereas the Surrogate school portrayed the island as essentially a pawn of the Kremlin in the USSR's superpower competition with the United States. Because both views are time-bound in the sense that they were interpretations of the Fidelistas' activities during the Cold War, they obviously have little relevance as explanatory tools today. Nevertheless some familiarity with them is useful for those interested in probing the historical evolution of the island's foreign relations.

The superclient concept, which was popularized by David Ronfeldt, holds that occasionally, due to its strategic location and/or other factors, a small developing nation can become such a valuable asset to a great power that it is able to extract from its patron significant political concessions including considerable decision-making flexibility in both the external

34 | Cuba's Foreign Relations in a Post-Soviet World

and internal realms), accomplishing all this despite the fact that it might appear to be locked into a relationship where it is the subordinate party.[13] Nor should the concrete material rewards involved be underestimated, for supercliency implies that in addition to the small country exercising considerable decision-making autonomy, extraordinary amounts of economic and military aid will be forthcoming.

Two countries frequently cited by this school as classic examples of superclients are Israel (vis-à-vis Washington) and revolutionary Cuba (with its special Soviet/socialist bloc ties). Rather than assuming the nonaligned stance so popular with many developing nations after World War II, both countries, so the argument goes, opted instead to move decisively into a Cold War camp. This decision was seen in Cuba's case as allowing it to capitalize upon and manipulate the competition between the United States and the Soviet Union, the result being the emergence of a relationship with Moscow that was more akin to a junior-senior partnership than the abject subordination that is traditionally assumed to flow from incorporation into a great power's sphere of influence.

While it is undeniable that Havana benefited, politically and especially materially, from its special relationship with the USSR and the socialist bloc, many observers (including the highly nationalistic Cubans) rejected the characterization of the island as a Soviet superclient, the main reason being that client status (super or otherwise) could be seen as implying that Moscow possessed and could readily exercise a policy veto with respect to the island's internal and external affairs. If true, this would mean that the Fidelistas, despite the latitude that they might on occasion be granted by the Kremlin, had in the final analysis surrendered their sovereignty on the altar of expediency. Such a depiction, insist the critics, grossly underestimated Havana's capacity for independent action and was therefore severely flawed as a mechanism for understanding the complex dynamics of the Soviet-Cuban Cold War relationship.

The Surrogate Thesis generated heated debate, primarily because it pulled no punches in castigating Havana as a puppet of the USSR, often portraying the Fidelistas as the Kremlin's overseas shock troops, and because it was employed as a partisan device to try to influence U.S. policy toward Cuba in the 1970s and 1980s. Advocates of this proposition insisted that Castro's revolution had long ago reached the point where it simply could not survive without the constant injections of massive economic and military aid that it received from the Soviet bloc. This severe dependency, the theory continued, gave the Russians so much leverage over the Fidelistas that Moscow was in a position to dictate the island's

Cuban Foreign Policy and Counterdependency Politics | 35

domestic and international agendas. According to this scenario, the Kremlin could and regularly did use the Cubans to spearhead its attempts to subvert and eventually dominate vulnerable Third World countries. In essence, then, the Surrogate Thesis denied that the Fidelistas charted their own way abroad, insisting instead that the USSR controlled their foreign policy. As Edward González put it, referring to Cuba's military presence in Africa, "Above all, this thesis rests on Cuba's high level of indebtedness to the Soviet Union, stemming from Moscow's willingness to subsidize the island's economy over the years . . . and to support Cuban armed forces with essential military hardware. Cuba's military operations in Angola and elsewhere in Africa can be seen as repayment of debts owed to Moscow."[14]

To hard-liners such as U.S. Senator Daniel Moynihan, the Fidelistas were nothing more than the "Gurkhas of the Russian Empire," stirring up trouble on Moscow's behalf and functioning as a vehicle for indirect Soviet aggression and eventual domination of targeted developing countries.[15]

The surrogate concept first began to acquire widespread publicity in the United States during the mid-1970s as a result of Havana's growing military involvement in Africa. Soon it became standard practice for opponents of the Revolution to portray practically all Cuban initiatives on the international stage in surrogate terms. This tendency not to distinguish between Cuban and Soviet foreign policies meant, of course, that any major expansion of Havana's influence could easily be perceived as threatening U.S. security by tipping the bipolar balance of power in Moscow's favor.

Despite its popularity in U.S. governmental circles and the mass media, most Cuban specialists in the academic community felt that the thesis was much too simplistic and ultimately untenable. González, for example, stated that "the surrogate thesis fails to account for Cuba's own domestic and foreign interests as an autonomous . . . actor in world affairs."[16]

Anthony Payne reached a similar conclusion with regard specifically to Havana's activities in the Caribbean (and by inference in the rest of the Western Hemisphere): "Whatever may be the case in respect to Cuba's African adventures, in the context of the Caribbean Cuba has to be seen as an autonomous actor in its own right rather than as a pliable agent of the Soviet Union."[17]

Overall, then, the general consensus seemed to be that while it was clear that the USSR had encouraged and materially supported Cuba's exploits abroad, thereby allowing it to take on more ambitious tasks and to carry

36 | Cuba's Foreign Relations in a Post-Soviet World

them out more effectively than might otherwise have been the case, it was likewise fair to say that Havana rather than Moscow exercised predominant control over the Revolution's foreign policies.

Developing the Concept of Counterdependency Politics

One unfortunate trait that Cuba shares with many other smaller countries is a vulnerability to external domination. As suggested in chapter 1, the island has fallen victim to this phenomenon throughout most of its history, with Spain controlling it for almost 400 years (1511–1898) followed by a 60-year period (1898–1958) during which the United States to a great extent managed its political and economic life.

Such superordinate-subordinate relationships have been conceptualized and labeled in many different ways over the years; both academics and politicians have at one time or another characterized them in terms of colonialism, empire building, imperialism, Manifest Destiny, hegemonic impulses, and the like. In the post–World War II era the dependency school emerged as the modern expression of this legacy, engendering in the process a heightened sensitivity on the part of nationalists in less developed countries to the nature of their ties with the world's economic centers of power. Contemporary Cuba, with a political culture incorporating a long tradition of struggle against foreign encroachment, has shared these concerns. Dependency has been widely seen as representing a real danger to the island's sovereignty, with the Fidelistas being especially worried about its potentially debilitating impact on their capacity to exercise effective control over the destiny of the Revolution. The pursuit of counterdependency politics has therefore emerged as a central thread in Havana's domestic and foreign policies.

The Nature of the Threat: Dependency Theory

Dependency theory attributes the plight of less developed countries primarily to external factors that have relegated them to an inferior and often exploited status in the international community.[18] The intellectual roots of the theory can be traced to three fundamental sources: classical Marxist writings on imperialism, especially by Lenin and his disciples; the promulgation in the postcolonial period, mainly by Third World scholars, of such concepts as neocolonialism and neoimperialism; and work done primarily during the 1960s by various Latin American economists associated with the United Nations Economic Commission for Latin America (ECLA).[19] This group, often called the Prebisch school after its leading exponent,

Raul Prebisch, was initially the most influential in refining Latin American dependency theory. Its scope of inquiry, however, was somewhat narrow, concentrating mainly on the negative developmental implications arising from the unequal terms of trade between the northern industrialized societies and the less developed countries (LDCs). According to this view, the Third World nations could not expect ever to improve their relative position significantly in the global economic arena as long as they remained locked into trade relationships whereby they mostly exported a few low-priced commodities to the industrialized states while simultaneously importing expensive manufactured products from those countries. Certainly prerevolutionary Cuba fit this profile, with the United States representing the metropole that dominated the island's economy both in terms of trade and as a source of foreign investment. But after 1959 the island no longer fit the classical dependency mold, for the Revolution's nationalization initiatives had succeeded in recapturing assets that had fallen under foreign (mostly Yankee) control, and the preferential treatment that it received from the Soviet bloc had neutralized most of its traditional trade imbalances. In the post–Cold War period, however, many of Cuba's basic economic vulnerabilities have reemerged, bringing with them the unpleasant possibility that the specter of dependency might once again appear on its horizons.

Defining dependency basically as the uneven development inherent in and promoted by such economic imbalances, ECLA analysts sought remedies in such strategies as diversifying Third World exports, import substitution (i.e., establishing domestic companies to service local consumer markets instead of relying on imports to do so), and regional integration. In short, they were inclined to perceive dependency as a technical problem rather than as the product of fundamental flaws within the capitalist structure of the international economic system. Consequently, the solutions they espoused essentially represented reforms geared toward more state involvement in the process of internal capitalistic development and heavier emphasis on economic nationalism (as opposed to free trade) in the relations of the LDCs with the industrialized world.

Eventually, the Prebisch school's basically moderate perspective was overshadowed by a more radical approach that went beyond the purely economic ties involved in dependency and began to explore the phenomenon in terms of the sociopolitical dynamics operative both within the LDCs and the developed nations and also at the level of their international linkages. In other words, this more comprehensive analysis viewed dependency as an inherent component of the global economy's capitalistic structure. Moreover, many radical *dependendistas*, believing that this situation was deliberately created and maintained by the industrialized countries to facilitate their systematic pillaging of the Third World, were skeptical and even contemptuous of solutions limited to economic reforms, insisting instead that the real heart of the issue is to be found in the broader configurations of power at the national and global levels.

A key element of this more complex picture that was beginning to emerge involved the interface between economic dependency and its political counterpart. Although there was general consensus that one type often functioned to spawn the other, differences of opinion often arose as to which form preceded the other. Some scenarios emphasized that the economic variety is most likely to be the first to develop. The origin of such dependency, it was said, can vary from case to case; it may, for instance, be the residue of a colonial experience or the fallout from such circumstances as becoming locked into unequal patterns of trade, allowing unrestricted private investment from abroad, accepting from other governments aid with strings attached, or running up a large foreign debt. But whatever the specific causes, the result is external control of a country's economy. At this point, it was argued, a crucial transfer of political power (defined as the capacity to determine the allocation of vital resources and values in a society) has also occurred, since the responsibility for making macroeconomic developmental decisions, normally considered to be the prerogative of a country's government, is now to a great extent being exercised by outsiders. In this view, political dependency has evolved as the natural corollary to economic dependency.

Other investigators were more inclined to reverse this sequence by stressing the primacy of political subservience. James Rosenau, although not a dependency theorist, contributed to this line of analysis through his innovative work on the notion of a "penetrated political system," which he explains as "one in which *nonmembers of a national society participate directly and authoritatively, through actions taken jointly with the society's members, in either the allocation of its values or the mobilization of support on behalf of its goals.* The political processes of a penetrated system are conceived to be structurally different from . . . those of a national political system. In the latter, nonmembers of a society do not direct action toward it and thus do not contribute in any way to the allocation of its values or the attainment of its goals."[20]

In a nation that has been penetrated, then, the role of foreigners is not limited merely to exerting exogenous influence. Instead, they are intimately involved in the society's internal decision-making processes. This

Cuban Foreign Policy and Counterdependency Politics | 39

relationship, according to the dependendistas, becomes one of political dependency when outsiders from the more powerful developed country become the controlling actors. The dominant industrialized center will, of course, materially benefit from this state of affairs, for the prevailing logic behind the pursuit of political hegemony has long been to exploit it for economic gain. Thus, from this perspective, the acquisition of political power sets the stage for the introduction of economic dependency.

A central feature of each set of political/economic dynamics summarized here, according to the radical dependendistas, is the development of a cooperative, symbiotic relationship between some metropolitan and Third World elites. While both parties, they argued, will actively seek such an arrangement, the main initiative frequently comes from sectors of the national bourgeoisie in the LDCs (often called the *comprador* class) who are willing to serve as local agents for or junior partners of foreign capitalist interests in order to be assured an ongoing piece of the exploitive action. In short, this alliance is seen as being based on a convergence of class interests, which subjects the masses in a dependent LDC to a complex pattern of oppression involving both internal and external dimensions.[21] From the radical perspective, the role played by the Third World clientele bourgeoisie cannot be overemphasized: Not only do these elements provide major assistance in facilitating exogenous penetration, but they also help to reinforce and protect the instruments of foreign domination. In other words, driven by their desire for self-aggrandizement, they function as enthusiastic promoters and defenders of dependency.

Within the Cuban context, the Batista regime of the 1950s would probably be considered by most radical dependendistas to be a prime example of this comprador phenomenon; it was corrupt and exploitive, it maintained and profited extravagantly from an inequitable distribution of societal wealth and power, and it capitalized upon a symbiotic relationship with Washington to protect its power and prerogatives. On the other hand, none of these characteristics would apply to the Fidelista revolution that overthrew Batista's tyranny.

The highest (and most controversial) stage of political dependency is reached when its purveyors go beyond the limited realm of decision-making participation based on an alliance with the comprador class and begin to use their power to prescribe the composition and nature of the government in a dependent country. At this point, the dominant center is usurping the right of national self-determination, which is a prerequisite for any people to exist as a truly sovereign nation. More subtle forms of such hegemony avoid the use of brute force, relying instead on various techniques of political manipulation to ensconce in power anyone—representatives of the comprador class, for example—willing to function as a subservient ruling elite acquiescing to the perpetuation (and even intensification) of a dependency relationship. Under certain conditions, however, the metropole may assume a more direct role in deciding exactly who will govern by resorting to covert operations or open military intervention in order to topple and replace recalcitrant regimes or to prevent radical nationalists from seizing power.

One can without too much difficulty find abundant evidence of such political dependency in the history of Cuba's stormy relationship with the Colossus of the North. One of the most egregious examples is the Platt Amendment, which was inserted into the 1902 Cuban Constitution at the point of U.S. bayonets and in effect gave Washington a blank check to intervene unilaterally in the island's affairs (by means up to and including armed force). Thus began a pattern of political meddling and control on the part of the United States that would continue, in one form or another, for more than half a century. For instance, operating under Platt's aegis, Washington dispatched armed forces to Cuba in 1906 and again in 1912 to crush dissident political movements and thereby to assure the survival of regimes that were acceptable to the United States and that would protect its interests on the island.[22] Abrogation of the amendment in 1934 did not signify the end of political buccaneering on Washington's part, as many Cuban nationalists hoped it would, but rather meant a shift away from crude gunboat diplomacy relying on the direct application of naked U.S. military force (sending in the Marines) toward more sophisticated tactics that sought to strengthen friendly elements within the country to the point where they would be able to acquire and maintain control of the government. The hallmarks of this new approach were financial/economic or military/security assistance programs that often included U.S. advisors to assure that the desired political outcomes were forthcoming. Numerous examples of such machinations can be found in Fulgencio Batista's checkered career, the most controversial being the security aid Washington provided during the 1950s to help battle Cuban "subversives" (including the young Fidel Castro), aid that served to enhance considerably Batista's brutal inventory of political repression. The Fidelistas' triumph in 1959 finally broke this legacy of subservience to the United States, which had characterized relations between the two countries since the island gained its independence, although Washington would continue (unsuccessfully) to try to regain control of the situation through such desperate maneuvers as the Bay of Pigs invasion in April 1961 and various attempts to assassinate Castro.

Latin American dependency theory, as the foregoing summary suggests, is open to various interpretations.[23] Thus it is difficult to reduce it to a concise delineation that is widely accepted. Ronald Chilcote probably did as good a job as anyone, particularly in highlighting the interface involved between developmental economics and international relations: "Dependency theory focuses on the problem of foreign penetration in the political economies of Latin America. Generally, this theory explains underdevelopment throughout Latin America as a consequence of outside economic and political influence. More specifically, the economy of certain nations is believed to be conditioned by the relationship of another economy which is dominant and capable of expanding and developing. Thus the interdependence of such economies assumes contrasting forms of dominance and dependence so that dependent nations might develop as a reflection of the expansion of dominant nations or underdevelop as a consequence of their subjective relationship."[24]

While willing to accept the broad outlines of Chilcote's formulation, the more radical wing of Latin dependendistas have insisted that the "dominant nations" to which he referred must be seen as the highly industrialized *capitalist* countries, especially the United States. These observers have been inclined toward a more ideologically partisan conceptualization viewing dependency as "the process of incorporation of less developed countries (LDCs) into the global capitalist system and the 'structural distortions' resulting therefrom. . . . This approach proceeds from a structuralist paradigm which focuses on the class structure in the peripheral country, the alliance between this class structure and international capital, and the role of the state in shaping and managing the national, foreign, and class forces that propel development within countries."[25]

Drawing on these two definitions as well as the more extended discussion preceding them, the term *dependency* is used here to refer to a phenomenon entailing so pervasive an external penetration of a Third World country's economic and political processes that ultimately crucial decision-making power is acquired and exercised by outsiders. In such cases, the developing nation has lost control over certain, often important aspects of its domestic and foreign policies. This loss of control, which has sometimes been portrayed as a lack of "effective sovereignty," represents the quintessential characteristic of dependency.

Focusing upon these shifts in power is the key to understanding the patterns of exploitation that, according to the dependendistas, are the main characteristic of dependent North-South relations. The fundamental dynamic involved, they say, is nothing particularly new—power is wielded in the interests of those who have competed successfully to possess it.

42 | Cuba's Foreign Relations in a Post-Soviet World

Although not always openly acknowledged, such selfishly motivated behavior has long been accepted in the United States, the pragmatic rationale being that it is an inevitable outgrowth of egocentrism, which is seen as an ingrained trait of human nature that serves (despite its potential liabilities) as a driving force behind individual and social progress. But when applied within the context of international power configurations, these rules of the game mean that it is the metropolitan centers, the industrialized states, that benefit at the expense of the less developed nations.

Basically, then, dependency emerges as the modern manifestation of classical colonialism.[26] Granted, the specific mechanisms of penetration and control have changed, but the essence of the imperial relationship remains unaltered and can perhaps be most simply described in terms of an informal empire: "The weaker country is not ruled on a day-to-day basis by resident administrators or increasingly populated by emigrants from the advanced country, but it is nevertheless an empire. The poorer and weaker nation makes its choices within limits set, either directly or indirectly, by the more powerful society and often does so by choosing between alternatives actually formulated by the outsider."[27] It is this specter of dependency and the threat of being incorporated into someone's informal empire (e.g., Washington's) that have rendered counterdependency concerns a leitmotif underlying many of revolutionary Cuba's actions on the international stage.

Key Elements of a Counterdependency-Oriented Foreign Policy

Based on this discussion of dependency as a threat that often confronts the world's less powerful nations, a counterdependency-oriented foreign policy agenda for a small developing country such as Cuba is conceptualized here as one in which the government assigns top priority to cultivating the capacity to *prevent exogenous penetration* of its decision-making processes and thereby *reduce its vulnerability* to external power centers to the point where its sociopolitical and developmental dynamics *are not* basically the product of a subordinate relationship with a stronger industrialized country, but rather are a reflection of a series of formally or informally negotiated relationships on both horizontal (South-South) and vertical (North-South) axes.

Obviously, the key to this whole counterdependency scenario hinges upon developing the wherewithal to prevent penetration and to reduce vulnerabilities. Although other formulas might be employed, the strategy that revolutionary Cuba (and others) have tried to use to achieve these ends involves two basic stages: first, the expansion of one's available political/economic space through diversification, and second, exploiting the opportunities that diversification presents to acquire and then assertively to wield (collective) bargaining power.

Diversification: Creating Political/Economic Space

Generating political/economic space through diversification is not a particularly difficult concept to address at the theoretical level, although the actual modalities of implementation can become complex. Basically it involves nurturing a multifaceted network of developmental ties rather than simply continuing to exist within a narrow circle dominated by one industrialized power or several, the ultimate goal being to push back as far as possible the constraining socioeconomic and political boundaries within which a government such as Cuba's must operate. William Demas summarized the stakes involved for LDCs: "Our degree of economic and other forms of effective independence is likely to be increased by a much greater geographical diversification of our trade and economic relationships than is now the case. . . . This issue of geographical (and therefore geopolitical) diversification . . . is fundamental. . . . It literally increases our options and degrees of freedom and can greatly reduce our trade and economic dependence."[28]

Such a scenario does not demand that one pull back from all ties to a great power with whom a dependency relationship has existed. Rather, what is normally advocated is *selective delinkage*, which means that certain aspects of a developing nation's international transactions that once transpired solely or primarily within the context of a dependency relationship should be gradually shifted outside that framework. When such restructuring assumes vertical (North-South) dimensions, the former client will put increased emphasis on expanding its connections with a broad cross section of industrialized nations. For example, if the LDC had previously traded almost exclusively with the United States, selective delinkage could be achieved by reorienting its import-export patterns in such a way as to direct a significant piece of the current action to European Union nations or Japan. The same general rules apply when functioning on the horizontal South-South plane, the only major difference being that there are probably greater opportunities for the restructuring to take the form of integration experiments. Such collective counterdependency initiatives might also entail the creation of jointly sponsored multinational corporations, research and development institutes, or producer cartels (e.g., OPEC) designed to raise and stabilize the world market prices of the raw materials that constitute the lifeblood of many economies in the less developed world.

Diversification will not, of course, eliminate the sensitivities of smaller states such as Cuba to external influence. Indeed the very nature of the contemporary world order, which is characterized by increasing economic and other forms of functional interdependence, makes it inevitable that developing countries are going to continue to be affected by events in the larger global community. What should happen, however, is that their vulnerability to penetration and domination by foreign powers will be reduced, they hope to a significant degree, by spreading their networks of international relations over a broad spectrum, for it has long been recognized that increased isolation translates into greater susceptibility to outside control.[29] In short, diversification provides the promise of some protection to countries like Cuba that would otherwise be heavily at risk should they have to stand alone in the often Hobbesian jungle of international politics against the predatory ambitions of powerful states pursuing policies that seek to create dependency relationships.

Criticisms have been leveled against a diversification strategy from various quarters. The notion is probably most distasteful to radicals who are convinced that dependency can only be combated effectively through revolutionary change resulting in global socialism and who therefore tend to look upon diversification as little more than a cosmetic rearrangement of an already seriously flawed international order. Others, while not as ideologically motivated, have also expressed some qualms about potential liabilities. Bengt Sundelius, for instance, contends that "the price for [multilateralization] is greater interdependence with the international system as a whole. While bilateral relations can be controlled, the diffusion of ties involves broader sensitivity to world-wide developments. Thus, the possibilities for unintentional societal disturbances may be increased. The use of many partners may reduce the risk of being manipulated by other governments but may also increase the overall threat to social and economic stability and prosperity."[30]

Such caveats notwithstanding, diversification remains an integral element, both conceptually and pragmatically, in the dynamics of counterdependency politics, for once implemented it provides a much larger array of foreign policy options. The change might be likened to the difference between playing a traditional harpsichord and a modern electronic synthesizer; both instruments produce music, but the synthesizer has an infinitely wider range. And just as the synthesizer expands the available artistic space by offering more choices, so can diversification increase a developing country's political/economic space.

Although perhaps not immediately apparent, the counterdependency implications of acquiring greater political/economic space are substantial. Specifically, if a government such as Cuba's succeeds in expanding its maneuvering room, it should at this point be able to be more enterprising in configuring (or orchestrating) its foreign relations and thereby enhancing its status as an independent actor on the global stage. The logic here proceeds as follows:

- A broader scope of international linkages translates into a greater ability on the part of a developing country to construct alternative scenarios and thereby to have more possibilities in terms of the ultimate course(s) of action it will pursue.
- Flowing from this scenario is the fact that the government involved has in effect gained more decision-making power, since a key component of one's ability to perform as a decision maker is the availability of choice—the larger the number of options, the greater one's opportunity and hence capacity to make decisions.
- Finally, and in many respects most important, an increase in decision-making power suggests more control over one's destiny.

Combining all these considerations, it would certainly appear that diversification has the potential to set in motion a chain reaction that can contribute significantly to the pursuit of counterdependency politics by helping to assure that effective sovereignty (as opposed to the "formal" variety that is characteristic of a heavily penetrated, dependent political system, where the decision-making power of the indigenous authorities is more symbolic than real) is the order of the day.

Enlarging political/economic space, however, is only the initial step in the two-stage model of counterdependency politics being developed here to analyze Cuban foreign policy. Diversification and all its ramifications do not represent ends unto themselves but rather can be seen more accurately as a set of preconditions that, once satisfied, place a developing country in an optimal position to proceed to the second and more crucial phase of the counterdependency agenda—the acquisition and especially the assertive use of collective bargaining power.

Assertive Bargaining: Maximizing Counterdependency Potential

Certainly one of the most significant aspects of diversification, at least from a long-term counterdependency perspective, is the positive impact it can have on the bargaining effectiveness of smaller countries like Cuba. Game theorists and others have established that the operational dynamics of the negotiating process can become extremely complex.[31] Yet the basic rules remain fairly simple; two important ones are (a) always put yourself in a position where others are vying with one another for your goods, services, or business, and (b) always be willing and able to walk away from a prospective agreement. Considerable maneuvering room is a crucial element in both of these scenarios—serious competition will probably not occur unless one has already developed a diversified network of contacts, and abandoning a particular deal is not likely to be feasible unless there are substantial opportunities to make alternative arrangements. When, on the other hand, these prerequisites have been met, an environment conducive to the acquisition of bargaining power exists.

Bargaining power, according to James Caporaso, is "the power to control the outcome of specific events."[32] Applied to the counterdependency paradigm, it can be seen as the ability of an LDC to negotiate the terms of its relationships with others, particularly the industrialized centers of power that represent potential threats with regard to penetration and dependency. Having reduced its vulnerabilities through diversification, as is being suggested here, an LDC should find the situation rather amenable to manipulating or renegotiating its external linkages in such a manner as to produce mutually beneficial rather than zero-sum configurations. Indeed, the capacity to do this is perhaps the most critical test of whether a developing nation can legitimately be said to possess effective sovereignty.

Yet acquiring the basics of effective sovereignty and the bargaining power that comes with it is hardly a guarantee of security, developmental or otherwise, in the often cutthroat arena of international affairs, for all forms of national power are relative in nature, and hence so also is any particular country's status in the global hierarchy of nations. For example, it can be expected that an individual LDC's foreign ties will continue to be asymmetrical when operating on the North-South plane since it will almost invariably be the weaker party and therefore will not enjoy the luxury of being able to bargain from a position of relative strength. This harsh reality poses major challenges for a developing state with regard both to using its existing bargaining power in the most assertive, productive ways possible and, perhaps more important, to being creative in enlarging the pool of bargaining strength on which it can draw when dealing with the larger world community.

Foreign relations diversification is not, of course, the only factor that can contribute to a Third World government's bargaining power and thereby allow it to be a more proactive practitioner of counterdependency politics. John Ravenhill, for instance, points out that success in these pursuits can be influenced by such domestic considerations as "the mobilizable economic resources of a country. . . . In addition, it is necessary to consider political and social variables such as the skills (and thus bargaining capability) of the domestic bureaucracy and the ability of the state to impose unpopular domestic policies on relevant domestic sectors who must bear the costs involved in capital accumulation (which would involve inter alia a consideration of the coercive capacity of the domestic government, its legitimacy, and its ability to mobilize the necessary constellation of class forces)."[33]

Moving once again onto the global stage, a developing country also may occasionally possess unusual bargaining power because another state is strategically dependent on it for something (e.g., industrialized Nation A relies heavily on a particular LDC to supply a scarce natural resource required by A's defense industries).[34] In practice, however, it is rare to find such fundamental weaknesses upon which smaller countries like Cuba can capitalize. Consequently, a more realistic international approach for such a country is to try to strengthen its hand by negotiating collectively. Some forays in this direction have already been launched, the mechanisms employed ranging from regional vehicles (an example in the Western Hemisphere is the Association of Caribbean States, which was formed in July 1994 with Cuba participating as a charter member) to commodity cartels (OPEC, the International Bauxite Association) to large, multi-issue organizations with worldwide membership (the Group of 77, the Movement of Nonaligned Nations). A common problem such multilateral initiatives have had to confront is the fact that the participants have not always been able to arrive at consensus regarding their overall priorities, the result being serious susceptibility to retaliatory divide-and-conquer tactics as disgruntled members become increasingly prone to breaking ranks and making their peace separately with the more (economically) powerful nations.[35] Conversely, the benefits that many former colonies of Western European states have achieved within the Lomé framework suggest that despite its faults, collective bargaining has immense potential as a means for nations such as Cuba to make major progress in pursuing counterdependency-oriented foreign policies.[36]

A Topical Overview

As in any country, revolutionary Cuba's foreign policies have been constantly evolving in response to both internal and external stimuli. For the sake of simplicity, this process can be broken down into four major eras, roughly delineated as

48 | Cuba's Foreign Relations in a Post-Soviet World

1959–72, In the Shadow of the Superpowers;

1972–85, Beyond the Superpowers: The Halcyon Days of Cuban Globalism;

1985–92, Engulfed by the Maelstrom: Cuba and the Passing of the Cold War; and

1992 onward: Cuba Confronts the Post–Cold War Order.

The examination presented here of the dynamics of Havana's actions on the world stage as it progresses through these phases will draw upon various analytical currents, such as the realist scenario and the impact of nationalism. Overall, however, the unifying theme is the concept of counter-dependency politics already set forth.

Primary attention, chronologically speaking, is devoted to Cuba's post–Cold War foreign affairs. The central concern is to probe the survival strategies Havana has been trying to implement—for example, economic diversification and initiatives to develop collective bargaining power via South-South coalition building—to deal in a general sense with the specter of dependency that has long stalked the island and in particular to neutralize the threat to the Revolution posed by Washington's resurgent hegemonic pretensions. The first three periods are surveyed rather quickly in order to provide a broad overview of the distinctive role that Fidelista Cuba has played on the world stage by taking the road less traveled and to establish a background against which to understand the island's current international situation.

3

In the Shadows of the Superpowers, 1959–1972

The revolutionary process in any country entails two basic phases, the initial one the period of insurgents struggling to seize power and the later one involving the creation and consolidation of the new social order for which they had been fighting. Normally it is the first stage—the drama of a people rising in revolt—that captures the public imagination and gets most of the attention, but it is after the shooting has stopped that the rebels face some of their most complex challenges.

Revolutions are invariably messy, confusing affairs. They are born out of chaos as the old system disintegrates, and then they must make their way through the uncharted waters of attempting to build a new society, often making numerous miscalculations along the way. In the process they suffer an almost constant barrage of criticism, denounced both by ideological foes whose hatred is unremitting and by former supporters who have somehow lost the faith, often because unrealistically high expectations have not been fulfilled or because people do not wish to travel the political paths chosen. It was this harsh reality that confronted the Fidelistas once the immediate euphoria of their improbable victory over Batista had run its course.

One problem that quickly emerged was the dogged persistence of some elements in Cuban society in their efforts to turn back the country's political clock. Despite broad popular support for the Revolution, there were still pockets of domestic resistance. These groups were opposed primarily to those aspects of the Fidelistas' program designed to obliterate the entrenched patterns of socioeconomic maldistribution in Cuban society, from which many in the island's upper class had long benefited (see table 1.1 for prerevolutionary income distribution patterns). Such elites, along with some of their middle-class allies, were willing to accept some political reforms (e.g., eradicating the brutality and especially the corruption that characterized the Batista regime), but their material self-interest rendered unacceptable any radical transformation of the island's old socioeconomic structures. When it became clear, through such initiatives as the May 1959 agrarian reform law, that the Fidelistas were serious about revolutionizing Cuban society and that this endeavor drew at least some of its inspiration from socialist ideologies, the battle lines were drawn.[1]

This polarization produced not only ongoing internal tensions but also an exodus, mainly to Miami and South Florida, of virulent Castro-hating exiles who were fanatically committed to destroying the Revolution and who, in pursuit of that goal, would enter into a long-standing, often highly controversial alliance with the U.S. government. Indeed, beginning in the latter half of the 1980s and continuing into the 1990s, this Cuban lobby (spearheaded by the Cuban American National Foundation—CANF) came to exert what many observers felt was a stranglehold over Washington's policies toward the island. The two crown jewels in its legislative campaigns were the 1992 Torricelli Law and the 1996 Helms-Burton Law (both discussed later).

Another consideration that complicated matters somewhat during the Revolution's early years was the young age of its leadership: Fidel was barely thirty-two when the rebels seized power, Che Guevara only thirty. Such youthfulness was an asset in the sense that it contributed to the charisma surrounding Castro's 26th of July Movement, but it also meant that the Fidelistas were inexperienced in the technical complexities of running a society and especially of managing the economy of a vulnerable developing nation. Consequently there was a greater than normal probability that blunders would occur as Cuba embarked on a revolutionary sojourn unprecedented in the annals of modern Latin American history. What is surprising is not that mistakes were made—one glaring example being the ill-conceived attempt in 1970 to bring in a 10-million-ton sugar harvest, which markedly disrupted the rest of the island's economy—but rather that serious errors were relatively infrequent.

It was in the rarefied and often cutthroat arena of international politics that the Revolution confronted its greatest and most dangerous obstacle— its clash with the Colossus of the North. There is still disagreement in some quarters as to which government was primarily responsible for the confrontation when it did explode. But regardless of how intellectually stimulating such arguments may be, the key historical fact is that the confrontation was almost inevitable, given the diametrically opposed political psychologies of the parties involved.

Basically two major currents converged to shape Washington's attitudes toward revolutionary Cuba: its traditional conception of the Caribbean as its "backyard" and its Cold War worldview. Historically the

United States has adopted a domineering posture with regard to Latin America, seeing itself as the ultimate arbiter of any issue that attracts its attention. Almost from the moment of gaining its independence, the United States looked upon the entire Western Hemisphere as its particular sphere of influence and set out to establish its supremacy.[2] In general, though, the most vigorous application of this scenario has taken place in the more limited confines of Central America and the neighboring Caribbean Basin, with Cuba the island nation that has tended to attract the most attention. Two of the most famous (and controversial) examples of this hegemonic mentality can be found in the theory of Manifest Destiny and in the Roosevelt Corollary to the Monroe Doctrine. The concept of Manifest Destiny, which first became popular in the mid-1800s as a rationale for the annexation of Texas and related frontier areas, was based on the belief that God had assigned the United States the mission of spreading its democratic and Protestant ideals westward across the continent. In other words, much like the Spaniards before them, these proselytizing Yankees viewed their territorial expansion as the logical outgrowth of a divine natural law operating to have "higher civilizations" (the United States) take charge of lands inhabited by "backward peoples" (indigenous North Americans and Mexicans).[3] By the end of the nineteenth century the geographic scope of the principle had been enlarged to include the Caribbean Basin, and it incorporated mechanisms of control that went beyond crude annexation to more sophisticated sphere-of-influence politics. These attitudes were reaffirmed in the 1904 (Teddy) Roosevelt Corollary to President Monroe's famous 1823 doctrine. As had the Platt Amendment with regard to Cuba, the Roosevelt Corollary claimed an unlimited unilateral right to intervene forceably in the affairs of Latin American states, proclaiming, "If a nation shows that it knows how to act with reasonable efficiency and decency in social and political matters; if it keeps order and pays its obligations, it need fear no interference from the United States. Chronic wrongdoing, or an impotence which results in a general loosening of the ties of civilized society, may in America, as elsewhere, ultimately require intervention by some *civilized nation,* and in the Western Hemisphere the adherence of the United States to the Monroe Doctrine may force the United States, however reluctantly, in flagrant cases of such wrongdoing or impotence, to the *exercise of an international police power*" (emphasis added). Although the Roosevelt Corollary was repudiated by the U.S. government in 1928, the basic idea that the United States should play the role of hemispheric policeman remained firmly embedded in Washington's policy psyche.

The Cold War in many respects internationalized attitudes that the United States had traditionally exhibited with regard to its perceived role in the Caribbean Basin. The theoretical rationale for such activism was rooted in the Realist school of international affairs, which had become influential in U.S. foreign affairs after World War II and had popularized the idea of international relations as a zero-sum game of power politics. This realist approach, buttressed by Washington's long-standing aversion to Marxist ideology, generated a foreign policy with the basic operating principles of *bipolarity* (the United States and the Soviet Union represented the world's only significant power centers); *macrolinkage* (practically all international political and security issues were considered integral to the bipolar struggle for power and had to be handled accordingly); and vigilant *containment* of communism (any expansion of which was seen as a victory for Moscow that enhanced its position within the global balance of power and thereby increased the security threat confronting the Western camp in general and the United States in particular).[4] Given the strategic significance that Washington has historically accorded to the Western Hemisphere and especially the Caribbean Basin, these areas became prime locales for the application of the Containment Doctrine; any challenges to the status quo that were considered communist in nature or simply leftist-inspired (a broadly defined term), and especially any challenges employing violence to seize power, were equated with threats to the policy of global containment and hence to the overall balance of U.S.-Soviet power. Washington felt compelled to bring its power to bear to restore stability and pro-Western political orthodoxy and felt justified in doing so. The 1954 overthrow of the Arbenz regime in Guatemala is generally considered to have been the first major instance of U.S. Cold War interventionism in the Caribbean Basin, but revolutionary Cuba would emerge as Washington's most enduring and most frustrating target. Indeed, even after the Cold War ended in the early 1990s, Washington continued to exhibit toward Havana a mentality that is a holdover from that era.

The Cuban Revolution has, of course, embodied elements that have been and continue to be fundamentally incompatible with these central currents shaping Washington's hemispheric and at times its global foreign policies. Foremost among these attributes are the nationalistic passions deeply engrained in the island's political culture and the Fidelistas' ideological radicalism.

From its inception, Castro's 26th of July Movement embraced Cuba's tradition of uncompromising nationalism. While such sentiments have led the Fidelistas to be cautious about any outside power or entanglement that might be seen as a potential threat to the country's sovereignty, history has taught them that they need to be especially wary when dealing with Washington. Thus a central principle of their foreign policy has been their refusal to acquiesce (by word or by deed) or even to give the slightest appearance of acquiescing to the idea that Cuba falls within the U.S. sphere of influence and must consequently defer to Washington's wishes and leadership. Any concession to this "backyard mentality" invites the resuscitation of an outmoded hemispheric order within which they will be relegated to the harsh dictates of a dependency relationship, as had been Cuba's lot for many years in the prerevolutionary period. Such counterdependency impulses, which to Cuban nationalists are fully understandable and completely justified, have often been interpreted in the United States as evidence of some sort of irrational anti-Americanism.[5] The result has been the creation of a climate that has served to reinforce Washington's hostility and that has therefore considerably enhanced the potential for confrontation between the two governments.

While nationalism represents a constant complicating factor in the dynamics of relations between the United States and Cuba, the issue of ideological radicalism is sui generis to the Fidelista period. There has been some controversy as to whether the philosophical orientation of the Revolution, especially as exemplified by Castro, was Marxist from the beginning. But whatever position one might take in this debate, there can be little doubt that the Fidelista mainstream was, at the very least, composed of idealistic socialists deeply committed to a program of reform that sought to create a more egalitarian society on the island. The key to this undertaking was to destroy the existing patterns of socioeconomic maldistribution that were rooted in the fabric of pre-revolutionary Cuba. Fidelista strategy in this campaign typically involved nationalization of a particular enterprise or even a whole sector of the economy, followed by a transfer of ownership either to a workers' cooperative or to the state itself, the latter option becoming standard operating procedure as the Revolution became increasingly radicalized. The problem on the international front was that Washington loathed these redistributive policies on both pragmatic and ideological grounds.

In terms of pure utilitarian Yankee self-interest, the radical reforms that Castro's government was implementing were unacceptable because their targets were often U.S. businesses or economic interests, which watched their assets in Cuba being seized by the new regime. Despite the fact that nationalization is absolutely permissible under international law (as long as "adequate compensation" is paid for the property involved), the United

54 | Cuba's Foreign Relations in a Post-Soviet World

States has traditionally been hostile toward the idea. The situation was further inflamed in the Cuban case because Havana refused to go along with the amounts that U.S. claimants were demanding for the reimbursement legally due them.[6] Hence, the United States insisted that Havana was engaging not in legitimate nationalization but rather in illegal expropriation.

The ideological factor, however, probably carried more weight in Washington's eyes, which saw Havana's actions as an assault on private property and, more important, on the sanctity of the capitalist model, from which flow the most cherished principles of U.S. thinking about economics and politics as well as convictions about the superiority of American society and culture. In the context of the times, such heresy was considered irrefutable evidence that revolutionary Cuba had embraced Marxism and therefore had given its allegiance to the Soviet camp in the global struggle for power. The Cold War logic driving this analysis revolved around the idea that communism was a tightly organized international movement controlled for the most part by the USSR. In other words, it was thought that Moscow set the strategic agenda that would then be carried out by communists and "fellow travelers" throughout the world. Implicit in this scenario was the notion that involvement in and loyalty to a Soviet-dominated movement precluded radical leftists like the Fidelistas from behaving in a truly independent fashion. Concerns or initiatives on their part were not seen as being motivated by legitimate nationalistic considerations but rather as deriving from the exigencies of international communism, and any concession to them would be the functional equivalent of a victory for the Kremlin in its struggle to weaken and ultimately to triumph over the Western world.

The convergence of all these factors strongly affected relations between the United States and revolutionary Cuba from the beginning, making a confrontation seem inevitable. Washington had already vividly demonstrated by its 1954 overthrow of the Arbenz regime in Guatemala that it would not hesitate to take strong measures against Latin governments that challenged its traditional hegemony, especially if they could be delegitimized on the basis of alleged pro-Soviet Cold War sympathies. The Fidelistas, on the other hand, were driven by both counterdependency and philosophical considerations that made them determined to pursue their own path irrespective of the disapproval or demands emanating from the Colossus of the North.

The clash that ensued meant that Cuba would, in effect, have to continue to operate in the shadow of the United States, although now it was playing the role of an antagonist rather than that of a docile client state. Following this course, however, was fraught with danger, for Washington's hostility posed a threat to the very survival of the Revolution. As events would later prove, the United States had at its disposal a daunting range of options, including assassination, economic warfare, and even armed intervention. At the heart of the dilemma confronting Havana was the harsh reality that it was lacking the resources necessary to be able to deal effectively with such a challenge on its own. Cuba's response was to turn to the Soviet Union for developmental and military assistance, for this seemed to be the only way to prevent Washington from reasserting its traditional domination. Yet Cuba would do so gingerly, not wanting simply to trade one dependency for another.

During this early period, then, the superpowers cast a long shadow over Cuba's foreign affairs agenda as it concentrated on managing the exploding confrontation with Washington while simultaneously trying to work out a relationship with Moscow that would contribute to the Revolution's security without sacrificing its independence. This delicate and often tumultuous balancing act monopolized much of Havana's attention as it sought to embark on an international odyssey never attempted by any other Latin American nation.

The U.S.-Cuban Confrontation Develops, 1959–1962

Latent Tensions

Although perhaps not readily apparent to the casual observer, relations between Washington and Castro's 26th of July Movement were strained even before the Fidelistas came to power. For many years, the United States had maintained highly cordial relations with the Batista regime, providing in the process rather substantial amounts of military aid, which was used against the rebel forces. But as it became increasingly evident that Batista's days were numbered, Washington reassessed its position and decided it would be prudent to begin to distance itself from its former client. This change of heart was most graphically symbolized in the announcement by the Eisenhower administration in March 1958 that it was suspending arms shipments to Batista (although U.S. military advisors did continue to work with Havana's armed forces).

While such gestures did serve to weaken Batista's position, they certainly were not designed to facilitate a Castroite victory. Indeed, the opposite was the case, as illustrated by the following excerpt from a memo to the White House written by Secretary of State Christian Herter in December 1958: "The Department [of State] clearly does not want to see Castro succeed to the leadership of the Government. We are therefore seeking, by all means short of outright intervention, to bring about a political solution in Cuba that will keep the Castro movement from power."[7] In essence, then, Washington was pursuing a strategy that became fairly common during the Cold War years—abandoning right-wing regimes that had become unviable in the hope that arrangements could be made for a successor acceptable to the United States. In Cuba's case, the United States tried to use its influence to assure that power would be transferred to a military junta with credentials that were both anti-Batista and anti-Fidelista. Understandably, such machinations did not endear Washington to the rebels who were to shortly take control of the island.

A Brief Interlude

Immediately after Castro came to power there was a short period during which both sides engaged in what might be termed a suspicious flirtation; clearly neither party was comfortable with the other, but each nevertheless seemed willing to explore the conceivable positives rather than accentuate the obvious negatives in their relationship. Accordingly Washington extended official diplomatic recognition to the new regime on January 7, 1959. Moreover, the U.S. ambassador, Earl Smith, who was perceived by the Fidelistas as being too closely linked to Batista, quickly resigned and was replaced by career diplomat Philip Bonsal, who in theory was better positioned to establish decent rapport with the new authorities in Havana.

Those who thought or hoped that increased cordiality was possible were encouraged when Castro accepted an invitation to visit Washington in April 1959 to make a speech to the Association of Newspaper Editors. Prior to the trip there were indications that the Cubans were interested in negotiating an economic aid agreement with the United States, a prospect that, if finalized, had the potential to serve as the foundation for an ongoing close association. Washington generally seemed amenable to the idea of working out such a package, although President Eisenhower refused to meet personally with Fidel to discuss the matter, and some elements in the administration, especially the Treasury Department, seemed inclined to demand hard-line policy concessions that Havana was unlikely to make (e.g., guarantees that foreign capital would play a major role in the Revolution's developmental plans). In any case, when Fidel and his high-powered delegation finally arrived, it quickly became apparent that they had abandoned their earlier position and were no longer inclined to pursue the aid question. Although both sides allowed this demonstration of their mutual wariness to pass without public or even private recriminations, the reality was that the political atmosphere had fundamentally changed and that tensions between the two governments were rising.

The Relationship Deteriorates

Certainly one development that triggered Cold War alarm bells in Washington was Castro's decision to explore the possible benefits (especially in the economic realm) of closer, more cooperative ties with the Soviet Union. As noted, this process began gingerly, particularly on the part of the USSR, since the Kremlin knew little about the rebels who had seized control in Havana and was highly skeptical of their socialist credentials. The Russians' qualms were reinforced by the fact that the orthodox, pro-Moscow Communist Party in Cuba had not supported Castro's 26th of July Movement and therefore had not played a central role either in the anti-Batista insurrection or in the revolutionary government that emerged from the struggle. Nevertheless, after some preliminary unofficial talks between Castro and a Russian journalist in the fall of 1959, events began to move quickly. In late 1959 Moscow accepted Fidel's suggestion that Soviet Deputy Prime Minister Anastas Mikoyan pay an official visit to the island in early 1960. Then, with Castro strongly promoting the idea, the Soviets expanded the economic relationship that they had initiated with two purchases of Cuban sugar (in August and September of 1959) by signing a trade agreement in January 1960. These events, however, were quickly overshadowed by the Cuban-Moscow connection forged during Mikoyan's trip.

The deputy prime minister arrived on February 4, 1960, for a whirlwind visit of approximately two weeks. The highlight was the announcement that a major economic accord had been reached, its main provisions being that the USSR agreed to (a) provide Havana with a credit line of $100 million (U.S.) to finance the purchase of Soviet goods and to support various developmental projects; (b) buy at current world market prices 425,000 tons of Cuban sugar in 1960 and 1 million tons per year from 1961 to 1965; and (c) sell oil to Havana at less than the going world rate.[8] Such arrangements, combined with others that would come later, would ultimately prove crucial to the Revolution's survival, for they gave Havana the wherewithal to withstand the economic warfare waged against it by Washington.

Juxtaposed against these cooperative links that Havana was developing with the Kremlin was an emerging pattern of increased bickering and mini-confrontations with Washington. Typically these feuds broke out when Castro's government began to implement various radical reforms viewed as too left-wing by Washington, which would then respond with some kind of retaliatory measures. The first major episode of this drama erupted in May 1959 when the Fidelistas unveiled their agrarian reform law, calling for governmental expropriation of the larger landholdings in the country. Although most owners of the great estates affected (mainly cattle ranches) were Cuban nationals, some U.S.-owned assets were involved. While never enthusiastic about "socialist experimentation" and concerned that this law represented just the first step in a larger Fidelista assault on private property and foreign—that is, U.S.—investment, Washington was willing to concede that Havana had the right to implement nationalization policies. It did, however, insist that any U.S. owners involved receive prompt and full compensation. But Cuba, its treasury seriously depleted by the pre-1959 civil war and by Batista's endemic corruption, was willing to offer only long-term government bonds, an option the United States considered unacceptable. Thus arose a major controversy over compensation, which triggered the worst suspicions that Washington harbored about the Castro government. No longer were the Fidelistas seen as reformers (perhaps misguided) who were engaged in somewhat distasteful but nevertheless legal nationalizations. Instead, they were increasingly perceived as radical "loose cannons" that had to be reined in before they spun out of control.

To demonstrate its growing displeasure with Castro and to bring pressure on him to conform with its policy preferences, the United States would turn to one of its most powerful economic weapons—the sugar quota. Sugar had long been and was still the mainstay of the island's economy; without the revenue earned from its sugar exports, Cuba faced the prospect of an economic disaster. A key element of this sugar-based economy was the U.S. quota system, which revolved around legislation guaranteeing certain foreign producers, including Cuba, a share of the lucrative North American market. In other words, the quota assured Havana of a captive market, year after year, for its sugar exports—in essence, an umbilical cord that based the well-being of the island's economy on its relations with its northern neighbor.[9]

Having toyed with the idea for several months, President Eisenhower finally made his move in March 1960, sending a message to Congress requesting that he be authorized to reduce the sugar quota of any country whenever he felt that national security considerations merited such action. Although Cuba was not specifically named in this action, everyone understood that revolutionary Havana was the intended target. Initially the powerful House Agricultural Committee was reluctant to agree, primarily because it was uncomfortable with the unrestricted scope (the power to adjust the quota for any country) of the White House's request. Ultimately, a compromise was reached whereby the committee agreed to grant the president discretionary authority to reduce Cuba's quota. On June 27, 1960, an amendment to this effect was attached to the Sugar Act that was pending in Congress.

As this drama was unfolding in Washington, increasingly tense U.S.-Cuban relations were further complicated by a confrontation over petroleum. On June 28, 1960, Havana sent a large shipment of Soviet crude oil that it had recently purchased to a U.S.-owned Texaco refinery on the island for processing. When the refinery refused, for both financial and ideological reasons, to accept the Russian oil, the Cuban government retaliated by seizing the plant. A few days later there was a repeat performance: with Washington encouraging the companies to take a hard line, a refinery owned by Standard Oil and a British one owned by Shell followed Texaco's lead and were likewise taken over on July 1.

This tit-for-tat scenario plunged forward with blinding speed, the first move occurring on July 3 when Congress passed the 1960 Sugar Act with the provision that gave the White House a free hand to determine the Cuban quota. Two days later, on July 5, Havana tried to match this expansion of Eisenhower's power by announcing that Castro's government had been given discretionary authority to expropriate any U.S.-owned property on the island. The next day President Eisenhower played the sugar card: he reduced whatever was left of Cuba's 1960 quota by 95 percent. Fortunately for Havana, the USSR stepped in to soften the blow by pledging on July 9 that it would purchase any sugar Cuba could not sell because of the U.S. boycott.

The stage having been set for a confrontation by these developments, the final act was not long in coming. Over the next few months (August–November 1960), as summarized by Jorge Domínguez, Havana upped the ante in this high-stakes political game by playing its expropriation card: "On August 7 the large U.S.-owned industrial and agrarian enterprises were actually socialized, and on September 17 all United States banks. . . . On October 24 Cuba socialized all U.S.-owned wholesale and retail trade enterprises and the remaining smaller industrial and agrarian enterprises."[10]

Perhaps even more unpalatable to Washington than such nationalizations was the military relationship that was developing between Moscow and Havana. Discussions between the two parties about possible arms

60 | Cuba's Foreign Relations in a Post-Soviet World

purchases and military aid programs had been taking place for several months, but in September 1960 actions replaced words as the first Soviet tanks arrived on the island. They would be followed over the next few months by artillery and other equipment as well as Russian military advisors. Meanwhile the White House was escalating the situation by first choking off the flow of almost all U.S. exports to the island and then announcing in December 1960 that no Cuban sugar would be allowed to enter the U.S. market in 1961; the quota was now zero.[11] Finally, on January 3, 1961, after Cuba had forced the United States to reduce drastically the size of its embassy staff in Havana, Washington severed all formal diplomatic and consular relations with Castro's government.

The Confrontation Explodes: The Bay of Pigs and Its Aftermath

While the falling out between Washington and Havana was a serious foreign policy matter, the process appeared to the general public to be playing itself out in a fairly normal manner. Behind the scenes, however, the atmosphere had for some time been turning increasingly nasty. The Fidelistas had hardly settled down in Havana before the United States began to ponder the possibility of resorting to much stronger means of dealing with them. Such sentiment was illustrated in March 1959 by a CIA proposal sent to the White House with the National Security Council's endorsement; among other things, the document suggested that a covert exile military force be created for possible future deployment on the island. In December the same year, CIA Director Allen Dulles approved a memorandum calling for the agency to explore its options with regard to "eliminating" (assassinating) Castro.[12] But such contingency plans were held in abeyance while Washington concentrated on firming up the political groundwork for a confrontation.

Within the Western Hemisphere, Washington's main initiatives to discredit and isolate the Fidelistas diplomatically, thereby rendering them more vulnerable to retaliatory action, focused on the Organization of American States (OAS). The Eisenhower administration understood that many Latin American governments were not anxious to be drawn into the U.S.-Cuban conflict, seeing it as a bilateral dispute rather than a situation that needed to be addressed by the regional community as a whole. Washington, however, recognizing that the underlying dynamics were moving toward some kind of forceful action on its part, wanted to create at least the appearance of prior hemispheric acquiescence to an anti-Fidelista position. At an August 1960 meeting of OAS foreign ministers in San José, Costa Rica, the United States was able to mobilize unanimous support for a declaration that, among other things, condemned any intervention or threat thereof, even if only conditional, by any outside power into the affairs of hemispheric states; denounced acceptance by any hemispheric government of the interventionist threats mentioned, labeling such action as a danger to hemispheric security; and reaffirmed that any form of totalitarianism was incompatible with the norms of the inter-American system.[13]

Although neither Cuba nor the USSR was specifically named in the document, everyone understood that these provisions were aimed at Havana and its evolving relationship with Moscow. So, despite the fact that Washington did not get the unequivocal repudiation of the Fidelistas that it would have preferred, it did nevertheless score heavily in the sense that the San José Declaration established a framework for portraying Havana and its policies and actions as a threat to hemispheric security. Over the years Washington would repeatedly employ this theme as a rationale for various anti-Cuban maneuvers.

The denouement of this whole chain of events was the Bay of Pigs invasion. The Eisenhower administration, encouraged by the easy success that it had experienced in 1954 in overthrowing Guatemala's Arbenz government with a CIA exile army, decided to employ essentially the same strategy against the Fidelistas. Anti-Castro Cubans were recruited, equipped, and trained by CIA overseers. By the time John Kennedy entered the White House in early 1961, the exile brigades were in their camps, primarily in Guatemala and Nicaragua, ready and anxious for deployment. The new president—reluctant to derail an operation that already had substantial momentum behind it and having in any case already embraced an intransigent anti-Castro line during the election campaign—opted to proceed with the plan. Central to its success was the assumption, based on CIA intelligence reports, that there was widespread anti-Castro sentiment in Cuba that would crystallize into mass rebellion once an exile landing had provided the necessary spark.

Havana was not sitting idly by as the storm brewed. It had managed to infiltrate the anti-Castro exile community heavily and was well aware that some kind of attack was in the works. Confirming these suspicions was an article that Tad Szulc had published in the *New York Times* on April 7, 1961, stating that an invasion was imminent.

Events came to a head on April 15. A CIA-orchestrated air strike was launched against strategic targets on the island, mainly airfields. Recognizing that the situation with Washington was now irreparable, and apparently hoping (in vain, as it turned out) that he might be able to get a commitment from the Kremlin to help defend the country if regular U.S. forces joined the assault, Castro publicly declared on April 16 for the first time that the Cuban Revolution was indeed socialist in nature. The next day, the exile invasion force hit the beaches at the secluded Bay of Pigs on Cuba's southern coast.

The whole affair quickly turned into a fiasco for Washington. Castro's forces, with Fidel assuming direct field command, quickly and effectively counterattacked, destroying the exiles' supply ships and pinning the intruders down on the meager strips of sand that they had seized. The larger uprising that the CIA had so confidently predicted never occurred; indeed, to the contrary, the Cuban masses rallied strongly behind the revolutionary government. With the situation on the ground unraveling badly, the Kennedy administration decided not to get more deeply involved. Specifically, the president refused to order U.S. combat units (especially the Air Force) into action to bail out the floundering operation. Within seventy-two hours (by April 17) the fighting was over, more than 1,400 of the invaders were prisoners of war, and Fidel's reputation as the Caribbean David who could outwit and frustrate the Yankee Goliath had been spectacularly launched.

Subsequently Castro would further infuriate Washington by proclaiming in December 1961 that he was a devout Marxist-Leninist and would remain so until the day he died. In the realm of foreign affairs, this radicalization of both the Revolution and its leader would be manifested most dramatically by Havana's growing proclivity to embrace guerrilla warfare as the primary tool to achieve the goals of its larger internationalist policies.

Revolutionary Internationalism and the Superpowers, 1962–1968

The ideological roots of the concept of revolutionary (or proletarian) internationalism reach back to Marx's famous call for unity among the workers of the world in the inevitable class warfare that he foresaw. His logic was straightforward: he viewed existing political boundaries as artifices that functioned to weaken the dispossessed masses by separating them into more manageable smaller units (the classic divide and conquer tactic), and he therefore concluded that victory in the struggle to achieve egalitarian social justice throughout the world demanded solidarity among all those truly committed to the cause. In other words, genuine revolutionaries had to be willing to join the fray whenever, wherever, and however their assistance was needed.[14] Perhaps the most vivid example of attempts to put this maxim into practice can be found in the experiences of the international brigades that fought in the Spanish Civil War during the 1930s.[15]

The Fidelistas began to dabble in the esoteric underworld of internationalist expeditions long before Castro formally proclaimed the Marxist nature of the Revolution. In 1959 they were allegedly deeply involved in launching guerrilla strikes aimed at the governments of Panama, Nicaragua, the Dominican Republic, and Haiti. Although it denied any complicity in the first two operations, Cuba's support for the two remaining campaigns was hardly a secret and indeed was eventually acknowledged by Havana. In the Dominican case a small rebel band, apparently trying to implement a strategy that was almost a carbon copy of the experience of the 26th of July Movement, infiltrated the country in June 1959. The effort failed miserably; the two landing sites were quickly overrun by government forces, with practically all the guerrillas being killed or captured. A similar fate befell a September 1959 expedition (which reportedly included Cuban combatants and was said to have had Che Guevara's personal sponsorship) against the Duvalier dictatorship in Haiti.[16]

It is tempting to interpret these exploits as evidence of a newfound Marxist-oriented militancy in Cuban foreign policy, but Havana was not doing anything particularly unusual since joint ventures to overthrow the region's worst tyrannical dynasties (the Somozas, Duvaliers, and Trujillos) had long enjoyed an aura of legitimacy. Highlighting this legacy was the formation in the late 1940s of the Caribbean Legion, a multinational unit formed by private individuals for the express purpose of attacking and destroying dictatorial regimes throughout the basin.[17] Among the legion's well-known participants, who helped to establish its credentials as a group of moderate democrats rather than wild-eyed leftist radicals, were José Figueres and Rómulo Betancourt, who later would be elected presidents of Costa Rica and Venezuela, respectively.

Whatever willingness to accept such activities by Cuba this tradition might have engendered in the late 1950s tended to dissipate in the early 1960s. Caribbean and other Latin American governments became less and less tolerant of Fidelista radicalism at both the domestic and international levels, sometimes because they had genuine qualms about the leftward drift of the Revolution and in other instances because they came under heavy U.S. pressure to adopt an anti-Cuban stance. Havana found itself confronting the specter of growing diplomatic and economic isolation within the Western Hemisphere.

The OAS quickly became the main arena in which Washington waged its anti-Fidelista campaign following the Bay of Pigs debacle, the primary U.S. goal being collective endorsement of its contention that revolutionary Cuba was an outlaw state that had to be treated as a pariah by the hemispheric community. This effort shifted into full gear in mid-1961 as the Kennedy administration dispatched various emissaries (e.g., UN Ambassador Adlai Stevenson) to lobby Latin governments for their support. Although there was still considerable reluctance to be drawn into the fray, Washington finally managed to get agreement for an OAS meeting to consider Cuba's status in the organization. Thus the Eighth Meeting of Consultation of Foreign Ministers of the OAS convened in Puente del Este, Uruguay, on January 22, 1962. The U.S. delegation arrived with specific orders from President Kennedy: oust Havana from the OAS! The key provisions of the resolution that was ultimately passed were as follows:

- Adherence by any member of the Organization of American States to Marxism-Leninism is incompatible with the inter-American system, and the alignment of such a government with the communist bloc breaks the unity and solidarity of the hemisphere.

- The present government of Cuba, which has officially identified itself as a Marxist-Leninist government, is incompatible with the principles and objectives of the inter-American system.

- This incompatibility excludes the present government of Cuba from participation in the inter-American system.[18]

Even while bringing heavy pressure to bear on various governments by making it clear that there would likely be a relationship between their votes at Puente del Este and the future availability of economic aid (via the Alliance for Progress and other programs), Washington did not get everything it wanted. In particular, it could not muster sufficient backing for a comprehensive package of economic sanctions against Cuba. It did, however, achieve its main goal—Castro's government was officially expelled from the OAS in mid-February 1962.

Despite some shortfalls, the U.S. had made major gains at the conference. Most important, it had succeeded in delegitimizing (at least by OAS standards) the revolutionary government in Havana and had thus orchestrated a situation in which its anti-Cuban offensive could be wrapped in a mantle of collective respectability with the claim that it was justified in light of the Puente del Este resolution. Having laid this groundwork, Washington in effect declared economic war on Cuba, announcing on February 7, 1962, that it was imposing its own trade embargo banning all U.S. exports to and imports from the island. Later the prohibitions of this blockade would be expanded to cover practically any economic activity that might conceivably be beneficial to Cuba, one major casualty being the highly lucrative flow of Yankee tourists. Attempts would also be made to globalize the blockade by persuading or coercing other nations to participate.[19] Such efforts finally paid dividends with respect to the previously recalcitrant OAS when, after concluding that Cuba had supplied some arms to guerrillas seeking to overthrow the Venezuelan government, all members except Mexico severed diplomatic relations with Havana and imposed their own comprehensive economic sanctions in July 1964.[20]

At this point, Havana's always simmering sensitivities about U.S. intentions had been inflamed by the cumulative impact of events over the past two years, crowned by the anti-Cuban vote in the OAS and the steps Washington took immediately thereafter to tighten its economic noose around the island. As noted, the United States had initially resorted to such extreme measures as an exile invasion and assassination plots in its efforts to drive Castro and his government from power. Now the strategy was shifting to a more subtle approach that emphasized efforts to block Cuba's ties—diplomatic and especially economic—to both the hemispheric and larger global communities, in the hope of an extended quarantine generating strains that would seriously destabilize the Revolution and lead to its demise. This new policy operated on the premise that a government's survival potential decreased as its international isolation increased. Havana was fully aware of the subversive logic involved. Thus, from its viewpoint, a threat to the Revolution's survival, along with the prospect of another chapter in the island's long history of dependency relationships with the United States, still loomed. The Fidelistas' most dramatic response was a call to the revolutionary barricades, especially in Latin America.

The vehicle announcing this shift to radical activism was the Second Declaration of Havana (February 4, 1962), which Castro issued immediately following the OAS decision to ban Cuban participation in the organization. Drawing on the tradition of the anticolonial wars of liberation waged by Simon Bolívar and José Martí, Fidel eloquently argued that it was once again necessary for the Latin American masses, who had been betrayed by governments that were little more than Yankee puppets, to join together in armed struggle—this time to free themselves from U.S. hegemony and exploitation. No hemispheric people, he said,

is weak—because each forms a part of a family of 200 million brothers, who suffer the same miseries, who harbor the same sentiments,

66 | Cuba's Foreign Relations in a Post-Soviet World

who have the same enemy, who dream about the same better future and who count on the solidarity of all honest men and women throughout the world.

Great as was the epic of Latin American Independence, heroic as was the struggle, today's generation of Latin Americans is called upon to engage in an epic which is even greater and more decisive for humanity. For that struggle was for the liberation from Spanish colonial power, from a decadent Spain invaded by the armies of Napoleon. Today the call for struggle is for liberation from the most powerful world imperialist center, from the strongest force of world imperialism and to render humanity a greater service than that rendered by our predecessors.[21]

Cubans, Castro indicated, would provide whatever support they could to this crusade, proclaiming that it was their obligation to do so because, in his famous phrase, "the duty of every revolutionary is to make the revolution."

As indicated, the Fidelistas' greatest hopes were focused on Latin America, where it was felt that conditions were especially favorable. As they looked about the Caribbean and surveyed the mainland from the Sierra de las Minas in Guatemala to Cape Horn, they found case after case in which the proper objective conditions for successful insurrection seemed to be present. What was needed to speed up the process, they thought, was a catalyst to unify the masses and galvanize them into action. Drawing on their own experiences in battling the Batista regime, they believed that small armed bands operating primarily in the countryside could provide this spark. Thus the cult of the Fidelista guerrilla was born, and the keystone of Havana's hemispheric policies became its ties to like-minded radicals dedicated to using violence to seize power.

Although Latin American affairs dominated Havana's internationalist agenda between 1962 and 1968, Cuba unobtrusively began developing a presence in Africa that would later become one of the centerpieces of its drive for Third World leadership. This saga started in 1963 when Havana sent advisors and a small contingent of combat troops to Algeria to help Ahmed Ben Bella's radical socialist government in its border dispute with Morocco. A cease-fire was signed before these forces became involved in any fighting and they were withdrawn shortly thereafter, but the fact that they were dispatched in the first place indicated that Cuba was indeed beginning to adopt a more ambitious conceptualization of its international role. At this time Havana also became involved in supporting various African national liberation movements, especially those struggling against Portuguese colonialism in Angola and Mozambique. Later it would take the unusual step for a small developing country of setting up formal government-to-government military aid missions in Congo-Brazzaville (1965) and Guinea (1966). Thus the seeds of Cuban Third World globalism that would bloom in Angola in 1975 were quietly planted in Africa during the 1960s.

Revolutionary messianics were undoubtedly an important element behind this decision on Havana's part to try to assume a vanguard role in promoting proletarian internationalism. But there were likewise key strategic and counterdependency considerations involved. The Fidelistas were highly attuned to the fact that the success of Washington's isolation policy placed them in an exposed position that was potentially dangerous. Proletarian internationalism, particularly in Latin America, was embraced in part as a possible antidote to this perceived threat of Yankee hegemonic pretensions. The assumption was that a rash of insurgencies on Washington's southern flank would inevitably trigger its Cold War obsession with containing the spread of leftist ideologies and movements. Consequently, if it rose to the bait and tried to respond to multiple challenges, the U.S. would no longer be able to focus all or even most of its counter-revolutionary attention on Cuba—the strategy of Che Guevara's exhortation to create "two, three, many Vietnams." Indeed some were so optimistic as to foresee rebel victories that would produce radical, highly nationalistic governments willing to ally themselves with Havana in fighting the threat of dependency posed by U.S. policy. Ultimately, however, this scenario would unravel as, one after another, the Latin American guerrilla offensives of the 1960s were smashed.

The impact on its superpower relations of Havana's commitment to revolutionary internationalism was not limited to its dealings with the United States, although here it certainly generated rather spectacular political theater as the melodrama of romantic pro-Castro guerrillas confronting the might of the Yankee Colossus played itself out in the mountains and jungles of Latin America. Less sensational but equally significant was the role that Fidelista radicalism played in the complex process of evolving Cuban-Soviet ties during the turbulent 1960s.

The intensification and apparent irreversibility of U.S.-Cuban hostility that emerged after the Bay of Pigs helped to create an environment in which both Havana and Moscow were inclined to explore the possibilities of deepening the patterns of cooperation between them that had already been established. Although it would probably be too simplistic to portray

Havana's motives for pursuing this path in terms of a single-factor analysis, its main incentive was quite obvious—Soviet bloc assistance would markedly enhance the ability of the Revolution to assure its military and economic security against the threats to its survival emanating from Washington. The Kremlin, on the other hand, saw the situation as a Cold War opportunity to capitalize on the anti-Americanism that had long been part of the island's political culture and thereby to establish a pro-Moscow outpost on the very doorstep of the United States. These favorable preconditions did not necessarily translate into a smooth courtship, however. Instead, the Moscow-Havana axis developed quite cautiously in some respects.

The most orderly progress occurred in such economic areas as trade, as illustrated in table 3.1, where the data indicate an overall growth rate of almost 7,300 percent during the first ten years of the Revolution. Supplementing this burgeoning trade relationship were the various economic and military aid programs that Moscow instituted. But the reservoir of goodwill that such camaraderie produced was not sufficient to forestall the emergence of suspicions and some nasty arguments in other areas.

Indeed, the Soviets had serious concerns about the Cuban Revolution from the beginning, the main one centering on what they felt to be a lack of commitment to orthodox Soviet-style Marxism on Havana's part, combined with a tendency to take unnecessary foreign policy risks (especially when dealing with Washington). The Fidelistas were likewise circumspect in moving toward the USSR, restrained by their fears of simply trading Yankee for Soviet dependency and uncertain about the depth of the Kremlin's commitment to defending the Cuban Revolution. Ultimately these currents converged to produce a bitter quarrel over the question of armed struggle in Latin America, with Havana seeking to assume independent leadership of the hemisphere's leftist movements by promoting its model of guerrilla warfare as the most appropriate strategy for them to use in seizing power. But as often occurs in such situations, one had to look beyond the immediate dispute to appreciate fully what was driving the participants. In this case it was the survival instincts of a small country— highly nationalistic and dependency adverse—trying to make the transition from the shadow of one superpower to engagement with another without sacrificing its security or its freedom of action.

The roots of this Cuban-Soviet dispute can be traced to Havana's growing frustration over its inability to obtain a definitive commitment from Moscow to use Soviet military power to defend the island from an external—that is, a U.S.—attack. The watershed event was the October 1962

Table 3.1. Cuban trade with the USSR, 1959–68 (in millions of pesos)

Year	Exports to USSR	Imports from USSR	Total
1959	13	-	13
1960	103	80	183
1961	304	263	567
1962	221	411	632
1963	164	461	625
1964	275	410	685
1965	322	428	750
1966	274	521	795
1967	367	582	949
1968	290	671	961

Source: José Luis Rodríguez, "The Economic Relations Cuba-USSR, 1960–1985," *World Economic Affairs,* no. 17 (1986), 20. This journal is published by the Center for the Study of the World Economy (CIEM) in Havana, Cuba.

Cuban Missile Crisis. The Fidelistas viewed the presence of Soviet missiles (the medium-range variety, capable of carrying nuclear warheads), along with the personnel and equipment necessary to maintain and protect the missile installations, as a crucial security resource. They served a crucial deterrent function, Havana felt, at both the practical and the symbolic levels. In a purely military sense, they were seen as providing the Revolution with a retaliatory capability that would serve to counterbalance any U.S. inclination to mount a direct military attack on the island (an idea that was seriously considered, but ultimately discarded, during the Bay of Pigs confrontation).[22] Psychologically the Soviet presence could be seen in a light similar to that associated with the deployment of U.S. troops in Western European countries—as evidence of the superpower's firm commitment to defending its friends against any external threat. It was therefore a terrible shock to the Cubans when Moscow negotiated a settlement to the Missile Crisis without including them in the process or even informing them about what was occurring. Indeed it was reported that the Cuban leadership knew nothing about the U.S.-Soviet agreement to end the confrontation until they read the news about it in wire service dispatches.[23]

The trauma produced in Cuban circles by the manner in which the Missile Crisis negotiations were handled was compounded by misgivings about Moscow's flirtation with the concept of peaceful coexistence with the United States. In general, says William LeoGrande, the notion made little sense to the Cubans in light of what they saw as Washington's ready inclination to resort to force in dealing with radical Third World regimes, with the growing conflict in Southeast Asia serving to reinforce Havana's skepticism. Not only, he suggests, "did peaceful coexistence seem unjustified [to the Fidelistas], but the USSR's dogged pursuit of it despite U.S. escalation in Vietnam deeply worried Cuba. If the U.S. was willing to expend such efforts in far-off Vietnam, would it not turn its military might on Cuba next? Could the USSR be relied on to defend Cuba at the expense of peaceful coexistence?"[24] With regard to the latter query, the consensus in Havana was an increasingly uncomfortable "no" that generated serious doubts about the USSR's trustworthiness as a potential ally.

From the Kremlin's perspective, of course, it made little sense to pursue adventures in Cuba (or elsewhere in the Third World) that might endanger its efforts to put its relations with the Western camp on a more even keel. Thus, while it clearly wanted closer, more cooperative relations with the Fidelistas, it was not willing in the process to do anything that would put its centerpiece Cold War policy of peaceful coexistence at risk. The Missile Crisis provided graphic evidence of exactly what Moscow's priorities were as it tried to juggle these two items on its international agenda. Initially it was willing to extend Havana the significant military aid of nuclear-capable ballistic missiles in order to help solidify the relationship, but, ultimately, the Kremlin chose to sacrifice its Cuban position (and concurrently the Fidelistas' confidence) to the exigencies of stabilizing superpower relations.

Throughout much of the 1960s, then, what appeared to many casual observers as a budding congenial partnership between Moscow and Havana was in reality a complicated situation with serious tensions roiling beneath the surface. Particularly from 1962 to 1964, the Fidelistas pushed the Kremlin to throw its support behind the Cuban Revolution, which in fact the Russians did in the economic realm. Moscow, however, was extremely reluctant to take any action that implied an open-ended political or security commitment since it felt that the firebrands in Havana often were too reckless when dealing with Washington. Moreover, Moscow seemed to think that the Cubans were somewhat "immature" as revolutionaries; they were seen as trying to do too much too fast, both at home and abroad, in their efforts to promote what the more staid Bolsheviks felt was an unrealistic brand of tropical socialism. These pressures finally exploded into a bitter quarrel over the question of Cuban-style revolutionary internationalism in Latin America, which emphasized support for armed struggle carried out by rural-based guerrilla bands who drew their inspiration from the Fidelista experience rather than from the politics of the hemisphere's orthodox, traditionally pro-Moscow communist parties.

As we have seen, Havana embraced the idea of revolutionary internationalism, motivated in part by security considerations centering on its desire to deflect Washington's hostility. But counterdependency concerns also entered the equation, focusing on Cuba's position as a new member of the international socialist community and the evolving relationship with Moscow that such status implied. From Havana's perspective, a pluralistic socialist community was infinitely preferable to one dominated by the USSR or any other power center. Theoretically, at least, revolutionary internationalism could contribute to this end by promoting the emergence in Latin America, and perhaps elsewhere, of independent Third World Marxist regimes that would support one another's autonomy within the socialist community. To the extent that such diversity existed, the probabilities would be reduced that Cuba's Moscow–Soviet bloc connection might develop into just another dependency relationship.

Moscow's attitude toward such revolutionary internationalism was less than enthusiastic, its position stemming from two basic concerns. First, as suggested, the Soviets were opposed on the purely pragmatic ground that the risk of severely antagonizing the United States was not justified by the potential gains. Second, on the question of leftist leadership in Latin America, they were not willing to accept the transfer of responsibility implicit in Havana's scenario from established (pro-Moscow) communist parties to Fidelista elements.

Havana's commitment during the 1960s to a policy of proletarian internationalism in the Western Hemisphere and the often bitter Cuban-Soviet quarreling that it engendered went through three distinct phases, says Raymond Duncan: 1962–late 1963, during which the Fidelistas insisted that armed insurrection represented the only viable path to revolutionary change in Latin America; late 1963–January 1966, which saw Havana moderate its position somewhat by stating that even though it still placed primary emphasis on paramilitary struggle, it was willing to concede that other options (such as assuming power via elections) sometimes existed; and January 1966–August 1968, which involved a return to the violent Fidelista hard line.[25]

The fairly tranquil middle segment to which Duncan refers could be characterized as a period of tentative Cuban-Soviet détente, with both parties content to deemphasize their differences and to concentrate instead on those areas where there was considerable potential for increased

72 | Cuba's Foreign Relations in a Post-Soviet World

cooperation (e.g., the expansion and solidification of Soviet bloc developmental and security aid programs). Evidence that a shift toward such moderation was under way surfaced when Fidel made his first state visit to the USSR in April 1963. Both sides adopted conciliatory positions in the negotiations that transpired. The Soviets, for example, sought to defuse Havana's anger about their behavior during the Missile Crisis by suggesting (although not guaranteeing) that henceforth they would be willing to defend the island against a direct U.S. assault.[26] The Cubans reciprocated by conceding that it might be legitimate for some Latin leftists—that is, for the established pro-Moscow communist parties in the hemisphere—to employ nonviolent strategies, including the electoral path, in pursuing power. A second Castro visit in January 1964 was likewise amiable, with the Cubans being particularly careful to demonstrate sensitivity to Moscow's position in the increasingly acrimonious Sino-Soviet dispute.

A turning point occurred in January 1966, when the Cubans convened a conference in Havana at which the Organization for the Solidarity of the Peoples of Asia, Africa, and Latin America, popularly known as the Tricontinental, was established. The Fidelistas apparently viewed the Tricontinental as a vehicle that would allow them to play a highly influential role among Third World revolutionary movements and thereby to establish an independent power base in world affairs. Integral to this strategy was the reemergence of Fidelista-style proletarian internationalism as a central pillar of Havana's foreign policy, especially in the Western Hemisphere. In the process, Havana's relations with both the orthodox communist parties of Latin America and their patrons in Moscow rapidly soured. In essence, says Jacques Levesque, "the Tricontinental inaugurated a period during which the solidarity that the Cuban Revolution had principally manifested toward the Latin American Communist parties and the socialist camp was shifted to . . . the Latin American guerrilla movements, regardless of whether they were Marxist-Leninist or not."[27] Aside from in the economic realm, where the situation remained fairly stable, Havana's disenchantment with Moscow had reached the point by mid-1967 where the overall relationship seemed to be at an all-time low. When Soviet Premier Aleksei Kosygin visited the island in June, having a few days previously concluded a cordial superpower summit with President Lyndon Johnson in Glassboro, New Jersey, the Cubans made little effort to conceal their displeasure with the Kremlin's policies. Indeed they even refused to extend the normal courtesy of issuing some kind of joint communiqué upon his departure.

Over the next few years the Fidelistas escalated the dispute over the issue of proletarian internationalism in Latin America on several fronts. Ideologically, they castigated Soviet moderation by heavily promoting Regis Debray's best-selling book *Revolution in the Revolution?* Based on long conversations with Castro, Debray endorsed the Fidelista contention that armed struggle led by rural guerrillas was the only viable option that true revolutionaries could choose.[28] Then, going beyond words to deeds, the Cubans created the Organization of Latin American Solidarity (OLAS) in August 1967 to facilitate their efforts to provide material aid and leadership coordination to pro-Castro insurgents throughout the hemisphere. Although these efforts were not particularly successful, OLAS during its two-year lifespan (1967–68) did serve as a vivid symbol of Havana's determination to assert its independence from Moscow in international affairs.

Consolidating the Soviet Connection, 1968–1972

By the late 1960s it had become increasingly apparent that Havana's strategy of trying to employ proletarian internationalism as its main policy vehicle for charting a complex survival course in the shadow of both superpowers was not working very well. Certainly with respect to the United States, the Latin American guerrilla struggles that Havana was championing were not producing anything even faintly resembling "new Vietnams" that might function to deflect some of Washington's attention from its obsession with destroying the Cuban Revolution by drawing the United States into protracted hemispheric quagmires. Likewise those struggles did not appear to have any serious prospects for relatively quick victories (like the experience of Fidel's 26th of July Movement) from which would emerge friendly governments that would serve to neutralize the U.S. effort to drive the island into a state of total hemispheric isolation. Instead, the insurgents suffered one setback after another. Either their organizations were completely smashed by government counteroffensives or they found themselves marginalized as political actors when they failed to expand beyond a fairly narrow base, often limited to a small geographical area (e.g., the "Red Republics" that existed in rural Colombia). Even the legendary Che Guevara fell victim to this cacophony of defeat: in October 1967 he was captured and murdered by U.S.-advised counterinsurgency forces while trying to foment a Fidelista-style insurgency in Bolivia. The bitter reality, then, was that Cuba remained isolated in the Western Hemi-

74 | Cuba's Foreign Relations in a Post-Soviet World

sphere as the 1960s came to a close, standing alone against a remorseless Washington, which, while probably not inclined to unleash a direct invasion of the island, was determined to wreak as much economic and political havoc there as it could in the hope that the Revolution might somehow self-destruct under the pressure.

The impact of the shortcomings in proletarian internationalism was also felt on Havana's Soviet front. Obviously the policy had not functioned as the Fidelistas had hoped it would—as a midwife for independent revolutionary states in the Third World that might contribute to the development of a more pluralistic socialist bloc within which a dependency-sensitive state like Cuba could feel more comfortable. What it did produce was increasingly strained relations with the Kremlin, the result being that Havana was in effect also becoming isolated within the international socialist community. And although the bickering over proletarian internationalism was a key element in the Russo-Cuban dispute, several other developments helped to heighten the tensions.

For example, while desiring aid from the USSR and its Eastern European allies, Cuba was not willing to adopt a Soviet-style developmental model for utilizing such assistance. Havana gave lip service to the idea, but in practice the free-wheeling Fidelistas operated without a detailed national budget, a comprehensive auditing system, or any of the other attributes normally associated with a centrally planned economy. Moreover, as opposed to the standard operating procedure in the Soviet bloc, there was no orthodox communist party playing a dominant leadership role in the island's affairs. Rather, the Cuban Communist Party (PCC)—formed in 1965 to unite the island's old-line communists, who operated within the Popular Socialist Party (PSP), with Castro's 26th of July Movement—was in fact dominated by Fidelistas and hardly functioned as a viable entity; its Central Committee rarely met, and it did not have its first official party congress until 1975. Looking across this economic and political landscape, the Kremlin's confidence in the Cuban Revolution was meager as it saw little that resembled its conception of a genuine Marxist society.

Another irritant in the Soviet-Cuban connection emerged in late January 1968 when Havana moved against what it called an unacceptable "microfaction" within the Cuban Communist Party led by Aníbal Escalante, a PSP member who had long maintained close and cordial ties with the Kremlin. Contending that this group had behaved irresponsibly by criticizing the Revolution's policies and by entering into relationships with foreign governments (those of the USSR and other Eastern European states) that served to promote their interests rather than Cuba's, forty-three alleged participants were brought to trial; thirty-five were ultimately convicted and imprisoned. The leitmotif of this incident was readily apparent to most observers—Havana was sending a signal to Moscow that it would not tolerate any Russian interference in its affairs and that it intended to pursue its own independent course in both foreign and domestic policies.

The USSR, while in some respects tolerant of Havana's assertiveness, was not unlimited in its patience. This was graphically illustrated in 1968 when the Russians made several gestures clearly intended to convey growing displeasure with the Fidelistas. For example, prior to the Escalante affair, in early January 1968 Cuba had to institute extensive oil rationing because Moscow was dragging its feet in making the vital petroleum deliveries that it had promised. Although the Kremlin insisted that the delays were caused by logistical problems, many observers saw them as a none too subtle reminder to Havana that it was highly vulnerable to economic retaliation, should it overly antagonize the USSR. What appeared to be a similar message was sent in March 1968 when Moscow, which had previously signed an agreement to increase its 1967 trade with Cuba by 23 percent, proved unwilling to go beyond a 10 percent expansion for 1968.

By mid-1968 it had become apparent that the Fidelistas' efforts to acquire more maneuvering space in relation to the superpowers were not working out as planned. This realization, combined with the ongoing strains in the Cuban-Soviet relationship, tended to generate on Havana's part a sense of growing political isolation and economic vulnerability, which in turn translated into intensified security concerns. Thus, as would often recur in the future, Cuba's pragmatism led it to reconfigure its international priorities.

Deemphasizing proletarian internationalism was one aspect of this retrenchment. Although not abandoning its long-standing dedication to the principle of supporting liberation and revolutionary movements, Cuba in practice reverted to its early 1960s stance, placing heavy emphasis on normalizing its relations with as many governments as possible. In other words, rather than applying strict ideological criteria that functioned to limit its political horizons to like-minded radicals, Havana became more flexible. In the Western Hemisphere, for instance, it proclaimed its willingness to cooperate with any regime that was "progressive," which it defined in a broad sense as being committed domestically to liberal reforms that would enhance social justice while pursuing internationally an independent foreign policy rather than operating as a U.S. client-state. Such tolerance for ideological diversity would provide Havana with a much broader range of options (which it would vigorously pursue in the 1970s and 1980s) in terms of cultivating opportunities for political and economic cooperation outside the shadow of the superpowers.

This Cuban shift to a more moderate, ecumenical position was but one element in a larger and dramatic reconciliation with the USSR that occurred during the late 1960s and early 1970s. Although Havana still refused to embrace the Kremlin's position on some issues, the bitter quarreling that had characterized the relationship for several years was finally put aside, and fence mending became the order of the day. The watershed event in the process was Castro's endorsement of the August 1968 Soviet intervention in Czechoslovakia and the subsequent Brezhnev Doctrine. Many people found it puzzling at best and outrageous at worst that Fidel, the fervent nationalist who had always condemned meddling by superpowers in the affairs of other—especially weaker—countries, would acquiesce to such muscle flexing on the Kremlin's part. But recognize, says William LeoGrande, that "the principle of the irreversibility of socialist revolutions and the willingness of the USSR to risk international crisis and opprobrium to support that principle constituted the linchpin of Cuban national security. Thus the Cubans probably viewed the intervention with reassurance rather than trepidation."[29]

When viewed from this perspective, and also taking into consideration such background factors as Havana's prior frustration over the Kremlin's reluctance to extend its defense umbrella to the island, Castro's position becomes quite understandable. In essence, it would appear that the Fidelistas were relieved to see that despite Moscow's commitment to détente with the United States, it was still willing to use its military power to guarantee the survival of socialist governments in other countries, potentially including Cuba. Such "backbone" was what Havana had been looking for ever since the Cuban Missile Crisis. Hence it supported, with some reservations, what was perceived as the USSR's new security assertiveness.

Cuban-Soviet rapprochement moved ahead swiftly after the Czechoslovakian breakthrough, with cooperation in the economic field leading the way. Trade relations expanded rapidly during the ten years following 1968, as indicated in table 3.2, the overall increase for the period being approximately 435 percent. Note in particular that after many years of running a trade deficit with the Soviet Union (1962–1974; see also table 3.1), Cuba in the latter half of the 1970s was finally enjoying a series of surpluses.

Such cooperation was enhanced by the fact that after suffering severe developmental dislocations as a result of its unsuccessful (and, said many

In the Shadows of the Superpowers, 1959–1972 | 77

Table 3.2. Cuban trade with USSR, 1969–78 (in millions of pesos)

Year	Exports to USSR	Imports from USSR	Total
1969	233	669	902
1970	529	691	1,220
1971	304	731	1,035
1972	224	714	938
1973	477	811	1,288
1974	811	1,025	1,836
1975	1,661	1,250	2,911
1976	1,638	1,490	3,128
1977	2,066	1,858	3,924
1978	2,496	2,328	4,824

Source: José Luis Rodríguez, "The Economic Relations Cuba-USSR, 1960–1985," *World Economic Affairs,* no. 17 (1986), 20. This journal is published by the Center for the Study of the World Economy (CIEM) in Havana, Cuba.

observers, foolish) attempt to bring in an unprecedented 10 million ton sugar harvest in 1970, Havana instituted various reforms that brought its economic structures and practices much more in line with the Soviet model. This process of economic détente culminated in 1972 when the island became the first non-Eurasian developing nation to be granted full membership in the Council for Mutual Economic Assistance (CMEA, the Soviet bloc's rough equivalent of the European Economic Community).[30] As Edward González noted, "Cuba's admission to the Soviet-led Council for Mutual Economic Assistance in July 1972 and the long-term agreements signed at the end of that year with the USSR . . . assured Havana of substantial and favorable levels of external support for the Cuban economy. The December 1972 agreements were especially important in that they deferred to 1986 repayment of Cuba's large debt to the USSR, provided new short-term Soviet credits, and set higher Soviet purchase prices for Cuban sugar and nickel exports."[31]

It should also be noted that the Kremlin's generosity extended to Havana's other main area of concern—defense. Just prior to joining CMEA, Castro visited Moscow in June 1972 and departed with the impression that the Soviet Union was willing to use its might to protect the island against external (read U.S.) aggression. These moves toward greater economic integration combined with concurrent increases in military aid and collaboration served as the crucible within which were forged the strong links that would typify Cuban–Soviet–East European relations throughout the 1970s and into the 1980s.

At this point, then, Havana's superpower relations settled down into a configuration that would essentially persist over the next thirteen years. Mutual suspicion and hostility continued to dominate the Fidelistas' U.S. front, while with respect to the socialist bloc there emerged a much more complex scenario, characterized in the next chapter as "dual tracking," which helped Havana to transform itself into a truly global player on the international stage.

4

Beyond the Superpowers

The Halcyon Days of Cuban Globalism, 1972–1985

Inherent in the Cold War were serious threats to the Fidelistas' security (in both the military and economic senses of the term) rooted in Washington's hostility toward the Revolution. Ironically, however, these tensions likewise engendered an international environment within which Havana was able to implement a sophisticated foreign policy that utilized *developmental coalition building* initiatives with the industrialized socialist bloc as the background against which to pursue a major campaign of *counterdependency diversification* with respect to its relations with the less developed nations, the ultimate goal being to acquire a position of Third World leadership.[1] Membership in CMEA (also known by its Russian acronym as COMECON) constituted the institutional linchpin of this strategy, providing Cuba assured access to a broad menu of socioeconomic and security aid programs that allowed it to achieve levels of development and a presence on the international stage comparable in some respects to those of the most modernized nations.

During the 1970s and continuing into the mid-1980s, the combination of these two elements—establishing a highly lucrative economic coalition with the socialist bloc that also included large infusions of military aid and expanding dramatically its relations with developing nations throughout the Southern Hemisphere in an effort to bolster its Third World leadership aspirations—was the defining hallmark both of Havana's overall foreign policy and of its counterdependency agenda. For purposes of simplicity, this complex exercise can be characterized as Cold War dual tracking. To some extent these two areas of activity were geared to servicing separate and indeed often traditional interests. The CMEA connection, for example, addressed such basic revolutionary concerns as survival and viability, while Third World diversification was linked to the basic counterdependency tenet that sovereignty must be maximized, in this instance by developing a political base outside any great power's sphere of influence. Ultimately the mutually supportive fusion of these various threads into an impressive strategic package allowed Havana to assume a high-profile, high-influence role in international affairs—a role that in many respects was almost totally unprecedented during the Cold War for a small developing country.

Overview: Cold War Dual Tracking

CMEA membership was pivotal to the Fidelistas' dual-track scenario, the key foreign policy by-products of this special relationship being that

- It provided the Revolution with a sense of military security that had been sorely lacking in the 1960s. Although Cuba never became a formal member of the Warsaw Pact (the Soviet mutual defense alliance that functioned as their equivalent of NATO in the West), the island was nevertheless widely considered to be "covered" by its deterrent umbrella. Moreover, Cuba received massive amounts of military aid from the socialist bloc, which transformed its armed forces into a formidable organization that even the Pentagon was not anxious to confront.[2] As such, Havana was able to jettison its prior obsession with the possibility of a U.S. attack and turn its foreign policy attention to other concerns.

- It significantly reduced Cuba's exposure to the economic warfare that the United States was trying to wage against the Revolution, thereby allowing Havana to concentrate on developing its own distinctive role in global affairs rather than being obsessive about responding to Washington's hostility, as had been the case.

- It enhanced the resources, both human and material, upon which rested the Fidelistas' capability to pursue an audacious global agenda, particularly in the realm of Third World affairs. In other words, Havana could now be more ambitious in terms of its international activities because it now had the power necessary to operate on a broader scale.

In effect, then, Cuba was tapping Eastern European resources to bolster its security, stabilize its economy, modernize its armed forces, and thereby put itself in a better position to explore new frontiers in its foreign relations.

As its CMEA ties were being consolidated, Havana began in the early 1970s to interject stronger South-South diversification into its international agenda. Cuba's foreign policy perspective began to expand beyond narrow Cold War parameters in which its status and role in international affairs were defined primarily in terms of its relations with the world's two superpowers. Probing these new horizons, the Fidelistas began to devote increased attention to launching initiatives designed to redefine and widen their contacts with other developing countries. For example, they made a concerted effort to reestablish Havana's respectability among Latin American and Caribbean nations, which led to its entry into various hemispheric functional organizations and which ultimately generated growing sentiment to lift the sanctions imposed on Castro's government by the Organization of American States (OAS) in 1964. It was, however, in Africa that Havana exploded most dramatically onto the international stage, establishing a major presence there by instituting numerous developmental and security assistance programs and by deploying thousands of combat troops who were decisive in winning two wars (in Angola in 1975–76 and, cooperating closely with the USSR, in Ethiopia in 1977–78). Cuba also assumed a substantially higher profile in the Nonaligned Movement, the pinnacle of its rise coming in 1979 when Fidel succeeded Sri Lanka's president as the sixth head of state to lead the organization.

The bottom line is that during this 1972–85 period, Havana emerged in a unique role on the global scene. Never before, at least not in the twentieth century, had such a small country exerted such influence on the international balance of power. Never before had a Latin American nation left such deep marks in world politics. While some observers were pleased with or at least tolerant of this unfolding drama, others were appalled at the remarkable foreign policy triumphs that the Fidelistas were posting. Secretary of State Henry Kissinger, for example, displayed both bewilderment and anger when in 1978 he fumed, "It is time to overcome the ridiculous myth of the invincible Cubans. Who ever heard of Cubans conducting a global foreign policy?"[3]

Whether Washington liked it or not, that is exactly what the Fidelistas were doing, with the flamboyance and charismatic style that had become the Revolution's trademark. This development was encapsulated in Jorge Domínguez's widely quoted observation that "Cuba is a small country, but it has a big country's foreign policy. It has tried to carry out such a policy since the beginning of the revolution, but only in the second half of the 1970s did it have conditions . . . to become a visible and important actor actually shaping the course of events."[4] Thus, just as in their unlikely victory over Batista and their David-versus-Goliath triumph at the Bay of Pigs, the Fidelistas were once again defying the odds, demolishing in the

82 | Cuba's Foreign Relations in a Post-Soviet World

process the old stereotype relegating nations deemed to be insignificant by the conventional measures of power to the outer fringes of global affairs. Indeed, much to the chagrin of the world's Kissingers, the Cubans' less traveled road ultimately led them to a position where they were firmly ensconced in the international spotlight.

Latin America: Balancing Normalization Initiatives and Radical Politics

Castro's government has been no different than any other in the sense that the precise configuration of its relations with other international actors has always varied from case to case. Such variety is to be expected, since no policy maker would ever be so naive as to assume that one formula applies to all situations. In a general sense, however, it is fair to say that a certain schizophrenia often characterized Havana's approach to its Caribbean and Latin American neighbors in the 1960s and 1970s, this situation emerging because the Revolution was conducting its foreign relations at two different levels. There were, of course, the conventional government-to-government dealings that routinely transpire between countries, especially those that have established formal diplomatic and trade relations. But a second sphere of activity also existed, involving party-to-party contacts between Cuban communists and their radical colleagues in other hemispheric nations, although here the lines were somewhat blurred since the convergence of the party and the government in the Cuban political system could create a situation where the linkages involved might be more accurately characterized as state-to-party. In any case, given this dualism, the island's attitude toward any particular country could be rather ambivalent: Havana could at the formal state level be maintaining correct and even cordial ties with an established regime, while simultaneously on the party side of the equation be supporting the efforts of indigenous rebels to overthrow it.

In contrast to its policies regarding most other areas of the world, where Havana placed primary emphasis on improving its position at the state level, its Latin American policies during the 1960s were heavily influenced by its commitment to proletarian internationalism, as we have seen in preceding chapters. It often tended to place more emphasis on championing the fortunes of various revolutionary movements than on normalizing its relations with hemispheric governments. In the 1970s, however, there was a reversal of these priorities as Cold War dual-tracking became the dominant theme in Cuban foreign affairs. Expanding Havana's formal diplomatic and trade ties was the main goal of the dual-track strategy, and

Beyond the Superpowers: Cuban Globalism, 1972–1985 | 83

since party-based internationalism often revolved around subversive activities that were detrimental to such diversification, it was for the most part downgraded during the 1970s. But beginning in the latter part of the 1970s, a mini-revival of Cuban radicalism occurred, focused on Central America and the eastern Caribbean. Essentially this reinvigoration of proletarian internationalism operated at the party-to-party level, although in the Nicaraguan and Grenadian cases the revolutionary movements with which Havana was closely associated succeeded in seizing power and thereby elevating their relations with Cuba to the state-to-state category.

Overall, then, Havana's hemispheric policies during this period represented a delicate, complicated balancing act involving both a broad normalization campaign and highly concentrated radicalism, with the former taking precedence.

Normalization Initiatives

Havana's first breakthrough in its campaign to escape the cocoon of isolation that the United States had spun around it occurred in the economic rather than the political realm, when Chile's liberal Christian Democratic government (led by President Eduardo Frei) decided in 1969 to resume trade and other commercial dealings with Cuba. Peru, whose highly nationalistic military regime was anxious to demonstrate its independence from Washington, quickly followed suit in June 1971.

Although Havana very much appreciated such reconciliatory gestures, they did not confer upon Cuba the main badge of political respectability that it was seeking—reestablishment of full formal diplomatic relations. This plateau was finally reached in late 1970, the catalyst being the November 1970 Chilean presidential election in which Salvador Allende, a Marxist who had long been sympathetic toward the Cuban Revolution, scored a remarkable victory. One of Allende's first moves after his inauguration was to reinstate the diplomatic relations with Cuba that had been severed in 1962 in accordance with the declaration expelling Castro's government from the OAS. This rapprochement with Chile was greeted as a critical milestone by the Fidelistas, for it appeared to Havana that after years of ostracism, the process of its reincorporation into the family of hemispheric nations had finally begun.[5] This optimism was reinforced in June 1972 when Peru, once again following Chile's lead as it had with regard to trade, also extended full recognition to Cuba. The year ended with the momentum behind hemispheric normalization receiving a major boost from a somewhat unlikely quarter—the English-speaking Caribbean, an area that had never been especially prominent on the Revolution's foreign policy agenda. That tradition was rudely shattered in December 1972 when Barbados, Guyana, Jamaica, and Trinidad and Tobago all reestablished formal state-to-state ties with Cuba.[6] The United States was not amused by these developments, for what had at first seemed only small cracks in the wall it had so assiduously built around Castro's Cuba now threatened to become large fissures with the potential to undermine the entire structure.[7]

Washington's anti-Cuban policies suffered additional setbacks over the next few years, as these countries normalized their relations with Havana: Argentina in mid-1973; Panama in August and Venezuela in December of 1974; Colombia in March 1975; Costa Rica in February 1977; and Ecuador, St. Lucia, and Suriname in 1979. But the fact that official ties were once more in place did not necessarily mean that congeniality followed. To the contrary, in the late 1970s and early 1980s various disputes arose to complicate Havana's dealings with Venezuela, Peru, and Ecuador. Although the bickering did not deteriorate in any of these three instances to the point where official diplomatic relations became one of the casualties, Cuba's links with the countries in question could be more accurately characterized as correct rather than cordial. The situation on the Colombian and Costa Rican fronts, however, was more volatile. Bogota, convinced that the Fidelistas were deeply involved in sponsoring attempts by the radical M-19 Movement to seize power, severed its diplomatic ties with Havana in March 1981. Later the same year, Costa Rica did likewise over a dispute regarding alleged Cuban mistreatment of political prisoners.

Havana's normalization and diversification initiatives in the hemisphere were not limited to bilateral (state-to-state) efforts, for participation in various multilateral intergovernmental organizations (IGOs) also entered into the policy equation. Indeed the Fidelistas, in what could perhaps be seen as an admittedly low-key manifestation of its proclivity to cultivate economic counterdependency options, seemed to gravitate especially to groups that concentrated on trade and related developmental issues. This attraction is illustrated by the fact that they were charter members of such consortiums as the Latin American Energy Organization (OLADE), founded in 1973; the Latin American and Caribbean Sugar Exporting Group (GEPLACEA), formed in 1974; and the Caribbean Multinational Shipping Company (NAMACUR), the Caribbean Committee of Development and Cooperation (CCDC), and the Latin American Economic System (SELA), all founded in 1975.[8] Beyond the material advantages that might be involved, there also seemed to be in these undertakings a political dimension related to the Revolution's long struggle against the United States, in the sense that Cuba seemed to be particularly interested in promoting the fortunes of groups like SELA, which explicitly prohibited U.S. membership, or those that seemed to have potential as vehicles through which Latin countries could achieve greater unity and would thereby be able to confront Washington more effectively.

Havana's enthusiasm for IGOs did not, however, extend to the OAS, despite the fact that there was growing sentiment within it to lift the sanctions it had imposed on Castro's government in the 1960s. Peru first broached this idea in 1972, submitting a resolution to rescind the July 1964 declaration that called on members to refrain from all political, economic, and other official state relations with Cuba. This proposal finally passed on July 29, 1975.[9] The Fidelistas' reaction to these developments was decidedly mixed. Obviously they were pleased that a major impediment to their normalization campaign had been removed. But they continued to be highly suspicious of the OAS due to its history of deferring to pressure from Washington, a habit which often led the Cubans to ostracize it as a "tool of U.S. imperialism." Ultimately this latter sentiment carried the day, with Havana refusing to make any move toward reactivating its membership and instead renewing its call for the creation of a purely Caribbean–Latin American body—that is, for an OAS that, like SELA, would exclude the United States.

Residual Radicalism

During the 1970s the Cubans experienced considerable success with their dual-track strategy in the Western Hemisphere, the resulting diversification sometimes entailing an overall normalization of state relations, while in other cases countries that did not extend Havana formal diplomatic recognition nevertheless resumed trading with the island. There were some setbacks, but basically the trend was positive.

The main regional departure from this generally successful pattern was Central America. Traditionally, with the exception of Costa Rica, most regimes there were notorious for their almost pathological hatred of anyone who did not embrace the extreme right wing of the ideological spectrum; for the atrocious brutality that they routinely employed to maintain themselves in power; and for their often incestuous relationship with Washington, whereby they traded political and economic concessions in return for U.S. policies geared to assuring their survival.[10] This environment was not favorably disposed, to put it mildly, toward any aspect of the Cuban Revolution, including its attempts at reconciliation with its hemispheric neighbors.

The tensions that had long been part of the body politic in the Caribbean Basin became even more pronounced in the 1980s. This situation could to a great extent be attributed to the convergence of two volatile currents, one the leftist insurgencies rooted in socioeconomic tensions (with Central America, which had a long tradition of political violence, exhibiting the greatest instability), the other the Reaganite groundswell in the United States. Ronald Reagan entered the White House in 1981 determined not only to pursue containment with a passion but also to incorporate into his repertoire an idea that had long been dear to his conservative constituents—the rollback of communism. Accordingly the new administration announced the formation of the Reagan Doctrine, which went beyond the traditional policy of extending (sometimes massive) security assistance to pro-U.S. governments that were confronting radical challenges. Henceforth, they said, the United States would provide strong support to insurgent movements that were fighting to overthrow Third World Marxist regimes.

Central America and, to a lesser extent, the Anglophone Caribbean quickly emerged as major theaters of Reaganite operations for both the old and the new versions of containment. Such virulent anticommunism had a sobering effect on many in the region, causing some governments that might otherwise have been open to cordial relations with Havana to begin to put some distance between themselves and the Cubans.

Combining the perception that there was little to be gained from normalization initiatives in Central America with the climate of ideological confrontationalism engendered by the Reagan Doctrine produced a situation in the Caribbean Basin where the Fidelistas, who had never completely abandoned the idea of proletarian internationalism, were often inclined to continue to practice the revolutionary politics that had been the mainstay of their larger Latin American policies in the 1960s.

Complete information about Cuba's activities at the party-to-party level has never been readily available, since some of these were conducted in a highly clandestine fashion. For example, controversy has always swirled around such questions as the extent of material aid (arms, money) that Havana provided to various movements and whether Cubans actually served as combatants in the armed struggles. In a general sense, however, it can be said that Havana defined its role primarily in terms of serving as a political broker with the top priority of unifying a country's various revolutionary factions into a comprehensive, flexible "popular front" organization. By adopting this stance, Cuba positioned itself to attack the problem of extreme fragmentation that had long plagued the

Latin American left and rendered it vulnerable to divide-and-conquer tactics (which were used with devastating results by the United States and its Latin allies in the 1960s). With Cuban assistance, however, this weakness began to be rectified. For instance, in 1977 and early 1978, Armando Ulises Estrada, one of Havana's top Central American specialists, played a pivotal role in consolidating the three major wings of Nicaragua's Sandinista movement. Cuba also hosted a December 1979 meeting at which three of El Salvador's main guerrilla bands formed the Farabundo Martí Front for National Liberation (FMLN). A fourth organization, the Popular Revolutionary Army (ERP), joined the coalition in late May 1980 after more discussions in Havana. Finally, under Castro's prodding, four Guatemalan groups gathered in Managua in November 1980 and negotiated an arrangement establishing the National Revolutionary Union (with a central directorate called the General Revolutionary Command).[11] These Cuban-brokered agreements, focused on establishing mechanisms for coordinating the political and military activities of radical leftists, generally functioned to make the Central American revolutionaries more formidable. The Sandinistas' victory in 1979 and the Salvadoran FMLN's ability to fight the government to a standstill throughout the 1980s, ultimately leading to a negotiated settlement of the conflict in early 1992, exemplified the effectiveness of Havana's efforts.

Ironically, however, the first victory scored by pro-Fidelista radicals did not come in Central America, where Havana had been most active in pursuing its policy of party-level solidarity, but rather on the tiny eastern Caribbean island of Grenada, where a group of young radicals calling themselves the New Jewel Movement (NJM) seized power in March 1979.[12] Many in the NJM, including its leader Maurice Bishop, had long been sympathetic toward the Cuban Revolution and had developed various kinds of fraternal ties with it. Nevertheless Havana, it was widely agreed, played no role whatsoever in the NJM coup. But as cordial state-to-state relations were quickly established and the NJM government made clear its need and desire for assistance in implementing its plan for socialist transformation, Cuba moved swiftly. It was soon involved in such diverse operations as a literacy campaign, various medical aid programs, and road construction.

Havana's most ambitious venture was the construction of a new airport, which the Grenadians considered absolutely crucial to their being able to expand their share of the lucrative Caribbean mass tourism market. Collaborating with various Western European countries, the Cubans agreed build the facility and to cover about half of its estimated $50 million cost. This project became a major bone of contention with the United States. The Grenadians, the Cubans, and even the Western Europeans involved insisted that the 10,000-foot runway and related facilities were necessary in order to accommodate the largest commercial planes and their passengers. Washington, however, complained bitterly that inherent in the airport's nature was a dual-use capacity that would readily allow it to be used (by its Fidelista patrons) for military purposes.

Putting aside the airport question, where interpretations of the facts differed considerably, it was true that the NJM government forged a number of security links with Havana and, to a lesser extent, with Moscow. The Cubans, for example, sent advisors to help reorganize the island's armed forces and to train them in using the arms and other equipment provided by the Soviet bloc. Whether such aid went beyond the Bishop government's legitimate defense needs was, as is often the case, a matter of perception. Certainly the Reagan administration concluded that it did, and consequently the United States treated the Cuba-Grenada relationship as a Cold War containment issue.

Grenada's radicalization was soon overshadowed by events in Nicaragua, where insurgents whose main leadership came from the leftist core of the Sandinista Movement (Frente Sandinista de Liberación Nacional, FSLN) finally won their long struggle against the Somoza dynasty on July 17, 1979. As was the case with the NJM government, Havana warmly embraced the new regime in Managua and began to provide it with both developmental and security assistance. By year's end approximately 50 Cuban military advisors and 2,000 civilian workers (mostly teachers and doctors) had arrived to help the Sandinistas consolidate their revolution and to rebuild a country shattered by the decades of abuse inflicted upon it by the Somoza dynasty.

Ultimately Sandinista Nicaragua would come to represent Havana's most extensive commitment to radical solidarity politics in the Western Hemisphere, as illustrated by the large number of support personnel that it dispatched. The developmental aid contingent peaked at about 5,300 in 1984, with a roughly equal contingent of 5,000 Nicaraguans undergoing professional and technical training in Cuba.[13] Comparable data regarding the number of Fidelistas dispatched to Managua to provide training and other logistical services to the Sandinista armed forces appear to be less reliable, for the estimates range from the lowest figure of 200 in 1984 to a high of 3,000 in 1985.[14] Given such disparity, it would appear that a reasonable middle-ground position was the 1985 statement attributed to Daniel Ortega, Nicaragua's Sandinista president, that there were almost

800 Cuban military advisors in the country, most of whom seemed to be assigned as instructors in the use of the Soviet bloc arms and equipment that Managua was receiving.[15]

Predictably, the Reagan administration reacted to these developments in a highly confrontational manner. In its view, the Cubans were functioning as the Kremlin's surrogates in establishing a beachhead in Nicaragua that the communist bloc would then use as a launching pad for subverting the rest of Central America. Reagan's secretary of state, Alexander Haig, sounded this domino-theory analysis when he insisted that the Russians had a "hit list" that included targets of opportunity (e.g., El Salvador and Guatemala) throughout the region, the ultimate goal supposedly being Mexico and its oil reserves. Consequently the Reagan Doctrine was unleashed. Operating through the CIA, Washington helped to organize, equip, train, and orchestrate the attacks of an anti-Sandinista guerrilla force known as the Contras. Thus began a highly controversial undeclared war against the Nicaraguan Revolution that continued until the Ortega government, having lost the 1990 presidential elections, peacefully transferred power to a generally centrist coalition party led by Violetta Chamorro.[16]

Ironically, the Cubans who were being portrayed by Washington as purveyors of irresponsible, wild-eyed radicalism in Central America were in fact counseling the Sandinistas to adopt moderate policies both at home and abroad. Do not put your revolution at risk by unnecessarily antagonizing the United States, the Fidelistas seemed to be saying. Such advice apparently was heeded. The Ortega government did not, for example, institute a totally state-controlled command economy along Cuban-Soviet lines, instead allowing a vigorous private sector to flourish, involving both domestic and foreign participation. Thus Nicaragua avoided or at least tried to minimize serious disputes over nationalization like those that had poisoned U.S.-Cuban relations in the early 1960s. Likewise, while not abstaining completely from involvement in the revolutionary armed struggles raging in neighboring countries (especially El Salvador), Managua tried to defuse tensions over the question by becoming progressively more supportive of Latin American efforts to achieve negotiated settlements of the Central American conflicts. This conciliatory emphasis was illustrated by the Sandinistas' July 1983 Central American peace proposal, which included, among other things, a prohibition on all outside aid (from Washington, Havana, or Managua) to guerrilla movements in the region and a pledge that no foreign military bases would be allowed in Nicaragua. The Cubans heartily endorsed this initiative, vowing that they would respect an embargo on the shipment of all arms to Central America and would remove their military advisors from the area as long as the United States guaranteed to do likewise (which it did not).

The Mid-1980s Balance Sheet

Havana's attempt in Latin America to combine conventional state-level normalization initiatives with an element of residual radicalism in implementing its dual-track strategy produced mixed results, as might be expected. In general, its forays into the uncertain waters of revolutionary politics were not fruitful. On the other hand, it often succeeded in establishing routine diplomatic and/or other kinds of relations (trade, cultural, technical) with a fairly broad range of hemispheric governments.

The eastern Caribbean emerged, in the 1980s, as the area where the Fidelistas found the ideological tides flowing most strongly against them. On the English-speaking islands, moderates and indeed often strongly anticommunist conservatives scored a string of electoral victories over left-wing parties (many of which were favorably disposed toward and in some cases had long-standing fraternal ties with Havana).[17] The most important race occurred in Jamaica, where Harvard-educated Edward Seaga won the October 1980 general election running on a right-wing platform that included harsh criticism of the incumbent Manley government's close ties with Cuba. Subsequently, in conjunction with a dramatic pro-Western reorientation of its foreign policy, Kingston broke relations with Havana on October 28, 1981, and ordered all Cubans to leave the country. Such proclivities were strongly encouraged by the Reagan administration, which made little effort to hide its determination to cut the Cubans down to size in the region. The precariousness of Havana's position was brutally driven home in Grenada where, in October 1983, the United States launched an invasion that destroyed the remnants of the New Jewel government (which had already been weakened by an internal power struggle between two factions led by Maurice Bishop and Bernard Coard) and led to the expulsion of all Cubans from the island. These developments, combined with the fact that most of Grenada's neighbors actively supported or at least quietly acquiesced to the attack, were extremely gratifying to Washington, for they indicated that its long-standing campaign to isolate Cuba politically and economically was proceeding nicely in the eastern Caribbean.[18] Such sentiment was further strengthened when, shortly after the assault on Grenada, Suriname's government decided, apparently in an effort to placate the Reagan administration, to distance itself from Havana by expelling Cuba's ambassador as well as canceling various agreements for cultural-educational cooperation that were symbolic of the previously cordial relations between the two nations. Overall, then, Havana's stock in the eastern Caribbean took a beating in the early 1980s as most governments there gave it the cold shoulder, including even those that continued to maintain formal diplomatic ties.

In Central America, where Havana made its heaviest investments in terms of supporting the armed struggles of revolutionary movements and trying to help the Sandinistas consolidate their hold on power, the situation essentially congealed into a stalemate. No party in any of the conflicts raging in Guatemala, El Salvador, or Nicaragua was able to make any major progress in the combat arenas, let alone a breakthrough that might have propelled a movement to the verge of victory. Consequently the center of action shifted to the negotiating table, with a number of Latin American countries that became known as the Contadora Group trying to play a mediatory role in the process. Cuba, whose policies had by this point come to place more emphasis on bargaining than on battling, supported these efforts to find a peaceful solution. Pragmatically this was the best course of action, but opting for it had a price: it meant that the Fidelistas were in effect no longer displaying any serious confidence in proletarian internationalism as a vehicle for advancing their basic dual-track policy.

Havana's diversification campaign fared better in the larger Latin American community, where normalization of conventional state-to-state relations (rather than revolutionary politics) received priority attention. These efforts were rewarded when these countries were added to the list of those that reestablished official ties with the island: Bolivia in January 1983; Uruguay in December 1985; and Brazil in June 1986.

The political dimensions of diversification were not the only aspect of the process that interested the Cubans. Equally important—and in some cases even more crucial than the resumption of diplomatic relations, normally symbolized by a formal exchange of ambassadors—were the potential economic benefits involved. At this point, of course, the Revolution's CMEA connection strongly dominated its network of trade and other commercial and financial transactions. But Havana's basic counterdependency instincts warned against allowing this situation to become too extreme. Consequently it was usually eager to capitalize on whatever possibilities presented themselves to diversify its economic ties. Indeed, such opportunities often emerged as a corollary to political normalization: diplomatic rapprochement served as the key to open the door through which trade and other forms of mutually beneficial relations could then flow.

The countries that Cuba courted most assiduously as economic partners were, not surprisingly, the Latin American "Big Three" — Mexico, Argentina, and Brazil. Havana's most extensive and lucrative arrangements were, as might be expected, with the Mexicans, since they had refused from the beginning to become a party to the U.S.-sponsored blockade of the island. In the early 1980s, for example, Cuban exports to Mexico were increasing rapidly, having grown from a rather meager 1–2 million pesos annually in the late 1970s to 185.6 million pesos in 1980. Similar expansion, notes Jorge Domínguez, was occurring on a broad scale: "By 1984 the two governments had signed sixteen agreements covering exchanges in technology, industry, culture, petroleum, tourism, and other areas; a new agreement, worth 400 million pesos to both countries, was signed in 1984 to promote collaboration in the steel, machinery, and sugar industries."[19] Panama was another important element in this panorama, for it served as a safe haven where the Fidelistas were allowed to set up holding companies and other operations that facilitated Havana's non-CMEA trade as well as often providing convenient "cover" for sometimes illegal or at least shady transactions with U.S. corporations.

Overall then, despite some setbacks, some outright failures, and the absence of any truly sensational exploits, Cuba made steady progress in its hemispheric diversification efforts during the 1972–85 period. But steady progress, especially in the often mundane realm of state-centered normalization-counterdependency politics, does not fire the imagination. Melodrama does, and the spectacle of Cuba's Cold War dual tracking leading it into the throes of war in Africa provided enough to satisfy most observers.

Cuba and Africa

Like many other Caribbean islands, Cuba has a large black and mulatto population descended from slaves who were imported to work its colonial sugar plantations, the combined size of these groups being such that many observers use the term *Afro-Cuban* to characterize the essential nature of the country's society.[20] The impact of this African community has been especially dramatic in the cultural realm; Cuban music, for example, draws heavily on the country's black roots, and its most popular religion is Santería, which is essentially an African creed that slaves "Europeanized" somewhat with cosmetic overlays of Catholicism. Traditionally, however, these historical-cultural links to Africa had never translated into a major foreign policy investment on Havana's part.

Shortly after Castro's triumph, the Fidelistas began to express greater interest in African affairs, their initial focus centering on North Africa where, as noted in chapter 3, they deployed military advisors and some front-line troops to Algeria beginning in 1963. This initiative did not evolve far because the urgency of the Algerian-Moroccan dispute that prompted it was defused by a cease-fire agreement eliminating any necessity for direct involvement by Cuban forces. Havana therefore recalled these combat units. Subsequently it would become more ambitious in supporting radical sub-Saharan national liberation movements (particularly those fighting the Portuguese in Angola and Mozambique) and would begin to dispatch official military aid missions to the continent, Congo-Brazzaville (1965) and Guinea (1966) being among the first recipients. Another indication of the Fidelistas' growing African orientation was the legendary Che Guevara's guerrilla adventure there. In April 1965, along with approximately 200 Cuban volunteers, he arrived to join insurgents who were trying to drive Moise Tshombe from power in the Congo (later known as Zaire). Having participated in the fighting for several months, Che's force withdrew in late 1965 at the request of their Congolese allies. Although Guevara was ostensibly operating on his own as a private citizen, having given up his Cuban citizenship as well as all of his posts in Castro's government, his sojourn there strongly suggests that African affairs were becoming increasingly prominent on Havana's international agenda during the mid- to late 1960s. They would move to center stage in the following decade.

Cuba's military forays into Africa during the 1970s, especially its Angolan and Ethiopian engagements, provide excellent examples of putting its policy of Cold War dual tracking into practice. As suggested, the Soviet bloc security aid that had poured in over the years had transformed Havana's troops into a formidable force. They were now armed with the most modern weapons; they were highly trained in battlefield tactics and related matters; and they had developed a logistical proficiency, especially with regard to transport and supply expertise, that allowed them to function effectively far from their home bases. These enhanced capabilities put the Fidelistas in the position of being able to expand the scope of their international activities (i.e., to diversify) into such a previously impractical theater of operations as Africa. A key consideration underlying such audacity was the potential to generate a commodity crucial to Havana's counterdependency agenda—bargaining power that could be brought to bear in its dealings with the superpowers.

Wolf Grabendorff explained this scenario as follows: "Cuba's greatest expectation [was] the possibility of gaining a *two-folded* bargaining power from its African involvement. On the one hand, it could enhance its position vis-à-vis the hegemonic USSR, since the Soviet Union [was] probably well aware of the fact that the military, organizational, and developmental achievements of Cuba could serve antithetical interests in the Third World. On the other hand, Cuba could also gain bargaining power vis-à-vis the United States. Its African card could become a useful trump in overcoming problems and resuming diplomatic relations with the United States."[21] Viewed from this perspective, what appeared to many to be absolute folly on Havana's part was in fact fully consistent with the overall logic of a foreign policy grounded in counterdependency considerations.

Angola, 1975–1976

The evolution of the Angolan conflict that burst onto the world stage in late 1975 was extremely chaotic and in many respects so shrouded in mystery that observers often could not agree on what the facts of the situation were. The main Angolan players were three anticolonial movements that had been involved, to one degree or another, in a brutal armed struggle to free the country from Portuguese control. These groups, each of which received assistance from outside powers, were the Popular Movement for the Liberation of Angola (MPLA), a radical left-wing party supported by Cuba and the USSR; the National Front for the Liberation of Angola (FNLA), supported by the United States, China, and Zaire; and the National Union for the Total Independence of Angola (UNITA), supported by the United States, China, and South Africa. The last two organizations were loosely allied against the MPLA, although eventually the FNLA would fade from the scene.

The pivotal year for the Angolan crisis was 1975, and the key development was the entry of both the South African and Cuban armies into the conflict. The chronological high points of this development can be summarized as follows:

- January—the Portuguese agreed to withdraw from the country, announcing that it would be granted its independence on November 10, 1975. Left unresolved, however, was the question of who would govern the nation following Portugal's departure. A civil war erupted as the MPLA and UNITA/FNLA turned their guns on each other in an attempt to position themselves to assume power in November.

- August—South Africa sent troops into southern Angola from nearby Namibia (a territory Pretoria controlled, having refused to transfer jurisdiction to the United Nations after World War II). The announced reason was to protect a hydroelectric plant that supplied power to both Angola and Namibia, but many observers felt that the move was in fact designed to provide a protective shield for UNITA and to facilitate increased South African covert aid to that group.

- October—South Africa openly entered the Angolan conflict, deploying thousands of elite troops from Namibia backed by heavy artillery and attack helicopters to fight beside UNITA.

- November—the MPLA declared on November 11 that it was now the government of an independent Angola; the UNITA/FNLA coalition did likewise on November 23.

At this point the MPLA, which initially had fared rather well in its campaigns against UNITA and the FNLA, was under siege. Although it controlled the Angolan capital of Luanda and adjoining territory in the central part of the country, momentum had shifted to its opponents. The primary threat was coming from the south, where Pretoria's troops, with their UNITA allies in tow, had launched an all-out drive that was surging northward toward Luanda in what was clearly intended to be the war's final offensive.

As this noose tightened, MPLA leader Agostinho Neto turned to his Cuban friends for help. Havana's response was electrifying. With Moscow providing some logistical support, front-line combat units were quickly dispatched to Angola and plunged immediately into the thick of the fighting.[22] Thus, to the amazement of many people and the dismay of some (particularly in Washington), the Revolution's armed forces proved themselves to be truly global warriors.

Exactly how many Cubans were deployed at this time was uncertain; Western intelligence agencies (including the CIA) put the number at around 20,000; Castro indicated in a December 1979 speech that the force peaked at 36,000. In any case, the Fidelista buildup that went into high gear in November 1975 was decisive in shifting the military balance irrevocably in the MPLA's favor. The Cuban troops stopped the various enemy columns that had been converging on Luanda and then launched their own counteroffensive, particularly against the South African forces, which constituted the greatest threat to Neto's government. By March 1976 the MPLA was clearly in charge; the South African forces had been driven back into Namibia, while the FNLA had been decisively defeated and would no longer be a major player in Angolan politics.

The Cuban/MPLA victory in the fighting in 1975–76 did not stabilize the overall picture to the point where Havana felt that it could disengage. Instead, the region's cauldron continued to bubble. The centerpiece in this new stage of the conflict revolved around U.S. and South African support for UNITA as it continued to operate in its southern Angolan strongholds, while simultaneously Havana and Angola were aiding the national liberation war of the Southwest African People's Organization (SWAPO) in Namibia.[23] Thus what might once have been envisioned as a short-term commitment dragged on, with the Cuban expeditionary force peaking at approximately 50,000; hundreds of thousands of Fidelista troops and developmental aid personnel rotated through Angola over the years.

Increasingly Havana came to see Namibia as the key to breaking this impasse, arguing that sovereignty for the colony would mean it could no longer be used as a staging area by Pretoria and its UNITA allies for attacks against Angola, and the Neto government would thus no longer need Fidelista troops to help guarantee the country's security. Finally, after protracted negotiations involving Cuba, Angola, and South Africa and mediated by the United States, an agreement was signed in December 1988 that led to Namibian independence in 1989 and the subsequent total withdrawal of Havana's combat forces from Angola.

Ethiopia, 1977–1978

The Cuban Revolution's second major foray onto African battlefields took place in support of Mengistu Haile Mariam's socialist government in Ethiopia, an impoverished country in a strategically important location: it borders the Red Sea, the route for an immense amount of the world's maritime cargo (including Persian Gulf oil) going through the Suez Canal. The path Havana traveled to reach this position was circuitous, to say the least. For years it had aligned itself with enemies of Emperor Haile Selassie's pro-American regime in Addis Ababa, especially the neighboring Somalis and rebels in Ethiopia's Eritrean region, who were fighting to establish their own independent country.

Ethiopia's political complexion began to change dramatically in September 1974 when a military coup drove Haile Selassie from power. Over the next few years Addis Ababa drifted steadily leftward as various elements jockeyed to control the government. Finally, in February 1977, a radical army faction led by Haile Mariam gained the upper hand. This new government, its sense of security enhanced by military aid received from Moscow in accordance with an arrangement made by prior authorities in December 1976, quickly upped the ideological ante by expelling all U.S. military advisors from the country approximately two months after assuming office.

These developments sparked a realignment of (Cold War) allegiances within the region. Both Moscow and Havana adopted an increasingly pro-

Table 4.1. Estimated numbers of Cuban troops in Ethiopia

1977	
December 13	400
December 21	650

1978	
January 12	2,000
January 25	2,500
February 10	3,000
February 24	10,000
March 16	11,000
April 1	15,000

Source: The table, based on U.S. State Department estimates, is from Nelson P. Valdés, "The Evolution of Cuban Foreign Policy in Africa" (paper presented at the 1979 conference of the International Studies Association in Toronto, Canada), 111.

Ethiopian stance, distancing themselves in the process from their previously close ties with Somalia and the Eritreans. Meanwhile the Somalis, seething with feelings of betrayal that were enthusiastically reinforced by the anti-Soviet regimes in Egypt and Saudi Arabia, decided to mend their fences with the Western powers. Washington responded positively, indicating its willingness to provide Mogadishu with weapons and other kinds of military aid.

Encouraged by its success in finding new allies and feeling that Haile Mariam's government was vulnerable due to the growing political instability that was afflicting Ethiopia, Somalia decided that the time was ripe to settle its dispute with Addis Ababa over the Ogaden Desert region, claimed by both countries but under Ethiopian control. The Somalis struck in July 1977, invading the Ogaden with 40,000 troops and quickly gaining the upper hand in the fighting. As the fortunes of the Ethiopian forces became increasingly bleak, and fearing that the survival of Haile Mariam's government might be at stake, Havana and Moscow launched a closely coordinated counteroffensive against the Somalis in late 1977. Basically the Fidelistas supplied the combat forces while the Kremlin provided logistical support, and Soviet officers commanded the overall joint operation. Havana's military buildup is summarized in table 4.1. The struggle was for all practical purposes over by March 18, 1978, when the Somalian army, which had taken a terrible beating from Cuban artillery and air attacks, began a final retreat to its own borders, although mopping-up operations continued for several more weeks.[24]

Developmental Aid and Counterdependency Dual Tracking

The military and security aspects of a country's foreign affairs almost always receive the greatest attention, for it is these policy areas that produce the great political dramas of nations locked in mortal combat that so captivate the media and the public.[25] Often overlooked in the excitement of the moment are the more mundane yet still extremely important dimensions of the overall pageant taking place on the international stage, such as economic relations and related developmental assistance initiatives. Numerous examples of this habit can be found in the U.S. context, for instance, the containment concept around which Washington's Cold War policies revolved. For most people, the term *containment* translates into military activity; it evokes images of the United States building a global network of anticommunist alliances, permanently stationing millions of troops abroad, and entering conflicts in places often totally unfamiliar to its citizens (Korea, Vietnam, Afghanistan). In reality, however, policy derived from the Containment Doctrine was a double-edged sword that also included a significant economic component, which often manifested itself in aid programs like the Marshall Plan for Europe and the Alliance for Progress in Latin America. Nevertheless, despite its importance, this latter part of the equation is often neglected in discussions of U.S. Cold War containment activities.

Similar myopia existed with respect to Cuba during this period. Those observing Havana's growing assertiveness in international affairs focused mainly on the more combative side of its image. Ledgers were filled with accounts of shadowy Fidelistas fanning out to promote guerrilla uprisings, of massive Cuban arms transfers to clandestine movements and revolutionary governments, and of the Angolan and Ethiopian wars. But just as the United States used its economic muscle in pursuit of containment, so also was Cuba astutely employing developmental aid as a tool to help achieve its counterdependency goals of diversifying its foreign relations, increasing its international influence, and thereby strengthening its bargaining position vis-à-vis the superpowers, especially the USSR.

In a move that was as unprecedented as was its combat role in Africa, Cuba, despite its small population and its lack of any significant natural resource base, created a remarkable package of socioeconomic programs for Third World nations, a package that in some respects equaled and even surpassed the efforts of more highly developed countries. By the mid-1980s, for instance, Havana was sending one civilian aid worker abroad for every 625 of the island's inhabitants, the comparable U.S. figure being approximately one Peace Corps volunteer or Agency for International Development (AID) employee per 34,700 U.S. citizens. Moreover, during the 1984–85 academic year, 22,000 scholarship students from eighty-two LDCs were attending high schools and universities in Cuba. In the United States, on the other hand, the federal government provided only 7,000 university scholarships for the Third World in 1985. A similar pattern emerges with respect to the USSR and its Warsaw Pact allies: In 1979, Cubans represented 19.4 percent of all Soviet bloc economic technicians working in the Third World, even though the island's population constituted only 2.5 percent of the combined USSR–Eastern Europe–Cuban total.[26] Proportionately, then, it would appear that Cuba's developmental aid efforts compared favorably with those of the two superpowers.

Revolutionary Cuba, unlike the highly industrialized nations, simply did not have the funds to finance major projects in the Third World, but it does have a well-educated population whose training and professional skills are often of the highest caliber. In the area of medicine and other health services, for example, its expertise and achievements rival those of the most developed countries. Unquestionably it is the Cuban people and their government that deserve the major share of the credit for these accomplishments. But Havana's Soviet bloc connection was an important contributing factor, for it gave the Fidelistas access to crucial human and material resources upon which they could draw in their drive to modernize their society. Thus, just as was the case with its programs of military and security assistance, Havana was dual tracking by capitalizing upon its Eastern European links to create the conditions whereby it was able to provide developmental aid to a large roster of Third World countries.

Cuba's developmental assistance efforts were almost always labor rather than capital intensive. Its basic strategy was to commit whatever human resources were necessary to get its initiatives off to a strong start and especially to conduct training so that local cadres would be able to take charge as quickly as possible. While Havana tended to concentrate on construction, education, and health care since it had large pools of highly trained professionals in those fields, it also provided help in such diverse undertakings as community development, agronomy and animal husbandry, communications, transportation, cultural affairs, applied marine biology and fishing, tourism, trade union organization, and sports.

Although Cuba dispatched contingents of developmental internationalists throughout the Third World, sub-Saharan Africa was its main theater of operations. During the heyday of such activity in the early 1980s, for example, 40.8 percent of all such personnel were posted to Africa in

1981, and that rose to 47.3 percent in 1984. Table 4.2 provides longitudinal and country data about these programs.[27] These in-country programs were supplemented by educational opportunities in Cuba that Havana made available through its extensive scholarship programs, the most innovative and ambitious operating on the old Isle of Pines, where prior to the Revolution the main inhabitants were prisoners (including, for a short time, Fidel himself). In a symbolic as well as a practical gesture, the Cubans transformed the former penal colony, now rechristened the Isle of Youth, into an educational showcase, which by 1985 was hosting approximately 12,000 foreign students in addition to a large Cuban contingent. Every Third World delegation, whose members were chosen by their governments and ranged from twelve to twenty years in age, had its own schools, each of which cost Havana about 1.2 million pesos per year to operate.[28] The main curricular emphasis was on vocational skills relevant to their nation's developmental plans. In this manner, the Cubans tried to assure that there would be a steady supply of trained personnel able to assume responsibility for the projects Havana's internationalists had launched back in their home countries.

All these multifaceted activities in Latin America and especially in Africa—aid to both revolutionary organizations and governments, participation in the Angolan and Ethiopian wars, and developmental assistance programs—firmly established Cuba as a major player in Third World affairs, but the Fidelistas were not content with a mere participatory role, no matter how significant. Instead they had leadership ambitions, which centered on the Movement of Nonaligned Nations.

Havana as a Third World Leader

Implementation of its dual-track strategy in Latin America, sub-Saharan Africa, and elsewhere involved elements of a larger policy mosaic that revolved around revolutionary Cuba's image of itself as primarily a Third World country rather than a member of the Soviet camp. This particular perception of its political personality led Havana to place increased emphasis during the 1970s on its role in the Movement of Nonaligned Nations (commonly referred to as the Nonaligned Movement or NAM). The NAM, which Cuba had joined in 1961 as the Western Hemisphere's only charter member, was established as an organization independent of (i.e., not aligned with) the two Cold War superpower blocs to serve as the main institutional vehicle for promoting cooperation among the world's developing states and for representing their interests on the international scene.

As the Fidelistas gradually assumed a higher profile in the movement,

Table 4.2. Cuban developmental aid personnel in sub-Saharan Africa

	1977	1978	1979	1981	1984	1986
Angola	4,500	8,500	6,500	6,500	6,000	6,000
Benin						35
Burkina Faso						15
Burundi						15
Cameroon						10
Cape Verde			13			15
Congo	20				140	85
Equitorial Guinea	150					10
Ethiopia	150	500	450	1,000	1,000	1,100
Ghana					40	35
Guinea		35	200	125	240	25
Guinea Bissau	45	85	40		75	85
Madagascar			25	50	35	5
Mali					10	15
Mozambique	100	400	600	1,000	900	900
Nigeria					5	5
São Tomé y Príncipe		140	200			60
Seychelles					20	20
Tanzania	425	200	80		150	25
Uganda						10
Zambia		20				15
Zimbabwe						55
Other		1,090	290	760	345	
(Total)	(5,403)	(10,970)	(8,385)	(9,435)	(9,060)	(8,540)
% change		+103.0	−23.6	+12.5	−4.0	−5.7

Sources: The 1977–79 figures come from H. Michael Erisman, *Cuba's International Relations: The Anatomy of a Nationalistic Foreign Policy* (Boulder, Colo.: Westview Press, 1985), 78–79. The 1981 figures come from U.S. Department of State, *Soviet and East European Aid to the Third World, 1981* (Washington: Department of State, 1983), 20–21. The 1984 figures come from U.S. Department of State, *Warsaw Pact Economic Aid to Non-Communist LDCs, 1984* (Washington: Department of State, 1986), 16. The 1986 figures come from U.S. Department of State, *Warsaw Pact Economic Aid Programs in Non-Communist LDCs: Holding Their Own in 1986* (Washington: Department of State, 1988), 12. *Note:* When a range of figures is given in the sources, which is common when estimates are being presented, or when two sources give different figures, I have used the average of the highest and lowest figures available.

opposition arose from some moderate members who felt that Havana's extremely close ties with Moscow and its radical left-wing ideology rendered it unfit for any kind of leadership position. Indeed some even questioned its membership credentials, suggesting that its CMEA affiliation and other links to the Second (Russian-led) World were such that it did not qualify as a nonaligned country. The Cubans responded by stressing that the movement had always taken the position that a country that was not a member of a multilateral military alliance concluded in the context of great power conflicts would be considered nonaligned. Revolutionary Cuba, they noted, was not and had never become a formal party to the Warsaw Pact. It did receive security assistance from the Soviet bloc, but other NAM members also received such aid from one superpower or another. As such, concluded Havana, it readily passed the litmus test for nonalignment.

In addition, the Cubans underscored the fact that their foreign policies had always conformed to and sought to further the international goals of the Nonaligned Movement. In particular, said Havana, Cuban revolutionaries had always stood at the forefront in the battle against Western imperialism and neocolonialism, at times even shedding their blood, as in Angola, to aid the cause of national liberation. Quite simply, then, the Fidelistas insisted that Cuba had always paid its political dues to the movement and therefore was indisputably a member in good standing. Ultimately these arguments prevailed, thereby clearing away a major obstacle to the realization of Third World leadership ambitions that the Fidelistas had been harboring for some time.[29]

These aspirations were finally realized in 1976 when the Nonaligned Movement unanimously selected Havana as the site for its next summit meeting. To be so chosen was not merely a symbolic honor. Rather the host government acquired considerable prestige and potential influence on the global stage by virtue of being assigned such responsibilities as setting the agenda for the upcoming summit and serving as the NAM's chief international representative until the next triennial conference. Thus, when revolutionary Cuba officially became head of the movement in 1979 (which meant that Fidel would serve as the organization's chairman until 1983), the occasion represented its acceptance into the innermost circles of Third World leadership.

What at first glance might have appeared to be essentially an exercise on Havana's part in enhancing its stature among developing nations also had important implications for its relations with the USSR. The central idea here, said William LeoGrande, was that "as Cuba emerged as a leader of the [Nonaligned] Movement, Cuba's value to the Soviet Union as a

Beyond the Superpowers: Cuban Globalism, 1972–1985 | 103

broker between the Third World and the socialist camp expanded tremendously."[30] Once this status as the key link between Moscow and the nonaligned community was established, Havana was in a favorable negotiating position to procure political and economic concessions from the Russians on a wide range of issues affecting the Revolution's foreign and domestic affairs. In other words, Cuba's Third World leadership initiatives translated into bargaining power that was then brought to bear when working out the terms of its relationship with the Soviet Union in particular and the larger socialist camp in general.

Havana's policies at this point represented counterdependency dual tracking in perhaps its most pristine form. The basic four-stage plan that Fidelistas devised can be summarized as follows:

- They would use their Moscow/CMEA connection to increase their ability to implement ambitious policies, including security and developmental aid programs, that would bolster their influence in Third World quarters and their prospects for playing a leadership role therein.

- The success they achieved in these endeavors would generate a reservoir of valuable political capital upon which to draw in their efforts to function as the key link or broker between the USSR and the nonaligned nations of the world.

- Assuming and executing such a linkage role would make Cuba a much more valuable ally in Moscow's eyes.

- Finally, they could use their strengthened position in both the nonaligned and socialist camps as leverage to assure that their evolving relationship with the Kremlin would become increasingly beneficial to them, thereby allowing the whole four-stage process to recycle itself.

In effect, then, what Cuba was able to do was to orchestrate astutely the interface between its Third World and Soviet bloc relations in such a way as to shift part of the burden of underwriting its counterdependency initiatives to Moscow's shoulders, an accomplishment somewhat akin to getting your opponent in a political race to finance your campaign.

Although the Fidelistas had some success in implementing this complex scenario in the 1970s, they were never really able to capitalize fully on the crown jewel of their endeavors—leadership of the Nonaligned Movement. Instead Havana experienced a dramatic reversal of its Third World fortunes when its Russian connection enmeshed it in the controversy surrounding the war in Afghanistan. The problem came to a head on January 14, 1980, when the United Nations General Assembly passed a resolution condemning the Kremlin's intervention, with NAM countries as well as other nonmember developing nations voting overwhelmingly in support.[31] It was strongly felt within the Nonaligned Movement that Cuba, as the organization's leader, was morally—if not legally—obliged to join in opposing what was seen by the Third World majority as aggressive, illegal intervention on the USSR's part into Afghanistan's internal affairs. But Havana, apparently under heavy pressure from Moscow, reluctantly chose to vote against the resolution, providing a rather convoluted explanation for its behavior that failed to placate its nonaligned colleagues.[32]

The backlash from this incident severely undermined Havana's ability to provide the assertive, flamboyant NAM leadership that many had anticipated, some with trepidation, others with relish. The fate of its campaign to win a seat on the United Nations Security Council, an honor that it had long coveted, stands as perhaps the most graphic example of the difficulty it now faced in trying to mobilize Third World support for its international initiatives. Prior to the Afghan crisis, the Fidelistas had become involved in a hotly contested battle with Colombia for the council's vacant Latin American slot. Washington, of course, was strongly backing Bogota. Although Havana had led on most of the early ballots (usually by a substantial margin), neither party had been able to muster the necessary two-thirds majority. After the Afghan debacle, however, it became obvious that enough opposition or at least indifference to Cuba's candidacy had developed within the nonaligned bloc to render a Fidelista victory impossible. Havana was therefore forced to withdraw from the race; Mexico emerged as the compromise selection. Such sentiment created an atmosphere in which Cuba had little choice but to adopt a fairly cautious, low profile stance in the NAM during its tenure as head of the organization, functioning essentially as a routine caretaker rather than playing the more familiar role of firebrand on the world stage.

Such problems, however, would pale into relative obscurity as the whole edifice of Cuban foreign policy was shaken to its core by one of the rarest of all political phenomena—a radical restructuring of the basic configuration prevailing in the international system, involving among other things the disappearance of some players and a significant revision of the informal rules governing relationships among states. This transformation, commonly referred to as the "end of the Cold War," was widely acclaimed as the dawn of a new era of global serenity. But for the Fidelistas, it meant the emasculation of the existing dual-track strategy that had been serving them well and the emergence of the Revolution's greatest crisis since the turbulent days of the early 1960s.

5

Engulfed by the Maelstrom

Cuba and the Passing of the Cold War, 1985–1992

The relative tranquility that had characterized Havana's Eastern bloc connections for approximately two decades was shattered in the late 1980s and early 1990s as turmoil engulfed the socialist camp. Communist governments with which the Fidelistas had cultivated a complex web of beneficial relations were driven from power and replaced by regimes that for the most part were at best indifferent to and in some cases quite hostile toward the Revolution. Probably the most dramatic development involved the German Democratic Republic, which had been one of the island's most important trading partners; it simply disappeared from the map as Germany was reunified. CMEA, which had been a lucrative source of developmental aid for the Cubans as well as providing privileged access to Eastern European markets, faded into obscurity, its official demise coming in June 1991. It was within the USSR itself, however, that the most important—and from Havana's perspective the most frightening—developments occurred: economic reforms were instituted abolishing the trade preferences and aid programs that had long helped to stabilize the island's economy and had contributed to its achieving a standard of living among the highest in the Third World. On the political scene, Mikhail Gorbachev, who seemed inclined to try to cushion the disequilibriating impact of such reforms as much as possible, was replaced in December 1991 by the much less sympathetic administration of Boris Yeltsin, whose disinterest in Cuban affairs meant that henceforth the island would be on its own in solving its economic and political problems.

As the shock waves of these convulsions spread out into the larger global arena, they spawned a new world order with political and especially economic dynamics that raised serious challenges to the future well-being of the Cuban Revolution. Indeed, the attitude in Havana toward this emerging situation often verged on the apocalyptic; officials repeatedly characterized it as the most serious crisis in the country's history.[1] Two broad international concerns attracted the most attention during this period as the Cubans struggled to deal with the maelstrom swirling about them:

- Trying to exert some significant damage control over the radical reconfiguration of their Russian–Eastern European ties involved in the transition to a post–Cold War environment, a key consideration being to minimize the negative impact on the island's economy. These endeavors were for the most part unsuccessful. Like a deer frozen in headlight beams, Havana found itself in a position where it could do little other than watch as havoc bore down upon it.

- Maintaining as much order and normalcy as possible in other key sectors of their foreign relations, with top priority being accorded to Western Europe and to Canada and Latin America. Efforts were also undertaken to mend Havana's Afghan-damaged fences with the nonaligned community.

The driving force behind all this activity was an idiosyncrasy that lay deep in the Fidelista psyche—fear of isolation. With its Soviet connection deteriorating, Havana knew that it had to protect its position on these fronts or face the prospect of being driven into a political and economic corner where it would be more vulnerable to attacks from its enemies.

A common thread running through this packet of foreign policy issues was the fact that the new rules of the emerging post–Cold War international game had engendered a growing tendency on Havana's part to conceptualize its security requirements in economic terms. For many years, as noted, the island's needs with regard to trade, credit lines, technical assistance, developmental programs, and the like had essentially been guaranteed by its privileged ties to the socialist bloc. This special relationship had crucial foreign policy implications in the sense that it significantly reduced (if not eliminated) Havana's vulnerability to the economic warfare that Washington had long been waging against it. But with that tie broken, developing other options to minimize Cuba's potential susceptibility to new offensives by its old nemesis became a matter of vital national interest.

Indeed in the late 1980s, Havana was experiencing economic difficulties that had little to do with the impending disintegration of the socialist bloc. Worker productivity was declining, export earnings were down, hard currency reserves were dwindling, debts owed to Western creditors were becoming increasingly unmanageable, and unemployment was emerging as another source of discontent. In short, the country was in the midst of a recession that then escalated to unprecedented crisis proportions by developments in Eastern Europe. These problems represented potential levers that Washington would try to use to destabilize Cuban society (like the anti-Allende campaign in Chile) in the hope that such pressure would, sooner rather than later, cause the Revolution to unravel completely.

Remarkably, despite all this adversity, Cuba continued its tradition of following the road less traveled, stubbornly maintaining its basic commitment to Fidelista socialism and refusing to compromise its nationalistic principles in any way in order to curry favor with the United States. Such defiance would not come cheaply, but as always Havana was willing to pay the price.

The Demise of Cuba's Soviet Bloc Connection

A somewhat deceptive calm characterized Cuba's Soviet bloc relations in the early 1980s. There was, for example, no serious public bickering on the political front (as had occurred in the 1960s), even though Havana harbored some resentment about the diplomatic damage it had incurred due to Moscow's intervention in the Afghan conflict. Instead, whatever differences of opinion or policy existed between the Fidelistas and their socialist colleagues tended for the most part to be handled in a discreet, low-profile manner.

The situation was particularly encouraging with respect to Havana's developmental efforts. In fact, the first half of the 1980s could in many respects be considered a boom time for the Revolution. The island's economy was expanding at a healthy rate, thereby providing a firm foundation for a standard of living that in certain respects compared favorably with that in the advanced industrial nations and in any case was the envy of most of its Latin American neighbors and much of the Third World at large.[2] Official Cuban government statistics for this period reported an annual growth rate in gross social product (GSP) of approximately 7.3 percent.[3] While there was some disagreement among observers about specific figures, Jorge Domínguez accurately summarized the overall scenario: "Although the Cuban government may [have overstated] growth rates for the early 1980s, economic performance was positive on average from 1981 to 1985, outpacing the economic growth of most Latin American countries for the first time since 1960. This good performance [was]

108 | Cuba's Foreign Relations in a Post-Soviet World

Table 5.1. Cuban trade with the USSR/CMEA (percent of total Cuban trade)

	1980	1985
Exports	66	86
Imports	76	80

Source: Comité Estatal de Estadísticas, *Anuario Estadístico de Cuba, 1986* (Havana, 1986).

explained to a large degree by Soviet and other CMEA support."[4] Remember, however, that Cuba's economic health, like that of practically any small island society, is heavily dependent on foreign trade; it has to bring in many commodities and goods that it cannot produce domestically, and it must be able to sell its products overseas in order to have sufficient currency reserves to finance these imports. By the early 1980s, as the data in table 5.1 illustrate, Cuba had become extremely dependent on its CMEA connection to service these needs.[5] As long as those ties functioned smoothly and in a manner that benefited the Revolution, the Fidelistas could and indeed did rest quite secure. But putting practically all one's economic eggs in a single basket is an extremely risky proposition, as would become painfully evident in the late 1980s and early 1990s.

The USSR, as might be expected, constituted the key element of Cuba's trade profile with the Soviet bloc (see table 5.2). Simple export-import data do not, however, tell the whole story, for a complex web of agreements with Moscow provided Havana with various subsidies, preferences, credits, technology transfers, and other forms of assistance. For example:

- The USSR was not only the major market for Cuban sugar, the island's most important export, but it also bought it at considerably above the going world market price.[6] Similar arrangements were made for the island's nickel exports. In effect, then, these preferential transactions functioned as a subsidy for the Cuban economy.

- As Havana's trade balances with Moscow shifted from surpluses in the late 1970s to deficits in the early 1980s (compare tables 3.2 and 5.2), the Kremlin provided loans on favorable terms—long-term, low-interest loans with payment in goods rather than cash—to cover the differences. In many cases these loans (as well as others) were essentially written off, as Moscow routinely agreed to extend or postpone repayment.

- The Soviets provided financing and/or technical aid for a wide variety of Cuban developmental enterprises, such as a petroleum refinery and nuclear power plant at Cienfuegos, an electric generating facility in east Havana, and a nickel-processing operation at Punta Gorda. Approximately 300 such major projects were under construction in 1983, says Jorge Domínguez.[7]

- One novel (and highly lucrative) aid program allowed Cuba to buy large amounts of Soviet oil on highly favorable terms and then sell on the open market whatever was left after its domestic demands had been met. This arrangement generated large amounts of hard currency that Havana then used to underwrite purchases of Western goods and services.

Such support contributed significantly to a solid performance by the Cuban economy in the early 1980s. But a rocky road lay ahead as the impact

Table 5.2. Cuban trade with the USSR/Eastern Europe, 1980–85 (millions of pesos)

Year	Exports to USSR	Imports from USSR	Total
1980	2,253.5	2,903.7	5,157.2
1981	2,357.5	3,233.9	5,591.4
1982	3,289.6	3,744.4	7,034.0
1983	3,881.8	4,245.3	8,127.1
1984	3,952.2	4,782.4	8,734.6
1985	4,481.6	5,418.9	9,900.5
	Exports to Eastern Europe	Imports from Eastern Europe	
1980	407.8	590.5	998.3
1981	570.1	717.6	1,287.7
1982	561.4	915.2	1,476.6
1983	639.9	988.7	1,628.6
1984	734.2	1,002.4	1,736.6
1985	619.9	1,088.1	1,708.0
Total exports/imports to USSR and Eastern Europe			
	1980	6,155.4	
	1981	6,879.1	
	1982	8,550.6	
	1983	9,755.7	
	1984	10,471.2	
	1985	11,608.5	

Source: Compiled from data presented in Anuario Estadístico de Cuba, 1988 (Havana, 1988).

110 | Cuba's Foreign Relations in a Post-Soviet World

of the radical restructuring of political and economic systems occurring in the Soviet Union and Eastern Europe engulfed the island.

The roots of this drama (which from a Fidelista perspective should more accurately be labeled a tragedy) can be traced to March 1985, when Mikhail Gorbachev assumed the reins of power in the Kremlin. After years of uninspired and indeed often insipid leadership by his predecessors, Gorbachev entered office convinced that reforms were necessary in order to revitalize Soviet society. He instituted in both domestic and foreign policies an ambitious menu of change revolving around two concepts: *glasnost,* which provided for more openness in political matters and greater tolerance for differing points of view, and *perestroika,* which sought to reinvigorate the USSR's overly bureaucratic command economy by interjecting some elements of a market system. In the process, he unleashed forces within the USSR and the Soviet bloc that ultimately swirled out of his control. John Rourke eloquently summarized what happened as follows:

> Gorbachev, among other things, . . . announced that the USSR was willing to let Eastern Europeans follow their own domestic policies. Eastern Europeans moved quickly to escape Moscow's orbit. This was symbolized most dramatically in East Germany, where the communist government fell rapidly apart. East Germany dissolved itself in October 1990, and its territory was absorbed by West Germany. . . . Other communist governments in the region also fell, and in February 1991 the Warsaw Pact dissolved.
>
> Although almost no one then could believe it might be true, the Soviet Union itself was doomed. Old-guard communists tried and failed to seize power in mid-1991 in an effort to reverse the tide of history. Within six months the USSR collapsed as its constituent republics declared their independence. On December 25 Gorbachev resigned his presidency of a country that no longer existed. Soon thereafter, at 7:32 P.M., the red hammer-and-sickle Soviet flag was lowered for the last time from the Kremlin's spires and replaced by the red, white, and blue Russian flag. . . . The Soviet Union was no more.[8]

Despite the turmoil boiling up around him, Gorbachev did not take precipitate action with regard to Cuban-Soviet relations. Inevitably, of course, there were some changes, such as a reduction in the level of aid provided by some programs. But overall it appears that Gorbachev's

Kremlin tried to move forward with its agenda, admittedly not always successfully, in a manner that would be minimally disruptive to its ties with Havana.[9] For example, while there was some overall decline from the 1985 high- water mark in the volume of the island's trade with the USSR and the Soviet bloc in general during the latter part of the 1980s (see table 5.3), these links were much more vigorous at the end of the decade than they had been at its beginning. The situation, in other words, had hardly reached crisis proportions. But this was soon to change.

The full force of the cataclysm exploded upon Cuba in the early 1990s as the old international order disintegrated. The watershed year was 1991; the following events represent some of the developments that contributed to the emergence of what would become known as the post–Cold War world.

June 28	CMEA (COMECON) formally disbands.
July 1	The Warsaw Pact formally disbands.
August 19	Communist elements opposed to Gorbachev's reforms mount a coup to remove him from office.
August 21	The coup attempt falls apart, with Boris Yeltsin (leader of the USSR's Russian Republic) playing a major role in frustrating it.
August 24	Gorbachev issues a series of decrees curbing the activities of the Communist Party; the party's Central Committee is dissolved.
December 8	Leaders of the Russian, Ukrainian, and Byelorussian republics declare that the Soviet Union no longer exists and proclaim the formation of a new "Commonwealth of Independent States" open to all Soviet republics.
December 21	Eleven republics of the USSR formally constitute themselves as the Commonwealth of Independent States.
December 25	Gorbachev resigns as president of the Soviet Union.[10]

Thus the passing of the baton was completed. Boris Yeltsin was now ensconced in the Kremlin, president of a scaled-down, noncommunist Russian state. The socialist bloc was gone as the political map of Eastern Europe was redrawn: communist governments throughout the area had been driven from power; various republics of the old USSR had declared their independence; and the two flagship organizations that Moscow had

Table 5.3. Cuban exports and their destinations and imports and their sources (millions of U.S.$)

	1985	1987	1989	1991[a]	1992
Exports and their destinations					
USSR	4,885.0	3,869.0	3,231.0		
Russia					632.0
Belarus					4.0
Kasakhstan					29.3
Albania	6.1	3.8	3.3		
Bulgaria	202.2	169.1	176.9		23.2
Czechoslovakia Slovenia	129.9	144.0	109.4	5.0	8.8
E. Germany	254.7	281.6	285.9		
Hungary	22.5	66.7	10.7	1.2	0.2
Poland	81.2	43.8	15.4	0.2	1.3
Romania	41.7	109.0	117.2	2.8	5.2
Total exports	6,531.0	5,402.0	5,392.0	3,550.0	2,030.0
Imports and their sources					
USSR	5,907.0	5,446.0	5,522.0		
Russia					191.0
Belarus					18.0
Georgia	-				
Kasakhstan					19.0
Lithuania					0.4
Albania	4.5	6.2	3.3		
Bulgaria	209.4	184.0	177.5		
Czechoslovakia	214.9	200.1	112.8	11.6	5.9
E. Germany	307.9	338.8	358.7		
Hungary	183.1	72.4	47.2	24.0	8.2
Poland	82.6	81.5	20.1	3.9	5.9
Romania	145.4	182.1	164.4	0.9	4.9
Total imports	8,758.0	7,584.0	8,124.0	3,690.0	2,235.0

Sources: Compiled from U.S. Central Intelligence Agency, *Cuba: Handbook of Trade Statistics—1992, 1995, 1997* (Springfield, Va.: National Technical Information Service, 1992, 1995, 1997).

a. 1991 was an extremely chaotic year for Cuban trade with the USSR/Russia, and good comprehensive data is not readily available.

Table 5.4. Basic Cuban economic indicators, 1989 and 1993 (in billions of pesos, unless otherwise indicated)

	1989	1993	% change
National product (GSP)	27.2	15.95[a]	–41.4
Gross domestic product (GDP)	19.6	12.8	–34.7
GDP per capita (in pesos)	1,865.0	1,177.0	–36.9
Soviet/CMEA aid	6.0	0	–100.0
State budget deficit	1.4	4.8	+243.0
Foreign trade transactions (total exports and imports)	13.5	3.4	–75.0

Sources: Based on official Cuban sources presented in Carmelo Mesa-Lago, "Prospective Dollar Remittances and the Cuban Economy," in Archibald R. Ritter and John M. Kirk (eds.), *Cuba in the International System: Normalization and Integration* (New York: St. Martin's Press, 1995), 59, and on Jorge F. Pérez-López, "The Cuban Economy in Mid-1997" (paper presented at the 1997 conference of the Association for the Study of the Cuban Economy, on the Internet at www.lanic.utexas.edu/la/cb/cuba/asce/cuba7), 3.
a. The estimated GSP ranged from 12.5 billion to 19.4 billion. The average of those two figures is used here.

employed to bind its camp together, CMEA and the Warsaw Pact, had disappeared, with some of their members seeking to join the European Union and/or NATO.

The demise of the old bipolar world order was widely applauded, especially by those who construed it primarily in terms of lessening the nuclear threat that had hung for so long over the global community. For Cuba, however, the negative implications in many respects outweighed the positives and were especially devastating in the economic realm. The catastrophic free fall of the Cuban economy that ensued (1989 is used here as the base comparative year) has already been widely documented and discussed.[11] A litany of dreary statistics has been presented to delineate the crisis, and the following are illustrative (see also table 5.4). The island's overall economy shrank by at least 40–45 percent, with its import capacity dropping from $8.12 billion (U.S.) in 1989 to $1.99 billion at its lowest point in 1993. Overall export earnings fell from $5.39 billion in 1989 to $1.28 billion in 1993 (a 76.3 percent drop). In 1992, petroleum shortages led to the suspension or curtailment of over 50 percent of all industrial activity, to a 70 percent reduction in public transportation, and to extensive electricity blackouts, especially in Havana and other major cities. Such an economic Holocaust was practically unheard of in the modern Western Hemisphere and certainly in Fidelista Cuba. Nevertheless, as its standard of living plummeted under shocks that would have produced at least blood in the streets and probably the total disintegration of many other societies, the Revolution persevered.[12]

The driving force behind this horror story was, of course, the destruction of Havana's preferential ties to CMEA and especially the Soviet Union and Russia. Trade flows that had been the lifeblood of the island's economy slowed to a trickle. Crucial imports nosedived, notes economist Andrew Zimbalist: "Oil imports from Russia decreased from 13.3 million tons in 1989 to 1.8 million tons in 1992; fertilizer imports plunged from 1.3 million tons to .25 million tons; and animal feed imports fell like a stone from 1.6 million tons to .45 million tons."[13]

The radically reduced trade remaining was conducted on terms highly unfavorable to Cuba (at least in comparison to prior practice). Moscow, for example, required that all commercial transactions—which had previously been conducted in accordance with comprehensive long-term agreements negotiated between the two governments, normally lasting five years—now had to be arranged on a case-by-case basis with individual enterprises, and they were shifted from a subsidized ruble basis to payment at market prices in hard currencies (which were and still are in extremely short supply in Cuba). Adding to Havana's woes was the fact that these market prices were often escalating dramatically. The cost of many crucial imported foodstuffs, for instance, skyrocketed over a two-year period (1991–93): cereal went from $80 to $130 a ton, chicken from $1,000 a ton to $1,500, and milk from $1,500 a ton to over $2,000.[14] Meanwhile, the prices of Cuba's two most important commodity exports—sugar and nickel—fell by 20 and 28 percent, respectively.[15] By 1993 the cumulative impact of such hammer blows had driven the Cuban economy deep into a depression.

As a result of developments in Eastern Europe, the world that Havana now confronted was indeed a daunting and in certain respects a frightening place. Some foreign policy formulas that had served it well in the past were no longer viable, the main casualty being the Cold War dual-tracking strategy that Cuba had employed with considerable success to enhance its military and economic security and to expand its influence on the international stage. Moreover, as these protective shields were peeled away, the U.S. threat loomed ever larger, for Washington had never abandoned its hopes of driving the upstart, fiercely nationalistic Fidelistas into a corner and ultimately bringing them to heel. Now, for the first time in many years, a real opportunity to do exactly that seemed to be emerging. Havana, knowing that it must never allow itself to fall prey to such isolation tactics, responded by devoting increased attention to trying to calm the waters as much as possible on other key international fronts. Such stabilization efforts were motivated not only by a perceived U.S. threat but also by the Fidelistas' need to buy themselves some time to make whatever policy adjustments (domestic or foreign) they felt were necessary to meet the challenges posed by a post–Cold War world.

Mending Fences with the Third World

In the early 1980s the Fidelistas' relations with the LDC community in general (Africa, Asia, and Latin America) and the Nonaligned Movement in particular were in considerable disarray. Such a situation was a marked departure from the 1970s, when Havana's political stock in these quarters had been high. As discussed, this reversal of fortunes, especially within the NAM, stemmed to a great extent from what was perceived as the overly pro-Soviet stance that Cuba had taken on the Afghan question. The sources of friction in the Western Hemisphere were more homegrown, centering on Havana's efforts to help consolidate the radical left-wing governments that had seized power in Nicaragua and Grenada and its involvement—the exact nature and extent of which was a matter of considerable controversy—in the Salvadoran conflict. These activities resurrected old fears in some quarters about subversion and militant ideological crusading (i.e., proletarian internationalism) on Cuba's part.

One initiative Havana launched that seemed to have some potential to revitalize its LDC vanguard status concerned the Latin American/Third World debt crisis that had exploded on the international scene in the early 1980s.[16] In 1985 Cuba began promoting a sweeping solution calling for the creation of an LDC cartel that would serve as the vehicle for persuading or pressuring creditors to accept an across-the-board default. Recognizing that a straight write-off would be unacceptable because it would likely lead to chaos in the Western banking community, Castro proposed that the governments of the industrialized nations guarantee repayment, arguing that the cost could easily be underwritten through a modest decrease in military spending (e.g., 10–12 percent), which he implied would be feasible within the context of a superpower arms control agreement involving some mutual force reductions. Also, contending that the root causes of the debt crisis could be traced to structural inequities in the existing system of global economic relations, he insisted that the New International Economic Order (NIEO) the Third World countries had long been demanding had to be part of the overall package. Although most countries proved unwilling to embrace Fidel's plan, the Cubans' ef-

116 | Cuba's Foreign Relations in a Post-Soviet World

forts did serve to demonstrate their eagerness to cooperate with other Third World governments on such widely shared concerns as debt relief, a reversal of the U.S.-Soviet arms race, and the establishment of mechanisms more conducive to balanced growth for all nations of the world.

But the factor that was probably most important in firmly reestablishing the Fidelistas in the mainstream of Third World affairs was the vital role that they played in helping Namibia to gain its independence from South Africa in 1989. Initially many LDCs had reservations about Cuba's decision in the mid-1970s to establish a strong military presence in Africa's southern cone by dispatching combat troops to Angola to defend Agostinho Neto's radical MPLA government against South African forces, for such a move ran counter to the long-standing Third World preference to avoid having their conflicts internationalized. Although the superpowers were the primary targets for such sentiment, it could likewise be aroused when countries were perceived (as Cuba sometimes was) as being "agents" of a Cold War alliance. Such misgivings took on added urgency when, as noted in chapter 4, the scope of Havana's involvement expanded beyond the Angolan theater to include the Namibian conflict.

Whatever qualms may have been generated by Havana's military exploits in Africa's southern cone, the ultimate outcome—a crushing defeat for South Africa and freedom for Namibia—was hailed by most Third World governments and as such served to enhance Cuba's international status. Certainly one solid indication that Havana had indeed regained some of the ground lost in the Afghan imbroglio was the strong support that it received from the developing nations when in October 1989 it again made a bid for a seat on the UN Security Council. In this instance, even though Washington once again mounted a major counteroffensive, Cuba prevailed with surprising ease, receiving the largest number of positive votes ever cast in such an election—146 out of a possible 156.[17] Such diplomatic gains suggested that entering the 1990s, Cuba was enjoying some success in rejuvenating its influence within what might be termed the general realm of South-South relations on its international political agenda.

Cuba's Changing International Economic Landscape

Most observers of the changes wrought by the end of the Cold War tended, at least initially, to concentrate on the drama involved in redrawing the world's political maps. Gone was the behemoth spanning eleven time zones that had been the Soviet Union, some of its old territory now being represented in world atlases by such newly independent countries as

Belarus, the Ukraine, Turkmenistan, Kazakhstan, and Kyrgystan. Czecho-slovakia split into two nations (the Czech Republic and Slovakia), while East and West Germany reunited into one state.

These developments required all countries, including Cuba, to devote attention to altering the configuration of their political relations. Diplomatic ties, for example, had to be established with sovereign nations that had recently emerged as actors on the global stage, and policy revisions were often necessary to deal with regime changes that had occurred, such as the rise to power in Eastern Europe of noncommunist governments (Poland, Hungary, and Romania).

In Cuba's case, however, the political ramifications of the post–Cold War order were overshadowed by economic considerations. Indeed, what became increasingly apparent as the maelstrom engulfed the Revolution was that the Fidelistas were confronting the daunting prospect of having to adjust to the loss of a highly lucrative network of ties with the socialist bloc, a network that had at its height sustained approximately 75–80 percent of the island's overseas commerce and perhaps as much as 40–45 percent of its entire economy. Understandably, therefore, trade and related questions tended to dominate the view from Havana.

Cuba's General Trade Profile, 1985–1992

Table 5.5 provides an overview of the main items involved in Havana's trade relations. On the export earnings side of the ledger, sugar remained king, with nickel a distant second. Not included in this information are the

Table 5.5. Composition of Cuban trade (millions of U.S.$)

	1985	1987	1989	1991	1992
Total exports	6,530	5,402	5,392	3,565	2,085
Sugar and by-products	4,841	3,987	3,914	2,670	1,300
Nickel	323	317	485	260	235
Fruits	157	163	139	100	50
Fish	129	141	127	115	120
Oil re-exports	574	308	213		
Total imports	8,758	7,584	8,124	3,690	2,235
Oil and fuels	2,871	2,600	2,598	1,240	835
Food	1,067	794	1,011	720	450
Machinery/equipment	2,637	2,354	2,531	785	475

Sources: Compiled from *Anuario Estadistico de Cuba, 1989* (Havana, 1989), and U.S. Central Intelligence Agency, *Cuba: Handbook of Trade Statistics, 1997* (Springfield, Va.: National Technical Information Service, 1997).

Cuba's Foreign Relations in a Post-Soviet World

Table 5.6. Cuban export profile, 1985–92 (millions of U.S.$)

	1985 (%)	1987 (%)	1989 (%)	1991 (%)[a]	1992 (%)
Total	6,531.0	5,402.0	5,392.0	3,550.0	2,030.0
W. Europe	426.0 (6.5)	343.2 (6.4)	361.5 (6.7)	353.1 (9.9)	316.9 (15.6)
E. Europe	5,617.2 (86.1)	4,683.2 (86.7)	4,064.8 (75.3)	9.2 (0.3)	651.8 (32.2)
Americas	79.5 (1.2)	81.6 (1.5)	157.9 (3.0)	235.3 (6.6)	269.3 (13.2)
Asia	290.3 (4.4)	207.4 (3.8)	379 (7.0)	349.4 (9.8)	303.4 (14.9)
Africa	28.5 (0.4)	12.5 (0.2)	111.4 (2.1)	99.9 (2.8)	85.9 (4.2)
Other	88.9 (1.4)	74.2 (1.4)	317.4 (5.9)	2,503.1 (70.6)	402.7 (19.9)

Sources: Compiled from U.S. Central Intelligence Agency, *Cuba: Handbook of Trade Statistics—1992 and 1997* (Springfield, Va.: National Technical Information Service, 1992, 1997).
a. 1991 was an extremely chaotic year for Cuban trade. Good comprehensive data were not readily available, hence the large "Other" figure.

income data from tourism. Suffice it to say, for comparative purposes, that gross tourism revenues were estimated to be $400 million in 1991 and $500 million in 1992.[18] But because there is considerable "leakage" of tourist dollars from the host country (e.g., to pay for external goods and services associated with tourism), these gross figures must be discounted somewhat. Using the average discount rate of 34 percent that is estimated for the Cuban tourism industry, which is in line with the average figure for Caribbean tourism in general, the net earnings would be $264 million for 1991 and $330 million for 1992.

Tables 5.6 and 5.7 provide a broad overview of the general patterns of Cuban export activity in the 1985–92 period. In many respects, such exports (especially the non-CMEA components) became the primary vehicle upon which the government relied in its efforts to adapt to the emerging post–Cold War international economic order. A strong performance in the export sector was crucial to financing the free market imports—either through the acquisition of hard currency or by providing a foundation upon which barter deals could be established—that the island's economy now had to have in order to function at any significant level of development and sophistication.

Table 5.7 focuses on Cuban export activity beyond its traditional CMEA–Eastern Europe center of gravity. The list of countries within the three geographical categories is not comprehensive, representing only Havana's leading customers in a particular region. The roster for the Americas is more eclectic in the sense that rather than being limited to Cuba's main export destinations, it incorporates a broader cross section of countries from the hemisphere.

Looking at tables 5.6 and 5.7, it becomes clear that the Western Hemisphere as a whole was definitely a growth area for Cuban exports in the difficult years of 1985–92, the gross dollar figures expanding at a healthy 238.7 percent rate that was unmatched by any other region. The Canadian figures were even more impressive, registering a percentage increase of 505.7.[19]

Within Latin America, the premier customers for Cuban goods and services during this period were Mexico and Nicaragua (although Managua's stock would drop dramatically by 1992, the 1990 elections having resulted in the radical, pro-Cuban Sandinista government being replaced by the conservative Chamorro administration). Indeed, the dollar volume of Havana's exports to Nicaragua was comparable to that for such highly developed nations as France, Germany, and Italy and frequently exceeded the figures for Britain.

This strong performance on the part of the Western Hemisphere, however, was somewhat late in materializing during the period when the inter-

Table 5.7. Cuban exports and their destinations, 1985–92 (millions of U.S.$)

	1985	1986	1987	1988	1989	1990	1991[a]	1992
Europe								
France	39.9	55.3	81	66.3	61.4	52.0	60.4	44.0
Germany	20.4	19.1	23.2	72.1	30.3	37.2	23.9	21.0
Italy	38.1	54.8	50.1	54.7	44.8	52.6	47.7	51.0
Netherlands	62.7	41.8	47.8	76.0	123	79.7	89.7	131.0
Spain	123.7	87.3	99.2	81.9	91.4	80.0	91.6	85.0
U. Kingdom	9.4	12.5	21.1	44.3	56.3	52.4	31.5	23.0
Asia								
China (PRC)	107.5	84.0	77.3	293.0	229.0	309.9	201.5	183.0
Japan	93.1	134.4	117.2	137.8	144.1	95.3	142.0	115.0
Americas								
Canada	35.0	55.2	41.0	77.9	57.7	122.7	146.7	212.0
Nicaragua	31.6	33.2	34.7	43.3	47.7	54.8	60.3	2.0
Mexico	2.3	2.4	1.5	8.9	23.6	95.5	105.0	7.0
Colombia	3.8	3.3	0.6	0.5	0.3	0.3	0.5	3.0
Venezuela	17.6	4.4	16.5	49.5	28.6	9.0	9.9	20.0
Argentina	0.3	1.2	0.9	1.1	1.3	0.8	0.9	2.0
Brazil	-	3.5	3.7	-	28.6	99.5	27.6	16.0

Sources: Compiled from U.S. Central Intelligence Agency, *Cuba: Handbook of Trade Statistics—1992 and 1997* (Springfield, Va.: National Technical Information Service, 1992, 1997).
a. 1991 was an extremely chaotic year for Cuban trade, and the data for this year must be viewed with some skepticism.

national system was being transformed into a post–Cold War configuration. During the 1980s, Cuba's exports to its hemispheric neighbors were fairly modest when compared to exports to most other areas, Africa being the sole exception. But in the 1990s this picture changed dramatically: the status of the Americas began to rival that of Western Europe and Asia. The main driving force behind this development, to the surprise of some observers, was Canada which was emerging as a major player in the island's economy. Illustrating this development was the fact that in 1992 only Russia exceeded the Great White North as a consumer of Cuban exports (compare tables 5.3 and 5.7). Also crucially important to Havana was the additional influx of considerable sums of money (not included in these export figures) coming from Canadian private investors and tourists; in both categories Canada established itself as one of Havana's most important economic partners.

The import side of the trade equation is summarized in tables 5.8 and 5.9. The profile in table 5.8 reveals that the Western Hemisphere was the only major region from which Cuba's imports actually *increased* in the 1985–92 period; the African numbers also grew, but the amounts involved were inconsequential. Comparing 1985 and 1992, the percentage changes (excluding the Africa and "Other" categories) were Western Europe = –14.7 percent; Eastern Europe = –96.9 percent; the Americas = +3.3 percent; and Asia = –58.5 percent.

During this time frame, the Western Hemisphere likewise significantly improved its relative position with regard to the gross volume of its goods and services flowing to the island. In 1985, for example, the Americas ranked fourth in the regional hierarchy of Cuba's import sources, lagging well behind both Eastern and Western Europe and even being eclipsed by the much more distant Asian suppliers, who had to overcome the disadvantage of higher shipping costs when competing for Havana's business. By 1992, however, the Americas had risen to second place, being "outsold" only by the Western Europeans.

In contrast to the export sector, where Canada increasingly overshadowed everyone else in the Americas in terms of trading activity with Havana, there was a more even distribution of major players supplying the island with imports, especially in 1991 and 1992 (see table 5.9). Although their relative positions changed over time, Canada, Mexico, and Argentina consistently played key roles in Havana's import scenario, with Buenos Aires occupying the top slot for four of the eight years in the 1985–92 era.[20]

Table 5.8. Cuban import profile, 1985–92 (millions of U.S.$)

	1985 (%)	1987 (%)	1989 (%)	1991 (%)[a]	1992 (%)
Total	8,758.0	7,584.0	8,124.0	3,690.0	2,235.0
W. Europe	718.6 (8.2)	508.4 (6.7)	723.3 (8.9)	851.0 (23.0)	612.8 (27.4)
E. Europe	7,054.8 (80.6)	6,511.1 (85.8)	6,360.1 (78.3)	40.4 (1.1)	216.4 (9.7)
Americas	413.7 (4.7)	294.3 (3.9)	634.4 (7.8)	506.2 (13.7)	427.2 (19.1)
Asia	532.7 (6.0)	239.3 (3.2)	308.9 (3.8)	280.1 (7.6)	220.9 (9.9)
Africa	3.2 (0.1)	4.2 (0.1)	7.2 (0.1)	14.5 (0.4)	5.4 (0.2)
Other	35.5 (0.4)	26.4 (0.3)	90.1 (1.1)	1,997.9 (54.2)	752.3 (33.7)

Sources: Compiled from U.S. Central Intelligence Agency, *Cuba: Handbook of Trade Statistics—1992 and 1997* (Springfield, Va.: National Technical Information Service, 1992, 1997).
a. 1991 was an extremely chaotic year for Cuban trade. Good comprehensive data were not readily available, hence the large "Other" figure.

Table 5.9. Cuban imports and their sources, 1985–92 (millions of U.S.$)

	1985	1986	1987	1988	1989	1990	1991[a]	1992
Europe								
France	105.1	53.8	54.7	72.7	46.9	68.2	62.5	90.0
Germany	105.2	106.0	69.6	90.3	124.4	259.5	123.4	59.0
Italy	63.0	67.2	63.8	93.3	81.3	109.2	156.9	104.0
Netherlands	29.8	29.9	38.8	50.0	40.6	39.8	38.2	42.0
Spain	291.0	291.6	192.7	210.0	216.2	302.4	283.3	199.0
U. Kingdom	75.9	86.6	67.5	55.4	87.1	71.9	50.1	50.0
Asia								
China (PRC)	116.8	95.6	79.4	155.5	212.3	252.0	224.2	200.0
Japan	303.1	296.4	115.5	116.9	54.1	73.0	35.7	18.0
Americas								
Canada	246.2	261.6	205.0	183.8	131.7	136.1	114.0	100.0
Nicaragua	1.0	1.1	0.9	1.1	1.2	1.4	3.0	4.0
Mexico	69.7	50.1	78.5	79.4	108.5	104.0	107.0	120.0
Colombia	4.6	2.2	0.9	9.2	26.6	19.9	21.8	14.0
Venezuela	16.5	8.5	328.5	15.9	28.0	30.8	49.0	79.0
Argentina	283.4	181.8	133.7	195.8	187.0	163.4	99.0	63.0
Brazil	-	1.3	3.0	23.2	76.7	78.9	66.0	17.0

Sources: Compiled from U.S. Central Intelligence Agency, *Cuba: Handbook of Trade Statistics—1992 and 1997* (Springfield, Va.: National Technical Information Service, 1992, 1997).
a. 1991 was an extremely chaotic year for Cuban trade, and the data for this year must be viewed with some skepticism.

Cuba encountered various difficulties in these efforts to diversify its international economic relations as its former anchor, the socialist bloc economy, disintegrated. One problem that quickly became apparent was that some countries were reluctant to trade with the island unless Havana made significant progress in servicing its debt to them in hard currency. But such preconditions involved a fatal contradiction: Cuba could only meet these obligations if it greatly increased its export revenues. In this futile circle, to refuse to trade until debts were serviced meant that the debts would not be serviced, since expanded trade was necessary for that servicing to occur.

Such frustrations have been fairly common in Havana's dealings with the highly industrialized states of the European Community, which were and still are among the island's primary creditors. But Latin American countries sometimes also entered this picture. In June 1990, for example, Peru announced that it was suspending a trade pact with Cuba due to Havana's failure to make a $5.2 million payment on its debt to Lima.[21] Similar difficulties arose with Colombia, Venezuela, Brazil, Argentina, and Mexico.[22]

Havana did implement some measures intended to help resolve such trade-inhibiting debt issues. The most common ploy was to agree to allow part of the revenue generated by Cuban exports to a particular country to be applied to paying off its existing debt. For example, in May 1992 Colombia and Cuba announced an arrangement whereby for every $10 worth of goods and services that the Colombians imported from Cuba, $5 would go to amortizing the island's Colombian debts.[23] The obvious attraction from Havana's viewpoint was the incentive thus created for the Colombians to maximize their Cuban purchases. Similar deals, which sometimes assumed quasi-barter forms whereby Cuba supplied goods (often medicines) and their value was then discounted from its debt, were struck with Venezuela (July 1992) and Brazil (February 1994).[24] Even more startling, when one considers the Revolution's tradition of comprehensive state ownership of the means of production, was the announcement of debt-for-equity swaps with Mexico. It must be noted that Havana had liberalized its laws on foreign investment and ownership significantly in 1982, but it had nevertheless up to this point consistently expressed skepticism about debt/equity swaps and had warned Latin American states against them (especially if the United States was involved).[25] Yet in December 1992, it was reported that a deal had been struck whereby the Mexican government would begin selling Cuban debt to Mexican investors at a discount, with Havana then buying back the debt by offering those investors equity interest in various Cuban enterprises (such as tourist hotels).[26] While it was never anticipated that such initiatives would completely resolve the island's debt/trade problems, they certainly were indicative of increasing flexibility and pragmatism on the Fidelistas' part.

Undoubtedly the greatest obstacle that Havana confronted in its efforts to expand and diversify its trade relations in general, and especially those with its hemispheric neighbors, was its old archenemy—Washington. As has been said, a central thread that has characterized the U.S. approach to Fidelista Cuba has been the idea of *isolation,* the basic premise being that the probability of the Revolution's demise is positively related to the degree of Havana's seclusion in both the hemisphere and the world at large. Such sentiment, at least among the most intransigent antirevolutionary elements in the United States, became even more pronounced in the early 1990s, for Havana was seen as being more vulnerable now that the socialist bloc no longer existed to function as a deterrent to and a neutralizer of Washington's hostility.

The typical tactics that the United States has used in attempting to incorporate hemispheric countries into this scenario have hardly been novel. There has been on the one hand the "carrot"—the prospects of trade, aid, and other benefits, with particular emphasis on the possibilities of preferential treatment for cooperative countries within the context of such programs as the Caribbean Basin Initiative (CBI) during the 1980s and the North American Free Trade Agreement (NAFTA) in the 1990s. On the darker side of the equation, there has been coercion and intimidation. Here, says Andrew Zimbalist, "threats and other pressure have been employed against other countries to deter economic relations with Cuba. Sometimes the threats are embodied in legislative initiatives that call for sanctions to be taken against countries that engage in certain types of transactions with Cuba. Sometimes the pressure takes the form of letters or phone calls indicating that the United States would look unfavorably upon Cuban participation in certain commercial activities."[27] A notorious example of such legislative initiatives was the 1992 Cuban Democracy Act (CDA, also known as the Torricelli Law), which raised the specter of various sanctions against any government that allowed a company that was under its jurisdiction and was a subsidiary of a U.S. corporation to trade with or invest in Cuba; that chose to extend trade preferences to Havana; or that pursued other policies that promoted closer economic cooperation with the island.[28]

It should be noted, however, that many of Washington's most stalwart trading partners, especially the Western Europeans and the Canadians, rejected the CDA and refused to work with the White House in implementing it. The primary bone of contention was the CDA's provisions concerning foreign subsidiaries of U.S. companies, which many felt was an unacceptable and illegal attempt by the United States to impose its domestic laws on other countries. But such complaints fell on deaf ears, for Washington remained irrevocably committed to its obstructionist tactics. This intransigence inevitably made it more difficult for Cuba to navigate the political and economic terrain as it tried to restructure its trade relations in the Western Hemisphere and elsewhere in response to the chaos caused by the disintegration of the Soviet bloc.

Exploring Hemispheric Economic Opportunities

As indicated, the Americas as a whole represented an area whose stock in the early 1990s was rapidly appreciating in Havana's emerging post–Cold War portfolio of economic partners. Concurrently, the campaign that had been under way for some time to normalize Cuba's political relations with hemispheric countries was proceeding smoothly. Indeed most Latin American and Caribbean governments had by this point reestablished diplomatic ties with Havana, and practically all the exceptions appeared willing to discuss the prospects for a rapprochement in the near future. In the CARICOM region, for example, formal links were established with Jamaica (broken in October 1981 and restored in July 1990); with Grenada (suspended in December 1983 and resumed in May 1992); with St. Vincent and the Grenadines in May 1993; and with Antigua and Barbuda in April 1994. Colombia, which had thus far been the only holdout among the three Caribbean Basin countries considered to be regional-influentials (the others are Mexico and Venezuela), finally reconciled with Havana in October 1993.

While strengthening and completing this process of normalizing state-to-state diplomatic relations remained a concern, trade and related issues moved increasingly to the forefront of the Fidelistas' hemispheric agenda.[29] Within this economic equation, Canada, which had joined Mexico in defying the rest of the Americas by refusing to break with revolutionary Cuba in the early 1960s, began to assume a position of growing importance. In the 1990s, Canada, driven by the combination of an aggressive business lobby, a steadily increasing number of joint ventures in Cuba, and a large share of the island's tourist market, would emerge as one of Havana's most important hemispheric economic partners.

As might be expected, the dynamics of improving trade relations unfolded somewhat unevenly; progress, problems, and prospects varied among subregions within the hemisphere. Moreover, as discussed in the next section, Havana's efforts often confronted a larger generic complication rooted in the fact that it was trying to expand its relations with Caribbean and Latin economies that often were too similar in their broad outlines to its own and therefore were limited in the export-import opportunities that they presented. This was a dilemma that Cuba would confront not only in the Western Hemisphere but also in its dealings with developing countries elsewhere in the world. These and other issues are addressed in the following subregional summaries of the restructuring process in the early 1990s.

Central America

Historically the Central American countries displayed little interest in developing vigorous trade and other relations with revolutionary Cuba. This situation could in a "technical" sense be attributed to the fact that Havana's political ties with most of these countries either had not been normalized or were at best at a minimalist stage of diplomatic formalities, which meant the foundation upon which solid economic cooperation is normally built was lacking. Such aloofness was reinforced by the extreme anticommunist sentiments that often pervaded the most powerful sectors of Central American societies and by their tradition of deference (many observers would characterize it more harshly as dependency-induced subservience) to Washington's hegemonic impulses in the hemisphere. In any case, the result was Central American power structures that often were not especially inclined to collaborate with the Fidelistas.

There was one glaring exception to this general rule in the 1980s and early 1990s—Nicaragua. It is, of course, hardly surprising that Cuban-Nicaraguan trade was brisk during the 1980s when the radical Sandinistas were in power (see especially table 5.7 and also table 5.9). But Managua became more aloof following the February 1990 Nicaraguan elections, won by Violetta Chamorro and her somewhat improbable anti-Sandinista coalition despite all the projections to the contrary.

But beyond the uncertainties of electoral politics, there were and still are some much more fundamental problems confronting Havana. The most basic, which in effect has represented a barrier to any Fidelista aspirations about expanding trade relations in this corner of the hemisphere, is that Cuba and all of these countries tend to export and import similar products (see table 5.10). The perfect textbook trade relationship is based on complementary comparative advantage, which when applied in a rudi-

126 | Cuba's Foreign Relations in a Post-Soviet World

Table 5.10. Cuban–Central American trade profiles

	Major exports	Major imports
Cuba	Sugar	Capital goods
	Nickel ore	Industrial raw materials
	Citrus fruits	Foodstuffs
	Fish products	Petroleum
Costa Rica	Coffee	Petroleum
	Bananas	Machinery
	Textiles	Consumer durables
	Sugar	Chemicals
El Salvador	Coffee	Petroleum products
	Sugar	Consumer goods
	Cotton	Foodstuffs
	Shrimp	Machinery
Guatemala	Coffee	Petroleum products
	Bananas	Machinery
	Sugar	Grain
Honduras	Bananas	Machinery
	Coffee	Chemical products
	Shrimp	Manufactured goods
Nicaragua	Coffee	Petroleum
	Cotton	Foodstuffs
	Sugar	Chemicals
Panama	Bananas	Foodstuffs
	Shrimp	Petroleum
		Capital goods

Source: Compiled from U.S. Central Intelligence Agency, *World Factbook 1990* (Washington, D.C.: Central Intelligence Agency, 1990).

mentary two-party scenario simply means that each participant will be highly efficient in supplying the goods needed by the other. An ideal hypothetical case would be Nation 1 exporting items A, B, and C and importing items X, Y, and Z, while Nation 2 exports X, Y, and Z and imports A, B, and C. But when almost everyone is in effect exporting commodities M, N, and O, as in the Cuban–Central American situation, the commercial prospects become bleak.

Recognizing that the key to transforming its trade with these and other developing countries into a vigorous growth sector is the development of new product lines, Havana began to target biotechnology, pharmaceuticals, and other health-related endeavors as particularly promising areas where it could provide goods and especially services to other LDCs as effectively as and often more inexpensively than could the industrialized nations. The world-class Center for Biotechnology and Genetic Engineering established in Havana, which has made significant progress in creating several varieties of interferon and streptokinase (a heart attack drug), became the flagship project in this campaign.

Nevertheless there remain many reasons to be skeptical regarding the extent to which the Central American states might represent significant customers for these new Cuban exports. Guatemala is the only nation in the area with a population size (estimated at 9.8 million in 1992) that makes it attractive as a potential market, but it traditionally has had an abysmal record in providing medical services to its people. Costa Rica has long had one of the finest health care systems in the Western Hemisphere and therefore could be seen as representing a viable outlet for Cuban medical products and services. The liability here is in the demographics: Costa Rica is the smallest nation in the region (approximately 3.2 million citizens in 1992), which has raised serious doubts about the extent of the demand that it could generate.

Basically the same comments made regarding the Central American region could be applied to Panama. Panama's economic utility to revolutionary Cuba does not appear ever to have taken the form of being a traditional trading partner. Instead, what Panama has provided is an operational base that Havana has often employed to frustrate U.S. efforts to restrict its commercial dealings with various third parties. For example, Donna Rich Kaplowitz indicates that Panama has been used as a channel through which British-based subsidiaries of U.S. corporations have done business with Cuba, thereby circumventing the ban on such subsidiary trade that Washington tried to impose with the 1992 Torricelli Law.[30]

Thus while Cuba would obviously respond favorably to any export opportunities that might develop in Central America, the prospects there did not at this point appear significant, and Havana understandably tended to concentrate on exploring the mass markets to be found elsewhere.

The CARICOM Region

Beginning roughly in late 1989 and early 1990, Havana embarked upon a major effort to expand and deepen its relations with the English-speaking nations of the Caribbean Basin, whose main regional organization is CARICOM (the Caribbean Community and Common Market, which had thirteen members in the early 1990s).[31] These ties, which had been

128 | Cuba's Foreign Relations in a Post-Soviet World

fairly robust in the 1970s, had for various reasons languished during much of the 1980s. One important reason for this development was the fact that the Reagan Doctrine (which committed Washington to providing strong material and logistical support for insurgent movements fighting to overthrow Third World Marxist regimes) began to be implemented, and the Caribbean–Central American region was a major theater of operations. Such intransigence—especially when combined with the 1983 Grenadian invasion, which demonstrated that the United States was willing to use its own troops to move against Caribbean governments that it perceived as being too radical and perhaps too closely aligned with Cuba—had a sobering effect in many quarters, causing some nations that might otherwise have been inclined toward cordial relations to begin to put some distance between themselves and Havana. Such tendencies were reinforced by the fact that Cuba did not always assign the Caribbean a prominent place on its international agenda during the 1980s, preferring to give higher priority to Central America and to nonhemispheric Third World affairs. This situation was summarized by Cuban Deputy Foreign Minister for American Affairs Ramón Sánchez Parody when he stated in a December 1989 interview that "Washington's hostile policy against the Cuban government has been a very important factor in the links with countries that are economically dependent on the United States. But we must also acknowledge that there was a lack of diplomatic work [on our part] and our foreign policy didn't give the [CARICOM] area adequate priority."[32] Having made this admission, Sánchez Parody indicated that Havana was now inclined to try to reenergize the Caribbean dimension of its foreign policy. Driven by the growing need to diversify its economic relationships as the Soviet bloc crumbled around it, in the early 1990s Havana began to devote serious attention to building new or stronger bridges to the Anglophone Caribbean.

The process began to gain momentum in late 1990 when, in response to Cuban overtures as well as CARICOM's desire to expand participation in the organization, the CARICOM heads of state decided at their eleventh summit conference (Jamaica, August 1990) to launch serious discussions with Havana regarding the possibilities for increased economic cooperation. A series of meetings followed in which significant progress was made toward an agreement covering a wide range of topics, but complications developed when objections were raised by some CARICOM members to expanding contacts and collaboration with Havana as long as tensions continued between Cuba and Grenada (which had severed all relations with the Fidelistas as a result of the 1983 crisis). Havana, once again demonstrating its interest in strengthening its CARICOM connections, responded by launching a campaign to resolve its differences with the Grenadian authorities. Following discussions highlighted by high-level meetings at the twelfth CARICOM summit (July 1991, St. Kitts–Nevis) and a February 1992 CARICOM conference in Jamaica, the two parties finally announced in May 1992 that they were reestablishing normal diplomatic ties.[33] With this obstacle removed, the restructuring initiatives moved forward swiftly on a variety of fronts. In late May 1992, for example, Havana established diplomatic relations with St. Vincent and the Grenadines.

More important, from an economic and even a symbolic perspective, was the June 1992 decision by the thirty-one members of the Caribbean Tourism Organization (CTO) to approve Havana's application for admission. Cuba had dominated the Caribbean tourism industry in the prerevolutionary period. It was only after the rupture of the island's relations with the United States and Havana's subsequent deemphasis of tourism as it concentrated on establishing alternative economic linkages with the socialist bloc that other Caribbean countries began to develop a truly significant presence in the industry.

The harsh economic realities of the emerging post–Cold War order forced Cuba to reassess its posture. No longer reviled as a seedbed of gambling, prostitution, and other forms of social corruption, tourism was now back in favor as an extremely productive source of the hard currencies that the island increasingly needed to service its import requirements.

This development was viewed with some trepidation in the CARICOM area, for it was recognized that Cuba could emerge as a formidable competitor in the highly lucrative Western European and Canadian markets (although the main prize—the United States—remained beyond its reach). Faced with the question of whether to close ranks against the island in an effort to frustrate its tourism aspirations or to enter into what might prove a mutually beneficial cooperative relationship with it, the CTO (within which the CARICOM countries are the most influential bloc) chose the latter course.[34]

The culmination of this essentially exploratory phase of Cuban-CARICOM rapprochement occurred at the thirteenth CARICOM summit conference (June 1992, Trinidad). Although the organization had traditionally restricted its membership to territories that were formerly part of the British empire, it was at this point becoming increasingly committed to broadening Hispanic participation in its activities. Normally the first step in this process was to grant official observer status to interested parties.[35] Similar initiatives were undertaken on Cuba's behalf at the thirteenth summit. While Havana's request for official observer status was not approved (due in large part, it was reported, to intense counterlobbying by the United States), CARICOM did take what was generally seen as an important first step toward eventual Cuban membership by voting to establish a joint commission to explore the prospects for greater CARICOM-Cuban cooperation in the areas of trade, developmental programs, and cultural exchanges.[36]

Although any such progress toward collaboration advanced Havana's larger counterisolation strategy, it was questionable whether in and of itself the CARICOM region of the early 1990s had much to offer Havana in terms of such tangible things as direct trade benefits. The organization's combined population at the time was roughly 5.8–5.9 million, not a particularly large market, although per capita income figures for the region were and are fairly high by LDC standards. It was true that Cuban commerce throughout the greater Caribbean (which includes such countries as the Dominican Republic, the Netherlands Antilles, Guadeloupe/Martinique, and St. Martin as well as the CARICOM community) was growing rapidly, the total figure doubling from $8.7 million in 1987 to S17.7 million in 1992.[37] But $17.7 million was a drop in the bucket in terms of the island's overall foreign trade, which according to tables 5.6 and 5.8 was $4.265 billion in 1992.

Trade was not the only area where restructuring had the potential to make an impact. It was conceivable, for instance, that CARICOM could provide an invaluable service to Cuba by functioning as a link (or "bridge") to other countries or regions with which Havana was interested in improving its economic relations. This proposition can be illustrated by looking at the implications of closer CARICOM ties with regard to possible Cuban involvement in the Lomé process.

The genesis of Lomé can be traced to England's decision to join the European Community (EC). London's pending entry sent out shock waves among the Third World members of the British Commonwealth, who feared that their privileged access to English markets was now in jeopardy. Consequently, when given the opportunity under the provisions of the January 1972 Treaty of Accession that ushered London into the EC to establish an institutionalized association with the *entire* European Community, the developing Commonwealth nations formed the ACP (Africa/Caribbean/Pacific) Group to serve as their agent. ACP membership quickly expanded to include the former colonies of other European powers (especially France), and the forty-six participating governments then entered into discussions in pursuit of a comprehensive new relationship with the EC. The result was the 1975 Lomé (I) Convention, which has subsequently been renegotiated every five years—Lomé II in 1980, Lomé III in 1985, and Lomé IV in 1990.[38] While the Lomé experience has not always lived up to the initial ACP expectations, it nevertheless represents a major accomplishment on the part of the Third World nations—specifically, the acquisition and exercise of collective bargaining power within the context of periodic negotiations over the exact terms of at least some important aspects of the North-South economic relationship.

Since the CARICOM countries have long played a highly influential role in ACP/Lomé affairs, and since Cuba has the basic credentials to join the ACP (being a former colony of an EC country), improved CARICOM ties could markedly enhance Havana's chances of becoming a party to the Lomé accords.[39] Such a move could contribute greatly to Havana's efforts not only to stabilize but also to expand its trade and aid links with Western Europe. Perhaps even more intriguing, however, were the possibilities that arose with respect to restructuring some of Havana's badly battered Eastern European connections. Practically all of the old COMECON nations were indicating that as part of their transformation toward more Western-style market economies, they wanted to become incorporated in some capacity into the EC framework. The former German Democratic Republic (East Germany) had already gained entry as a result of reunification with an existing EC member; Hungary, Poland, and Czechoslovakia were usually considered to be the next most likely candidates. But even if the Eastern Europeans were not involved in the equation, the remaining CARICOM/ACP/Lomé/EC linkages represented potential restructuring opportunities for the Cubans.

The Regional-Influentials (Mexico, Venezuela, Colombia)

As the export data show (see table 5.7), Mexico emerged in the late 1980s as a major consumer of Cuban goods and services. Colombia's purchases, on the other hand, were at this time minuscule, as might be expected since relations between the two countries were not fully normalized until October 1993. Venezuela occupied the middle ground, although its general trend as a Cuban customer was rather sharply down in the early 1990s (compared with the 1988 high water mark, the value of Cuban exports to Venezuela was down by 80 percent in 1991 and by 59.6 percent in 1992). In many respects it was Venezuela's role in the triangular oil trade involving Havana, Caracas, and Moscow that was its most important contribution to Cuba's economic well-being. The arrangement here called for the

USSR to provide oil to Venezuela's customers in Europe while Caracas reciprocated by supplying Cuba an equal amount of oil, which otherwise would have had to be shipped from the Soviet Union. The basic idea was to reduce transportation costs for all parties involved. In Cuba's case, such savings in effect increased the purchasing power of the oil credits or subsidies that it was receiving from Moscow. This scheme unraveled in the early 1990s along with the Soviet economy, when Moscow was no longer able to guarantee deliveries to Europe, and subsequently the noncommunist elements that assumed power in Russia showed little interest in resurrecting it.

The patterns on the import side of the ledger were similar: Mexico was a major supplier for Cuba while Venezuela and Colombia lagged much farther behind (see table 5.9). However, despite the large differentials in the volume of Cuban trade between Mexico on the one hand and Colombia and Venezuela on the other, Havana in the early 1990s often registered higher trade deficits with the two smaller trading partners.

Looking ahead, it seemed unlikely that there would be any radical change in the near future in the basic configuration of Cuban economic relations with these three countries. Mexico, despite uncertainties regarding the possible impact of its entry into NAFTA on its ties with Havana, continued to be the regional middle power that seemed to offer Cuba the greatest prospects for future trade and other forms of economic cooperation.[40] Indeed, a more Machiavellian perspective might even see Mexican membership in NAFTA working to Havana's advantage, providing a "back-door mechanism" that Cuba could exploit to carry on disguised trade with the United States or at least to undermine the Torricelli Law by developing or resuming ties with Mexican subsidiaries of U.S. companies interested in doing business with the island.

Beyond the normal import/export activities, Mexico also was emerging as a major source of investment capital for Cuba. Havana had significantly liberalized its laws regulating foreign private investment and was vigorously promoting joint ventures with foreign entrepreneurs. As of late 1993, the Spanish and Canadian business communities were the leading respondents to such overtures, but the Mexicans were not far behind.[41] One of the most ambitious projects at this time involved Mexican businessman Mauricio Fernandez Garza, who announced in November 1992 that he had concluded a deal for joint operation of fifteen existing textile plants in Cuba that would employ approximately 35,000 people. Mexican investors were to be the senior partners with a 55 percent share, the Cuban government holding the remaining 45 percent. Fernandez Garza and his associates made an initial $55 million investment in the venture, the eventual total being estimated at $611 million.[42] Moreover, the Monterrey-based Grupo Domos was indicating that it was interested in seeking a fifty-five-year concession to operate a major telephone company in Cuba, suggesting that it could provide $500 million of the estimated $1.5 billion operation.[43]

Aid initiatives on the part of the Mexican government (or its two regional power counterparts) were not, however, part of this basically encouraging scenario. This exception was made clear to Havana at an October 1991 meeting between Castro and the "Big Three" heads of state in Cozumel, Mexico, where he was informed that no developmental assistance programs or special oil deals would be forthcoming.[44]

The Southern Cone ABC Powers

Of Argentina, Brazil, and Chile (the ABC powers), Brazil was the one that had the most solid track record as a consumer of Cuban goods and services as the Cold War era ended, as table 5.7 reveals.[45] Note that the 1990 figure for Havana's exports to Brazil, almost $100 million, represented an unusual "bulge" attributable to a special one-time massive purchase of Cuban anti-meningitis vaccine. But even discounting this anomaly, Brazil still was a vigorous and often profitable trading partner for Cuba, with the island enjoying trade surpluses in 1986, 1987, and 1990.[46] Conversely, Argentina and Chile represented next to nothing in terms of markets for Havana. Indeed, Chile's position was so insignificant that it often did not merit an entry on charts and tables summarizing Cuban economic activity.[47]

But even on the generally robust Brazilian front, there remained problems that complicated progress toward closer trade relations. For example, Havana was not particularly successful in procuring the kind and quantity of credits that are often a necessary component of major commercial transactions. Moreover, said Luiz Vasconcelos, "Cuban products have been poorly received by Brazilian clients, relative to their purchasing power. Only biotechnological products purchased directly by the Brazilian government have been positively received so far. Sales of other products, such as processed ores, light electromechanical products, rum, and tobacco, have not yet fulfilled the expectations of Cuban exporters."[48] Even Cuban biotechnology sales encountered some resistance; the Brazilian government's health commission recommended in early 1994 against future purchases of the anti-meningitis vaccine that Havana had previously supplied in large quantities, until questions about its level of effec-

134 | Cuba's Foreign Relations in a Post-Soviet World

tiveness were resolved. At roughly the same time, however, Brazil signed contracts to purchase $30 million of other Cuban health products.[49] In the final analysis, although there would inevitably be setbacks and failures, the immense size and complexity of Brazil's markets guaranteed that they would continue to attract Havana's attention.

Turning to Argentina, its role was overwhelmingly one of selling goods, primarily foodstuffs, to rather than buying them from Havana (compare tables 5.7 and 5.9). At least in part, the one-sided nature of this trade relationship was attributable to noneconomic factors. The bilateral political atmosphere within which the two countries operated was somewhat strained in the early 1990s, with Argentine officials being rather vocal in their criticism of Cuba's human rights record and their demand that Castro institute political reforms that would establish a Western-style political system revolving around multiparty elections. Not surprisingly, the Fidelistas were no more willing to bow to pressure emanating from Buenos Aires than they were when it came from Washington. Basically, then, the situation was that Buenos Aires was content to make money from its food sales to the island but reluctant to assist Havana economically by taking any dramatic steps to open its markets to Cuban exports.[50] Primarily political rather than commercial considerations likewise led Chile to be inclined to sit on the sidelines as far as trade relations with Cuba were concerned.

The Canadian Case

Canada has always had an unusual relationship with Cuba.[51] It resisted official requests from Washington to break relations with Castro in the 1960s and even criticized the Kennedy government's actions during the October 1962 Missile Crisis. Prime Minister Pierre Trudeau was the first leader of a NATO nation to visit Cuba (in 1976), and during his tenure agreements covering fishing, tourism, air service, hijacking, and communications were established. Business boomed, as Canadian exports reached $400 million in 1980.

Even during the conservative Mulroney period (1984–93), when Ottawa overwhelmingly supported the foreign policies of Washington while promoting the continentalist Free Trade and NAFTA deals, Canada maintained fairly consistent relations with Cuba. As indicated in table 5.11, bilateral trade continued to develop despite the economic crisis that engulfed the island in the early 1990s. Indeed, Canada represented an exceptional case during the extremely difficult 1991–92 period in that it was one of the few trading partners with whom Havana enjoyed a healthy surplus.

Table 5.11. Canada-Cuba trade (in millions of Canadian$)

Year	Exports to Cuba	Imports from Cuba	Total
1985	330,327	44,345	374,672
1986	368,019	72,614	440,633
1987	274,459	51,472	325,931
1988	230,613	87,117	317,730
1989	154,600	62,100	216,700
1990	170,500	130,200	300,700
1991	127,900	152,800	280,700
1992	113,000	256,100	369,100

Source: Caribbean and Central American Relations Division, External Affairs and International Trade, Canada; International Trade Division, Statistics, Canada.

It was during the Mulroney years that the Canadian government introduced legislation blocking the impact of the Torricelli Law on multinational companies operating in Canada, voted against the U.S. blockade of Cuba in a key vote held at the UN General Assembly in November 1992 (although it abstained on a technicality the following year), and extended to Havana official humanitarian assistance (food and medicine). Moreover, Mulroney's secretary of state, Joe Clark, emphasized the need for Cuba to be readmitted to the OAS—a theme his Liberal counterpart subsequently echoed.

Notwithstanding profound ideological differences, joint ventures along with other types of economic relations began to blossom during this period and would continue to grow dramatically. By 1993, for example, Canada's 130,000 visitors represented approximately 28 percent of all tourists going to Cuba, and its corporations had entered into the second-largest number of joint ventures (Spain was the leader in this area).[52] In addition, the island's largest single foreign investment in the early 1990s was made by a Canadian mining company (to be discussed), and Canadian firms carved out a leading role in oil exploration and development. In short, from the new air terminal at Varadero to much of the food sold in the hard currency stores, from oil exploration in Matanzas to hotel management in Oriente, the Canadian influx was unmistakable.

Of particular significance was the increasingly dominant position of Canadian investors in the Cuban mining industry. Within this key area of economic development, the role of Alberta-based Sherritt Incorporated stood out. Sherritt first became seriously interested in doing business with Cuba in 1991. Negotiations ensued on a number of fronts, with a Sherritt oil subsidiary launching the company's first in-country operation when it opened a Cuban office in March 1992. The major breakthrough in cooperation came in June 1994, when Sherritt signed a contract with Cuba's General Nickel Company whereby the two firms would join to mine, refine, and market throughout the world the island's cobalt and nickel resources. Using the major Moa Bay plant in Cuba and Sherritt's refinery in Alberta, this unique mutual ownership agreement soon came to be viewed by Havana as probably its most valuable joint venture initiative.[53]

Canada's strengthening of its Cuban relations in the early 1990s would accelerate over the next few years. Among the measures to be undertaken were the authorization of large quotas to Cuban vessels fishing off the Atlantic Coast of Canada (an agreement that in 1993 supplied the island with 23,000 tons of badly needed protein) and the provision on several occasions of emergency developmental assistance. Together with the endeavors of individual Canadian entrepreneurs (who were extremely keen on doing business in Cuba for several years before Ottawa showed any interest) and the ever-increasing number of Canadians seeking relief on Cuban beaches from the long winter, it became clear that even closer ties would almost inevitably ensue as the twenty-first century dawned.[54]

The Economic Powerhouses: Western Europe and the Far East

In contrast to those with many other parts of the world, Havana's relations with Western Europe have for the most part tended to be relatively tranquil. Naturally there have been occasional tensions and disagreements, but such problems have seldom escalated to crisis proportions. A key factor contributing to this legacy has been the reluctance of the Europeans to join Washington in its efforts to isolate the Revolution. Consequently Cuba has been able not only to maintain normal diplomatic ties with Western Europe but also has developed a fairly vigorous pattern of trade.

Political disputes inevitably impinged to some degree upon Cuba's commercial relations with Western countries; the French kept Havana at arm's length during the early 1960s, for example, due to its sympathy for the Algerian independence forces, and West Germany reacted similarly once the Fidelistas established cordial ties with the German Democratic Republic. Generally, however, Cuba preferred to try to push such considerations into the background and to concentrate instead on doing business. Such pragmatism was graphically illustrated in its evolving links with Spain.

After a stormy beginning in the early 1960s, when the Castro and Franco governments were embroiled in a number of disputes, it became apparent to both countries that reconciliation would serve their mutual self-interest. As part of this process, a three-year trade treaty was signed in 1963. Subsequently commerce flourished between Castro's Marxist revolution and Franco's vehemently anticommunist, fascist regime, with Spain becoming the island's premier trading partner in Western Europe. In a symbolic gesture underscoring the importance of its Madrid connection in its efforts to maximize its economic space, Havana observed a period of official mourning when Franco, one of the most widely despised dictators of his time, died in 1975. Despite occasional political disagreements, these cooperative relations were by and large maintained with the democratic Spanish leadership that succeeded Franco.

Rather than politics or ideology, the primary factor clouding this Western European picture from the mid-1980s onward was the Revolution's growing problem of debt. Although the island had normally experienced some deficits in its European trade balances, it had been able to manage them and hence to maintain a respectable credit rating. Eventually, however, Cuba had to announce in July 1986 that it was suspending all interest and principal payments on the hard currency debts it owed to Europeans while it attempted to negotiate a comprehensive rescheduling package. Although some temporary arrangements were made, the hemorrhage of red ink continued unabated as Havana's overall arrears swelled from approximately $3 billion (U.S.) in late 1986 to an estimated $6 billion in 1990.[55] Trade relations can, of course, proceed even under such adverse conditions and indeed continued to do so in this case; Cuban sugar and other exports still flowed into European markets while Havana continued to make purchases there as best it could. But what remained extremely problematical as long as the debt crisis persisted was Cuba's ability to convince its European associates to grant the credits that it urgently needed in order to expand its imports of machinery and other crucial items that its old CMEA suppliers were no longer willing or able to deliver.

One major mechanism with which Cuba had earlier begun to experiment in order to reinvigorate and strengthen its Western European economic ties was joint ventures. As noted, Havana markedly liberalized its laws governing such undertakings in 1982, in an attempt not only to attract substantial amounts of foreign investment but also to gain access to marketing, management, and other kinds of expertise that it sorely needed in order to be able to compete more effectively in the highly developed free market sectors of the global economy. Among the main (and in many respects quite generous) incentives offered to prospective partners were absolute freedom from government interference for the joint enterprise in appointing its board of directors and management personnel, in setting its production plans, in establishing prices, in hiring and firing workers, in entering into contracts with national or foreign companies, and in choosing the accounting system that it considers most appropriate (which could produce important tax benefits); unrestricted repatriation of the foreigners' share of the profits generated by the company's normal operations or its sale; a temporary waiver of taxes levied on profits; and, perhaps most important, majority ownership by the foreign investors in exceptional circumstances. The response to these overtures was rather encouraging; Havana announced that 173 joint venture projects with foreign companies (many of them European-based) were fully operative as of December 1994, while many others were in various stages of negotiation or preliminary implementation. Tourism-related enterprises were especially attractive and clearly had an impact, with the number of visitors to the island more than doubling in just four years (from 300,000 in 1990 to 630,000 in 1994, with 800,000 estimated for 1995).[56]

In contrast to Cuba's long historical tradition of rather strong ties to Europe, the Far East was an area that had received relatively little attention prior to the Revolution. Gradually, however, both ideological and economic considerations led the Fidelistas to begin to gaze more attentively toward the Far East.

On the political front the Cubans quickly developed a strong affinity for Ho Chi Minh's revolutionary movement, extending it whatever assistance they could during its long struggle against Washington and its South Vietnamese clients. Such Cuban solidarity was not merely an exercise rooted in the old maxim that "the enemy of my enemy is my friend." Instead, Havana tended to look upon communist Vietnam as one of the few members of the international Marxist community that it could legitimately consider a "natural ally," in the sense that Ho and his followers shared the Fidelistas' commitment to stubborn ideological independence and especially to the establishment of a truly pluralistic socialist bloc within which the smaller participants would not be subjected to hegemonic pressures from the strong. Such congeniality, however, did not always characterize Havana's relations with the region's communist giant— the People's Republic of China.

Beijing's initial response to Castro's victory was unusually positive when one considers that he was not yet a declared communist, and the two countries quickly established strong ties. In fact, so cordial was the connection that the Maoists were soon praising Cuba as a glorious model of revolution and encouraging others to follow its example. While Havana's strident anti-Americanism certainly resonated well with the PRC, the main factor reinforcing China's friendliness was almost certainly the growing tensions during the 1960s between Cuba and the USSR. In essence, the Chinese saw Havana as a potentially useful Third World ally in their bitter dispute with Moscow. This honeymoon lasted until the Cubans began to mend their fences with the Kremlin in the late 1960s and especially the early 1970s. Cuban-PRC bickering over a variety of issues ensued, and the firestorm signaling that the relationship was in almost total disarray erupted in 1976 when Beijing in effect allied itself with the United States and the South Africans by supporting efforts to destroy Agostinho Neto's MPLA government in Angola. The Cubans viewed this as treachery of the worst kind and proceeded to pillory China as an unscrupulous imperialistic power that would stoop to anything in its attempts to bring vulnerable LDCs under its influence.

Surprisingly, these political tensions in the Sino-Cuban relationship generally had little negative impact on trade issues. Indeed, from 1975 to 1983 China occupied a position comparable to that of Japan as a Cuban trading partner.[57] Subsequently, as both governments moved swiftly and effectively to put aside the rancor that had previously characterized their political dealings, this already well-established pattern of commerce became even more dynamic. There was, for example, constant traffic between the two countries as various delegations explored the prospects for increased economic cooperation. As a result of such activities, the island had by the end of 1990 emerged as the PRC's most important trading partner in all of Latin America.[58] The total value of Cuban-Chinese trade for 1990 was approximately $561.9 million (U.S.), as shown in table 5.12, the expectation being that the trend would be sharply upward in the near future, but such anticipated expansion did not materialize. Instead, the figure was down 24.2 percent (to $425.7 million) in 1991 and then dropped an additional 15.4 percent (to $383 million) the following year, for a two-year decline (1990–92) of 31.8 percent.

Moving beyond the Asian socialist societies, Cuba, like practically all other nations (both developing and industrialized) that were making pilgrimages to the Orient in search of trade and aid, inevitably found itself drawn to the brightest star in the Asian economic constellation—Japan.

The two islands had maintained vigorous trade relations going back to the early 1960s, with the volume involved often exceeding the figures generated in Havana's dealings with Canada and some of its main Western

140 | Cuba's Foreign Relations in a Post-Soviet World

Table 5.12. Cuban trade with Japan and China (in millions of U.S.$)

		China	Japan
Cuban exports to	1985	107.5	93.1
	1988	293.0	137.8
	1991	201.5	142.0
	1990	309.9	95.3
	1992	183.0	115.0
Cuban imports from	1985	116.8	303.1
	1988	155.5	116.9
	1990	252.0	73.0
	1991	224.2	35.7
	1992	200.0	18.0
Export/import totals	1985	224.3	396.2
	1988	448.5	254.7
	1990	561.9	168.3
	1991	425.7	177.7
	1992	383.0	133.0

Sources: Based on figures in tables 5.7 and 5.9.

European partners. But as table 5.12 shows, the Japanese were steadily losing ground to the Chinese in the late 1980s and early 1990s. Despite this erosion, there were several factors (beyond the obvious attraction exerted by Japan's market potential and its vast investment resources) that functioned to sustain Havana's interest in a Tokyo connection. Among these were Japan's accommodating stance on the issue of technology transfers—Japanese business executives recognize that LDCs want an infusion of the most advanced technology available and, in contrast to their counterparts in many other industrialized societies, the Japanese have often been willing to make concessions to such desires as an unavoidable cost of doing business. Further, the Japanese have shown a willingness not characteristic of many Western investors to enter joint ventures as junior partners, thereby alleviating the Cuban fears of neocolonialism that are often triggered by the idea of foreign majority ownership. Finally, being at the time under heavy pressure to recycle some of the country's immense trade surplus, Tokyo tended to offer foreign aid on terms that were often much more favorable that those of many other donor countries.

China and Japan (with perhaps a few of the so-called Asian Tigers like Singapore also added to the list) appeared to offer some safe harbors where Cuba might find respite from the stormy economic seas that were engulfing it in the later 1980s and early 1990s. On the other hand, the history of Asia is littered with the shattered expectations of Westerners. But the exigencies of conquering the crisis posed by the emerging post–Cold War order demanded that the Fidelistas explore every possible avenue of relief open to them. Thus, despite the uncertainties involved, the Far East came to occupy a status somewhat akin to that of the major Latin American countries and Western Europe on Cuba's international economic agenda.

6

Cuba Confronts the Post–Cold War Order, 1992 Onward

Revolutionary Cuba has exhibited, as emphasized throughout this work, a fondness for taking the road less traveled by other countries, especially by its neighbors in the Western Hemisphere. Consequently, it has assumed the aura of a political trailblazer. In this vanguard role, it was the first hemispheric nation to embrace Marxism as its official ideology and the only one to become formally affiliated with the Soviet bloc. It is the only Latin American country to have established a significant military presence abroad, the most dramatic manifestations of this policy coming in the Angolan and Ethiopian wars. It rose to a position of leadership and influence within the Nonaligned Movement attained by only a few other developing nations. And it has over approximately the last forty years demonstrated an almost uncanny ability to frustrate Washington's intense efforts to eradicate all vestiges of Fidelismo from the island.

As the twentieth century drew to a close, Cuba continued this trailblazing tradition by emerging as the most prominent member of the now-defunct CMEA community making a serious effort to maintain some semblance of its former socialist order within the often unfriendly confines of what has become known as the post–Cold War world. Rendering this task doubly daunting is the fact that small island nations like Cuba confront some serious developmental obstacles, which are often subsumed under the broad rubric of the "size versus viability" dilemma.

Admittedly, the mere fact that a country is comparatively small (measured in terms of physical area and/or population) does not necessarily mean that it will be weak or somehow severely handicapped. However, limited size often involves some inherent liabilities:

- a local market that may have limited capabilities for supporting a modern, diversified domestic economy;

- a meager endowment of the natural resources normally associated with a strong development industrialization potential (resources sometimes called "strategic minerals");
- high per unit costs for both exports and imports;
- high per capita costs for public services and for the development and maintenance of a solid economic infrastructure; and
- difficulties in retaining high-quality administrators, managers, scientists, and technicians.

Indeed, some observers have questioned whether nations exhibiting such vulnerabilities even have the capacity to function as viable economic entities in the modern world; Hans Vogel suggests that they are likely to succumb to what he calls a self-increasing deficit of autonomy rooted in the kinds of structural scarcities described.[1] This situation has been severely exacerbated in Havana's case by Washington's economic blockade, which at a minimum has been designed to complicate the island's development efforts and ideally has sought to trigger such pervasive economic chaos that the Revolution would be totally destroyed.

The Castro government's response to these exigencies has been broadly (and somewhat simplistically) conceptualized here in terms of two basic counterdependency survival strategies: political and economic diversification and developmental coalition building. These two approaches are not mutually exclusive and indeed can be complementary, although as a rule successful coalition building is the more pressing and more beneficial of the two exercises. During the Cold War era Havana managed to pursue both policies quite effectively, as we saw in chapter 4, but beginning in the early 1990s the dynamics of post–Cold War systemic transformation forced it, at least initially, to rely almost exclusively on the diversification option. Whether Cuba will henceforth be able to go beyond political and economic diversification to the establishment of effective new developmental coalitions stands as one of the greatest challenges on its current international agenda.

The pivotal role that Cuba's CMEA affiliation played during the Cold War (in terms of both economic and national security affairs) meant that the North-South plane was at that stage uppermost in the Revolution's developmental coalition-building considerations. In other words, Cuba's main concern was to establish and then strengthen its institutional connection with a group of *industrialized* nations—that is, with the Eastern European socialist bloc. In the post–Cold War era, however, the horizontal (or South-South) axis has moved to the forefront, with Havana focusing almost all its attention on other *developing* states as potential coalition partners. Beyond such tangible benefits as the increased trade and investment opportunities that should be forthcoming, the issue of enhanced (collective) bargaining power can be a crucial element in the South-South equation. The basic idea here is to use such coalition building as a mechanism for the member LDCs to formulate a master plan for their dealings with the centers of global economic power (either individual countries, such as the United States, or groups, like the European Community), thereby putting themselves in a position where it is likely that they will be able to negotiate more advantageous North-South developmental arrangements than would be the case if each was operating independently. But, as often applies with such promising grand scenarios, there can be devils that lurk in the details of implementation.

A common problem that such multilateral initiatives have had to confront is the fact that the participants have not always been able to maintain consensus regarding their overall priorities, the result being serious susceptibility to retaliatory divide-and-conquer tactics as disgruntled members become increasingly prone to break ranks and make their peace separately with outside countries or groups. Conversely, the benefits that many former European colonies have achieved within the Lomé framework suggest that despite its faults, collective bargaining has significant potential as a means for developmental coalitions to make major progress toward establishing a viable position in the emerging post–Cold War international economic order. Certainly for small countries like Cuba, such a coalition-building strategy would appear to be preferable by far to attempting to deal individually with the economic powerhouses of the world.

However, in contrast to the situation faced by most of its colleagues in the Third World at large and especially in the Caribbean–Latin American region, the road upon which Havana's foreign policy travels continue to be abnormally rough, and the primary cause of the potholes, detours, and other obstacles that it confronts is the United States. The demise of the Cold War radically transformed the larger global arena within which U.S.-Cuban relations are played out, the most dramatic development being Moscow's disappearance as a major third party factor affecting the attitudes and actions of the two central players. But these momentous events did not radically alter the climate within the Colossus of the North, or at least within the Washington Beltway where foreign policy decisions are ultimately made. Instead, opinion on the key issue of normalizing relations with revolutionary Cuba continued to be badly split.

The hard-line school in this debate has taken the position that with the disintegration of the Soviet bloc, the radicals in Havana have now found themselves in a situation where they are more isolated and therefore more vulnerable than perhaps ever before. Consequently, for those espousing this viewpoint, the time was now ripe to go for the jugular by increasing dramatically U.S. pressure on the island, aiming thereby to achieve the unfulfilled dream of driving Castro from power and aborting Cuba's attempt to implement a socialist revolution. Their primary tactic in pursuing this agenda has been to promote congressional legislation that would intensify the U.S. economic blockade against Cuba, two examples of such initiatives being the Torricelli and Helms-Burton laws (discussed in more detail later).

Opposing this increasingly confrontational scenario have been those advocating some degree of normalization. Within this group there tend to be two main currents of thought. The first includes those who wish to use the normalization process to bring about internal change in Cuba, the main goals being a transition to a full-fledged market economy and the institution of political reforms that would result in a Western-style system with multiparty elections (which, it is hoped, would usher Castro and his supporters from power).[2] In many respects, then, the political agenda of this group has been similar to that of the hard-liners; it is the strategy to be utilized that has differed. What has been proposed here is an approach emphasizing the carrot rather than the stick, on the assumption that progress toward normalization—probably in small, incremental steps— would occur only after Cuba began to institute "genuine" (which usually means acceptable to the United States) economic and political reforms.

The second group has tended to approach the normalization question on the basis of the merits and interests involved rather than seeing it as a mechanism for leveraging change in Cuba. For example, there has been growing sentiment for normalization within the U.S. business community, where some segments feel that continued intransigence on Washington's part is causing them to lose trade and investment opportunities to foreign competitors whose governments have established and maintain regular relations with Havana.[3] Others can see no reasonable rationale whatsoever (e.g., Cuba as a security threat) for an ongoing hard line and therefore argue that normalization should be pursued as a matter of routine foreign policy principle.[4] They point out that despite some strident domestic opposition, it has been both possible and useful for Washington to mend its fences with such former antagonists as Beijing and Hanoi, and they contend that there is no logical reason to treat Cuba as an exceptional case.

Basically, then, two interrelated themes have dominated Cuba's post–

146 | Cuba's Foreign Relations in a Post-Soviet World

Cold War foreign policy: (1) continuing the restructuring of its network of economic relations that began in the early 1990s, with increasing attention to exploring the prospects for coalition building in the Western Hemisphere; and (b) somehow—either by a negotiated normalization of relations or by a carefully calibrated campaign of counterdependency politics—defanging what the Fidelistas see as the Yankee imperialists who have continued to stalk the Revolution and who, if given the opportunity, would not hesitate for a second to force the island once again into a neocolonial status. What was at stake was, perhaps, no less than the Revolution's very survival.

Trade Restructuring and Coalition Building

The passing of the bipolar world order represented at best a decidedly mixed blessing for Cuba. The policy area that was most positively impacted, at least in the short run, concerned Havana's efforts at political and economic diversification. For many years Cold War considerations had led some countries, particularly in the Western Hemisphere, to be extremely hesitant to normalize their relations with Havana. And even when official diplomatic ties were established, it was not unusual for governments to be reluctant to go beyond pro forma protocol into the realm of genuine cordiality. In other words, there was little inclination to do anything that might benefit the Cuban Revolution significantly, either politically or economically. Sometimes such sentiment was rooted in sincere misgivings about the Fidelistas' close ties to the Soviet camp, while in other cases it represented a crassly expedient response to pressure from Washington for support of its global crusade against communism. At the heart of both of these positions was a Cold War rationale that was rendered irrelevant by events of the late 1980s and early 1990s. Consequently governments that had previously kept their distance from Havana often became more forthcoming and friendly.

Overall, however, the economic negatives of the new international order far outstripped any diplomatic positives as far as the Fidelistas were concerned. The unraveling of the island's economy, beginning roughly in 1989, is discussed in chapter 5. But, finally, after Cuba took a series of terrible hits in the early 1990s (with 1993 representing the year of greatest suffering), the situation began to improve somewhat from 1994 onward as the impact of various economic reforms began to be felt. A few examples of initiatives taken by the government with the general goal of increasing national productivity were the enactment in 1995 of a new and more generous foreign investment law that sought especially to attract overseas capital into the tourism and extractive industries; giving permission for some citizens to establish small private businesses; enhancing the food supply by allowing farmers to sell some of their produce in public markets; and legalizing U.S. dollars as a freely circulating currency (clandestine use by many people had previously undermined the authorities' ability to regulate financial flows). In essence, then, Havana was moving toward the creation of a mixed economy, drawing inspiration from similar experiments being undertaken by the PRC and Vietnam. Like any other nation, Cuba would experience some setbacks and disappointments in its revitalization efforts, but at least the worst of its nightmare seemed to have passed.

The pivotal year of 1994 saw modest growth in the country's basic economic indicators, with the overall gross domestic product expanding by 0.7 percent. While hardly representing a spectacular improvement, the figure suggested that the economic free fall of previous years had finally bottomed out and that maybe recovery was on the horizon. Such confidence was vindicated in following years as the GDP grew by 2.5 percent in 1995 and 7.8 percent in 1996.[5] Admittedly these gains were calculated on the basis of years in which economic productivity was low by Cold War Cuban standards, and they might therefore have looked more impressive, especially in 1996, than they actually were. In any case, the robust 1996 performance was not repeated in following years; in 1997 Cuba registered a 2.5 percent GDP increase, and although officials optimistically projected a similar 2.5–3.5 percent boost for 1998, the actual growth was closer to 1.0 percent.[6]

Despite clear evidence that the island has weathered the worst of its crisis and that its situation has been improving, many observers have remained doubtful that the Revolution has any realistic chance in the foreseeable future of regaining the high levels of development and the standard of living that Cuba enjoyed during its boom years in the 1970s and particularly the early 1980s. Such skepticism is based on the fact that even at a fairly strong annual GDP growth rate of 5 percent, for example, and assuming the island's post–Cold War decline was no more than 40 percent (a figure some observers feel is too low), it would take at least seven years to recoup the losses. A more feasible annual average of 3 percent would stretch the time frame out to approximately twelve years.

It must be remembered, of course, that from the Fidelista perspective, these economic issues can also take on serious security connotations. Although Havana has periodically expressed fears that Washington might be tempted to launch a military strike against the island now that Soviet counterforce no longer looms as a viable deterrent, few observers feel that this is a likely scenario. Such a conclusion does not apply on the economic front, where the island's post–Cold War problems represent potential levers that could be used by the U.S. government and its allies among the vehemently anti-Castro elements of the Cuban exile community to try to destabilize Cuban society (like the anti-Allende campaign in Chile) to the point where the Revolution completely unravels. It is such considerations that have conferred an aura of special urgency upon Cuba's efforts to develop and strengthen its post–Cold War network of international economic relations, in terms of both trade diversification and South-South developmental coalition building.

Trade Diversification

Havana's initial response to the crisis it was confronting was to assign top priority to the pursuit of what appeared to be (given CMEA's disintegration) the only viable remaining component of its established dual-track strategy—political and especially economic diversification. The campaign to expand its network of trade and related ties was supported by such major initiatives as a drive to develop new export product lines (e.g., in the biotechnology field) and efforts to attract foreign investors by further liberalizing the laws governing joint ventures on the island. However, in contrast to the strong South-South orientation that had tended to characterize Cuba's diversification policies in the 1970s and 1980s, greater emphasis was now being given to expanding the island's trade and investment relations with such industrialized power centers as Canada and the European Union. Beyond these horizons, Latin America was the only southern region that continued to draw serious Cuban attention; the position of the Far East, once felt to have considerable potential as a trading partner, suffered significant erosion.

A global overview of post–Cold War Cuban export-import activity is presented in tables 6.2 and 6.4. Admittedly the data are often less complete than one might prefer. This shortcoming is exemplified by what appear to be the excessive numbers consigned to the "Other" category. While it may be necessary to use this designation as a temporary classification for some incomplete findings due to problems in the reporting process, the practice may well distort the total picture until the ambiguities are resolved and the information can be moved to its proper station.[7]

Nevertheless the general patterns that emerge are indicative of the terrible blows the Cuban economy suffered in the 1990s and provide a good

Cuba Confronts the Post–Cold War Order, 1992 Onward | 149

Table 6.1. Cuban export-import performance

	Percentage decline	
	Exports	Imports
1985–93	80.4	77.3
1989–93	76.4	75.5

Sources: Calculated from tables 5.6, 5.8, 6.2, and 6.4.

outline of Havana's evolving trade partner priorities as it has attempted to respond to the exigencies of a new international economic order.

In 1993 Cuba's trade figures hit rock bottom. The devastation that this contraction produced can be illustrated by a performance comparison that measures 1993 against 1985 (which was the Revolution's best year in two decades) and 1989 (when the winds of change began to blow through the USSR and Eastern Europe) (see table 6.1). While such developments would be a matter of serious concern for practically any government, they almost invariably translate into a disaster of epic proportions for island countries such as Cuba, where economic health tends to be heavily reliant on international commerce.

In many respects, exports represent the vital bottom line toward which most of the Revolution's economic reforms in the 1990s have been aimed and upon which Havana has been relying as the vehicle that will allow the nation to make a successful transition to a post–Cold War world. A strong performance in the export sector is crucial to financing, either through the acquisition of hard currency or by providing a foundation upon which barter deals can be established, the imports that the Cuban economy must have in order to function at any significant level of development and sophistication. Tables 6.2 and 6.3 break down the 1992–97 evolution of Cuba's export profile along the same lines as were used in chapter 5.

There are key generalizations that can be drawn from these data:

- Within an overall context of export recovery during the period, Western Europe emerges as the most dynamic area of activity, followed by the Americas. The 1992–97 percentage change in terms of *gross* export dollars was a spectacular +77.0 for Western Europe and a robust +32.2 for the Americas, as opposed to -42.2 for Eastern Europe and -25.5 for Asia, with Africa essentially holding steady. Turning to the data on "market shares" of Cuban exports (table 6.2), Western Europe had by 1997 surged comfortably to the

Table 6.2. Cuban export profile, 1992–97 (millions of U.S.$)

	1992 (%)	1993 (%)	1994 (%)	1995 (%)	1996 (%)	1997 (%)
Total	2,030.0	1,275.0	1,375.0	1,627.0	2,000.0	1,850.0
W. Europe	316.9 (15.6)	266.1 (20.9)	275.4 (20.0)	474.0 (29.2)	541.0 (27.0)	561.0 (30.2)
E. Europe	651.8 (32.2)	456.3 (35.7)	318.2 (23.1)	249.0 (15.3)	522.0 (26.1)	377.0 (20.3)
Americas	269.3 (13.2)	156.3 (12.3)	159.8 (11.6)	329.0 (20.2)	394.0 (19.7)	356.0 (19.2)
Asia	303.4 (14.9)	132.7 (10.4)	185.0 (13.5)	312.0 (19.2)	218.0 (10.9)	226.0 (12.2)
Africa	85.9 (4.2)	60.6 (4.8)	8.1 (0.6)	41.0 (2.5)	48.0 (2.4)	87.0 (4.7)
Other	402.7 (19.9)	203.0 (15.9)	428.5 (31.2)	222.0 (13.6)	278.0 (13.9)	247.0 (13.2)

Sources: Compiled from U.S. Central Intelligence Agency, *Cuba: Handbook of Trade Statistics—1998* (Springfield, Va.: National Technical Information Service, 1998).

Table 6.3. Cuban exports and their destinations, 1992–97 (millions of U.S.$)

	1992	1993	1994	1995	1996	1997
Europe						
France	44	39	44	57	50	48
Germany	21	14	25	31	22	26
Italy	51	33	50	54	38	19
Netherlands	131	89	101	172	230	264
Spain	85	65	78	96	132	123
U. Kingdom	23	13	16	13	30	25
Asia						
China (PRC)	183	74	121	214	138	100
Japan	115	51	63	89	67	109
Americas						
Canada	212	132	142	234	294	255
Nicaragua	2	3	1	1	2	1
Mexico	7	4	12	6	23	36
Colombia	3	3	13	20	21	28
Venezuela	20	3	5	2	2	0
Argentina	2	2	48	7	8	4
Brazil	16	10	57	40	32	22

Source: Compiled from U.S. Central Intelligence Agency, *Cuba: Handbook of Trade Statistics—1998* (Springfield, Va.: National Technical Information Service, 1998).

head of the pack, with Eastern Europe and the Americas running essentially neck and neck for second place honors, although they were traveling in different directions, since the general trend over the whole six-year period was upward for the Americas while Eastern Europe's share was sliding. Indeed, comparing the 1992 and 1997 market shares reveals that the Americas had expanded their position by 45.5 percent while Eastern Europe's had shrunk by 37 percent. Western Europe, of course, posted the largest market share gain at 93.6 percent, while Asia lost 18.1 percent.

- The Asian category was especially vulnerable to severe fluctuations because Cuba's trade in the region was highly concentrated in two countries; Japan and the PRC normally accounted for least 94 percent of Havana's overall Asian sales. Therefore any significant decline in exports to one of those partners would translate into a precipitous regional drop unless there was a counterbalancing increase with the other. Basically, then, Cuba still had a long way to go in implementing a diversification program in the Far East.

152 | Cuba's Foreign Relations in a Post-Soviet World

The even harsher reality was that Havana suffered significant export setbacks with both of its key Asian partners. Comparing the 1988 (high water mark) and 1993 figures in tables 5.7 and 6.3, the erosion over this period totaled $305.8 million (-71 percent); if the less draconian 1997 is used as the post–Cold War comparison year, the comparable figures become $221.8 million and -51.5 percent.

- In Western Europe, on the other hand, Havana's efforts at export diversification seem to have been more successful. Table 6.3 shows that while there has been some concentration at the top of the group, with the Netherlands and Spain consistently outpacing their colleagues by a large margin as consumers of Cuban goods and services, the distribution of trade thereafter becomes rather even. Italy and France, for example, have routinely alternated in the third and fourth positions as destinations for Havana's exports, with Germany and the United Kingdom following closely behind.

- Within the Americas (see table 6.3), the island's premier post–Cold War customers have been Canada and Brazil. In general, the dollar volume of exports to these two countries has compared favorably to that for the highly developed European Union (EU) nations. Indeed, since 1992 Canada has routinely outstripped all EU members (except the Netherlands in 1997) as a consumer of Cuba's exports, while Argentina in 1994 and Colombia in 1995 joined the Brazilian pattern of normally outspending both Germany and Great Britain.

The broad contours of the island's evolving import situation (see tables 6.4 and 6.5) parallel in many respects the general trends found in its exports, the major exception in terms of the regional categories being Eastern Europe's much weaker position relative to Western Europe and the Americas. If the time frame is extended back to 1989, the status of CMEA–Eastern Europe as a source of Cuban imports plummets from a 78.3 percent market share in 1989 to 8.9 in 1997 (a percentage decline of 88.6). In short, the numbers confirm what even the most casual observer could have predicted—that as a result of CMEA's demise and with it the trade preferences that Havana had enjoyed (discount prices, lucrative barter deals, etc.), Eastern Europe would pale into relative obscurity on the Revolution's import profile.

Asia, in contrast to the other three major regions with which it was competing during the post–Cold War period (Africa being excluded as a serious player), registered a pattern of significant erosion in its position as

Table 6.4. Cuban import profile, 1992–97 (millions of U.S.$)

	1992 (%)	1993 (%)	1994 (%)	1995 (%)	1996 (%)	1997 (%)
Total	2,235.0	1,990.0	2,025.0	2,807.0	3,355.0	3,560.0
W. Europe	612.8 (27.4)	591.5 (29.7)	671.2 (33.2)	913.0 (32.5)	1,010.0 (30.1)	1,032.0 (29.1)
E. Europe	216.4 (9.7)	12.1 (0.6)	261.2 (12.9)	262.0 (9.3)	502.0 (14.9)	318.0 (8.9)
Americas	427.2 (19.1)	543.9 (27.3)	297.7 (14.7)	817.0 (29.1)	934.0 (27.8)	732.0 (20.6)
Asia	220.9 (9.9)	210.8 (10.6)	189.3 (9.3)	226.0 (8.1)	223.0 (6.6)	223.0 (6.3)
Africa	5.4 (0.2)	9.9 (0.5)	5.8 (0.3)	0 (0)	33.0 (1.0)	40.0 (1.0)
Other	752.3 (33.7)	621.8 (31.3)	599.8 (29.6)	589.0 (21.0)	659.0 (19.6)	1,214.0 (34.1)

Sources: Compiled from U.S. Central Intelligence Agency, *Cuba: Handbook of Trade Statistics—1998* (Springfield, Va.: National Technical Information Service, 1998).

154 | Cuba's Foreign Relations in a Post-Soviet World

Table 6.5. Cuban imports and their sources, 1992–97 (millions of U.S.$)

	1992	1993	1994	1995	1996	1997
Europe						
France	90	127	133	148	193	216
Germany	59	40	41	70	70	57
Italy	104	64	63	81	114	122
Netherlands	42	55	50	71	54	50
Spain	199	191	289	396	465	474
U. Kingdom	50	21	40	30	38	32
Asia						
China (PRC)	200	177	147	146	101	156
Japan	18	18	24	19	24	21
Americas						
Canada	100	107	84	200	197	260
Nicaragua	4	NR	1	3	3	1
Mexico	120	189	271	355	369	327
Colombia	14	20	35	18	23	19
Venezuela	79	120	90	112	119	21
Argentina	63	72	48	65	125	NR
Brazil	17	19	25	42	43	50

Source: Compiled from U.S. Central Intelligence Agency, *Cuba: Handbook of Trade Statistics—1998* (Springfield, Va.: National Technical Information Service, 1998).

a Cuban supplier. Its market share contracted by 36.4 percent in the 1992–97 period (from 9.9 percent of the total to 6.3 percent, as indicated in table 6.4), far outstripping Eastern Europe's more modest decline of 8.2 percent. Meanwhile the Western European (+6.2 percent) and hemispheric (+7.9 percent) import market share performances were replicating their positive counterparts on the export side of the Fidelista trade ledger, although at less spectacular levels.

Numerous considerations almost always influence any buying decision, but it can be assumed here that all other factors being roughly equal, transportation is a major cost variable operating against Asian suppliers. An item purchased in Asia (particularly Japan, which as an industrialized nation has fairly high labor costs) will overall probably be more expensive for a Cuban customer than a similar item bought in the Americas or even in Europe due to the longer supply lines involved. Certainly such considerations have become salient in Japan's case; its exports to Cuba plummeted from a pre-crisis high of $303.1 million in 1985 (see table 5.9) to only $21 million in 1997 (see table 6.5), a 93.1 percent reduction. As long as the Fidelistas' special relationship with the USSR gave them access to substantial amounts of hard currency, they may have been more willing to absorb the higher cost of Japanese products.[8] But Havana's hard currency reserves have shrunk drastically in the post–Cold War era, requiring it to concentrate on more cost-effective partners among the highly industrialized market economies, such as the Canadians and various EU nations.

The comparable Western European figures (1985 versus 1997) would appear to reinforce this analysis. As opposed to the across-the-board declines in Cuban imports from its two primary Asian sources, the figures actually *increased* (by a total of $373.1 million) for four of Havana's six main Western European suppliers (thereby more than offsetting the total decline of $92.1 million registered by the two remaining major EU nations). For Canada the pattern was somewhat uneven; its exports to Cuba dropped precipitously from $246.2 million in 1985 to a low of $84 million in 1994 but then rebounded nicely by 1997 to finish slightly ahead of the 1985 mark. Certainly the trend during the post–Cold War years (see table 6.5) has been sharply upward — +160 percent from 1992 to 1997. Indeed if 1993, the low water mark for Cuba's total imports, is used as the base post–Cold War year, then Canada's gross increase as well as its percentage gain through 1997 were greater than those of any Western European country except Spain.

Overall, then, the picture emerging from the post–Cold War data is that Havana's efforts at serious trade diversification, which began in the late 1980s, have moved steadily forward to the point where it would appear that such restructuring has become firmly and, at least for the foreseeable future, irrevocably embedded in the fabric of its international economic relations. Gone is the near-monopolistic position, rooted in the Revolution's developmental coalition with CMEA, that Eastern Europe once occupied (see table 6.6 for a country-by-country summary of Cuba's post–Cold War trade with its former CMEA associates). In its stead has emerged a much more complex web of economic relations, with the most multifaceted threads radiating out to Western Europe and the Americas, where Havana has developed a fairly varied menu of trading partners. Admittedly some pockets of concentration where the regional profiles tend to be dominated by a limited cast of characters have continued to exist in Asia (Japan and the PRC). On the other hand, the status of the Eastern European and Asian countries within the overall Cuban trade hierarchy has been declining during the post–Cold War period. Both groups lost ground in the 1992–97 period as destinations for the island's

156 | Cuba's Foreign Relations in a Post-Soviet World

Table 6.6. Cuban exports and their destinations and imports and their sources (millions of U.S.$)

	1992	1993	1994	1995	1996	1997
Exports and destinations						
Russia	632.0	436.0	301.0	225.0	406.0	352.0
Belarus	4.0	7.0	1.0	0		
Kazakhstan	29.3	3.5	0			
Kyrgyzstan				12.0	23.0	
Bulgaria	23.2					
Czechoslovakia	8.8					
Czech Republic		1.0		1.0	1.0	1.0
Slovakia						1.0
Hungary	0.2	0.1	0	0		
Latvia			14.0	0	11.0	4.0
Poland	1.3	0.5	1	1	2	
Romania	5.2	7.7	17.0	37.0	63.0	18.0
Total exports	2,030.0	1,275.0	1,375.0	1,627.0	2,013.0	1,850.0
Imports and sources						
Russia	191.0	-	249.0	237.0	465.0	284.0
Belarus	18.0	5.0	0	3.0		
Georgia		1.0				
Kazakhstan	19.0		0			
Kyrgyzstan			0	19.0		
Lithuania	0.4		1.0	0	1.0	2.0
Czechoslovakia	5.9					
Czech Republic		4.0	2.0	4.0	6.0	7.0
Hungary	8.2	2.5	2.0	0	1.0	0
Poland	5.9	3.1	2.0	3.0	4.0	
Romania	4.9	4.9	9.0	36.0	20.0	21.0
Total imports	2,235.0	1,990.0	2,055.0	2,805.0	3,355.0	3,560.0

Source: Compiled from U.S. Central Intelligence Agency, *Cuba: Handbook of Trade Statistics—1998* (Springfield, Va.: National Technical Information Service, 1998).

exports: Eastern Europe dropped from the first to the second slot, while the Far East went from third to fourth position, and Asia's position as a supplier of Cuban imports likewise slid from third to fourth.

Recognize, however, that thus far these achievements in restructuring trade patterns have functioned primarily as a defensive mechanism for Cuba. Specifically, they have served to contain and to soften somewhat the hammer blows that have rained down upon the island as a result of the disappearance of the developmental coalition component (i.e., CMEA membership) from the dual-track strategy that the Fidelistas had employed so successfully during the Cold War era. There are key payoffs that such diversification has not produced—and indeed probably does not even have the potential to deliver, at least within the current context of a global international economic system characterized by intense free market competition:

- A degree of developmental security.

  The more diminutive states like Cuba are usually highly susceptible to serious setbacks and even disaster when trying (either by choice or under the duress of circumstances) to operate as autonomous actors in an international economic system where cutthroat strife is the norm. Unless they are lucky enough to control large reserves of some strategic commodity (e.g., oil) or enjoy some truly unique competitive advantage, it is likely that they will be handicapped by the size versus viability dilemma discussed previously.

  Trade diversification may spread somewhat the risks that these countries face, but high exposure to radical shifts in the economic winds remains. This phenomenon is starkly illustrated by the volatility in Cuban-French commerce: Havana went from slight surpluses in 1987 and 1989 to major deficits that ranged from approximately $90 million a year in the 1993–95 period to $168 million in 1997. Such vulnerability is not uncommon in these cases and obviously serves to undermine the trade stability that governments prefer.

- Bargaining power and the developmental momentum that can flow from it.

  Smaller developing nations like Cuba are not likely to possess much individual bargaining power, especially when dealing with the industrialized centers of the world. The obvious alternative is to operate via collective mechanisms, which requires transcending the more limited horizons of bilateral economic and political diversification.

These considerations inevitably led the Fidelistas to confront the crucial issue of supplementing their existing defensive diversification with proactive (South-South) coalition building. Admittedly, it is unlikely that Havana will be able in the foreseeable future to achieve the degree of socioeconomic development and protection that its CMEA membership provided, but any significant movement beyond a conventional trade diversification agenda would constitute a major contribution to its ongoing

158 | Cuba's Foreign Relations in a Post-Soviet World

search for enhanced power and (counterdependency) security in the post–Cold War world.

Developmental Coalition Building

Like other forms of international relations, developmental coalition building can be pursued on a number of levels, the simplest occurring on a bilateral basis. Usually, however, a more ambitious multilateral approach is adopted that can involve double-digit participants (e.g., the fifteen-member European Union or the twenty-five-member Association of Caribbean States). In any case, the most common forms of economic coalition building are as follows (ranked from the least to the most complex):

- Free trade compacts

  The key element in such arrangements commits those involved to lowering radically or ideally removing all major impediments to trade between them, such as tariffs and related barriers. Participants retain control over their economic relations with countries and organizations that are not covered by the free trade agreement. Accordingly a signatory could, for example, enter into bilateral or even multilateral preferential trade arrangements with countries outside the free trade area or could impose whatever tariffs it pleased on goods or services originating outside the boundaries of the free trade zone.

- Customs unions

  A customs union is similar to a free trade agreement, but it adds the establishment by its participants of common external tariffs with regard to commerce with nonmembers. In other words, a greater degree of centralized regulation of external economic relations is added to the equation at this stage of coalition building; members are no longer totally free agents with respect to their economic dealings with the rest of the world, but instead they must be prepared to adhere to the "uniform code" of external tariffs that normally emerges from negotiations among all members of the customs union.

- Common markets

  A common market adds various provisions to a customs union structure, the most important being assurances that there will be an unimpeded flow of labor and capital among participating countries. When this point is reached, the process of integration has

Cuba Confronts the Post–Cold War Order, 1992 Onward | 159

begun to make the transition from mere coordination of certain economic policies (e.g., tariffs) to the realm of nurturing the emergence of a new economic actor on the international scene.

- (Complete) economic unions

These entities incorporate all the traits mentioned in the previous three categories and then factor in provisions that function to centralize control over the monetary and fiscal policies of all participants. Within this context, it is also common to supplement and eventually to replace the national currencies of members with a common currency (e.g., the EU's movement toward adoption of the European Currency Unit—popularly known as the Euro—as its uniform currency).

At this stage, then, the previously separate (but coordinated) national economies of the member states begin to be integrated into a single unit, the ultimate goal being the creation of a new, larger, and more powerful center of economic activity that will have greater developmental potential than its previously fragmented parts and will be more competitive in the global arena.[9]

Whatever the options that might theoretically be open to revolutionary Cuba today, it is virtually guaranteed that Havana will not be able to pursue a multilateral North-South coalition-building agenda in any of these forms and definitely not in a manner that would rival the breakthrough it made in 1972 when it was admitted to CMEA. Certainly EU or NAFTA membership is absolutely out of the question. Likewise, bilateral free trade agreements with industrialized countries (e.g., Canada) do not appear to be likely. Hence it would seem that the Fidelistas' only viable developmental coalition-building opportunities rest on a South-South axis and that within these parameters, the Latin American–Caribbean region emerges as the most promising.

There is a fairly extensive list of multilateral developmental coalitions in the Western Hemisphere. Among the major groupings are the Southern Cone Common Market (MERCOSUR), founded in 1991 with Argentina, Brazil, Paraguay, and Uruguay as its participants; the Andean Group, created in 1969 with Bolivia, Colombia, Ecuador, and Peru actively involved since its inception and Venezuela having joined in 1974 (Chile was a charter member but withdrew in 1976); and the Caribbean Community and Common Market (CARICOM, formed in 1973 as a successor to CARIFTA, the Caribbean Free Trade Association, which had operated since 1968), currently with fifteen participants, three associate members, and nine observer countries.[10] The Association of Caribbean States (ACS), organized in 1994, is the most recent addition to the list of hemispheric developmental coalitions. Its scope is rather large with twenty-five full-fledged members and three holding associate status.[11]

Not included among the bodies mentioned are the Latin American Economic System (SELA) or the Latin American Integration Association (ALADI), in both of which Cuba participates. Havana joined SELA as a charter member in 1975 and was admitted to ALADI in November 1998, having held official observer status since 1985.[12] The reason for this exclusion is that neither group, at least as constituted in 1999, neatly fits any of the profiles of multilateral developmental coalitions summarized at the beginning of this section. This characterization applies especially to SELA, which does not define itself as a free trade organization, a customs union, or a common market but rather as a vehicle for "consultation, coordination, and joint economic and social promotion."[13] In other words, SELA seeks to serve as a forum or a caucus in which members aim to achieve some consensus on developmental issues, especially in preparation for large international conferences on North-South economic relations. ALADI, on the other hand, does aspire to become a free trade federation at some time in the future. Indeed it was created as a successor to the Latin American Free Trade Association (LAFTA), the track record of which proved disappointing to its members.[14] Currently, however, it concentrates on the more modest goal of encouraging limited commercial and related agreements among its members with the hope that this foundation will serve as the basis for a comprehensive free trade accord at some undefined future point.

Returning to the list, the specific geographical orientations of MERCOSUR and the Andean Group preclude any foreseeable prospects for full-fledged Cuban participation. Consequently CARICOM and the ACS have been the main foci of Havana's hemispheric efforts at multilateral coalition building. The key issue that needs to be examined in both cases is, of course, their viability as vehicles for Cuban development and the acquisition of collective North-South bargaining power.

CARICOM

As noted in chapter 5, in the early 1990s Havana began to explore seriously the prospects for closer cooperation with and eventual membership in CARICOM. Having encountered and overcome some initial obstacles, these endeavors began to bear fruit at the thirteenth CARICOM summit conference (Trinidad, June 1992), where it was decided to create a Joint Commission to promote and oversee the collaborative process. A formal

Cuba Confronts the Post–Cold War Order, 1992 Onward | 161

agreement setting up this body was concluded at the fourteenth CARI-COM summit (Bahamas, July 1993). Since that time, however, a somewhat mixed picture has emerged with regard to Cuba's multilateral coalition-building and related developmental initiatives in the region.

Economic cooperation has been moving forward in various functional areas, one key example the travel industry (see chapter 5 for details regarding Cuba's 1992 admission to the Caribbean Tourism Organization and related matters). Also, the expansion of trade has been considerable, as illustrated by the data in table 6.7. But recognize that the figures for both 1996 and 1997 must be approached with some caution, for they are inflated by the fact that they include a large amount of petroleum produced outside the Caribbean that the Fidelistas purchased through West Indian brokers. Such transactions, although obviously benefiting both parties, did not represent "trade" in the purest sense of the term since the product that Havana was buying was not produced in the Caribbean country that was selling it. Although good longitudinal information that excludes brokered oil was not readily available, it is probably safe to say that such entries would be at least half of those presented here for 1996 and 1997. Even assuming this to be the case, the upward trend in Cuba-CARICOM trade (especially in percentages) during the 1990s would be impressive. Upon closer investigation, however, one can discover some serious imbalances. For example, the 1996–97 total is composed of only $36 million in Cuban exports to CARICOM countries, as opposed to imports of $405 million. Thus, while the overall volume of trade was increasing, its configuration was such that Havana was running a major deficit of $369 million with its Caribbean neighbors (in contrast to 1996 surpluses of $63 million with Asia and $58 million with Eastern Europe).

Table 6.7. Total Cuban trade with CARICOM, selected years (millions of U.S.$)

1992	17.7
1995	30.0
1996	400.0
1996–97[a]	444.0

Sources: "Cozying Up to the Caribbean," a summary of news reports from the Cuban newspaper Granma that was provided via electronic mail from Havana by the Grupo de Video Joven (April 26, 1993); "Cuba Tops Caribbean-Canada Agenda," a Reuters news report provided via electronic mail by the Cuba-L listserver (March 4, 1996); and "Cuban Trade with CARICOM Totals $440 Million," CubaINFO, vol. 10, no. 1 (January 8, 1998): 6–7.
a. Twelve-month period covering the latter part of 1996 and the early months of 1997.

Counterbalancing such trade shortfalls are, of course, the potential benefits to be reaped in other dimensions of the relationship. For instance, the private sector in CARICOM countries could serve as a significant source for the foreign investment capital that Havana has been assiduously courting. Ideally such entrepreneurs, in addition to their money, would bring with them various spin-off benefits like access to modern corporate technology (e.g., the computerized workplace) and managerial skills.

One other important aspect of CARICOM's activities involves participation in the Lomé process. As noted in chapter 5, Lomé provides a mechanism whereby a long list of former European colonies known as the Africa/Caribbean/Pacific Group negotiate formal accords with the European Union that regulate economic exchanges between the two parties. These Lomé agreements have provided ACP members with preferential access to EU markets as well as various types of aid programs. Cuba, on the other hand, was in the unenviable position as the 1990s drew to a close of being the only Latin American country that did not have an official trade agreement with the European Union. There have been periodic negotiations to rectify this situation, but failure to resolve certain key issues—such as resuming payment of the island's existing debts to European countries as well as concern in some quarters (e.g., Spain) about Havana's human rights record—precluded any comprehensive settlement.

Consequently participation in Lomé represents an attractive proposition to the Fidelistas. The most obvious material incentive is the opportunity for Havana to establish trade and developmental relations, with Western Europe as a whole, that would be more stable (and probably more extensive) than has been the case in the past. But equally significant from a strategic perspective is that fact that Lomé status would constitute a major breakthrough for the Fidelistas in post–Cold war counterdependency politics, because they would then in effect have acquired the power to bargain collectively with one of the world's major centers of economic power. Such an accomplishment might be seen in counterdependency terms as something akin to the triumph of a wildcat oil prospector who, after years of hard toil, finally brings in the big gusher.

For Cuba, full CARICOM membership would seem to represent the optimal means for cementing all these considerations (enhanced trade and investment, functional cooperation, Lomé access, etc.) into a truly coherent package.[15] Thus far, however, its efforts along these lines have not borne fruit. It has not gained entry to the organization's inner circle, nor have its requests for official CARICOM observer status, which normally functions as a prelude to full membership, been granted. Likewise, its campaign to conclude a free trade agreement with the group was rebuffed (at least for the time being) in August 1996, the main explanation being that such a move might unnecessarily antagonize Washington during the volatile U.S. presidential season.[16] But this reticence continued even after Bill Clinton had been reelected, as illustrated by CARICOM's failure to consider the question of Cuban membership at a February 1997 meeting in Antigua.[17]

More recently, however, CARICOM has played a major role in opening Lomé's door to greater Cuban involvement. The instrument that it has wielded in this exercise has been the Caribbean Forum (CariForum), which is the body used by CARICOM to formulate and represent its interests in the APC Group's negotiations with the European Union to update the Lomé Accords.[18] In late March 1998 Havana formally applied (with strong support from France) for admission to the CariForum as an observer, a designation that would allow it to join the group's preparatory activities in a nonvoting capacity and to monitor closely any subsequent formal talks with the EU. Cuban foreign trade minister Ricardo Cabrisas described this request as "the beginning of a process that could lead to the island becoming the sixteenth Caricom state, which would be of highest interest to us."[19] CARICOM approved this petition in May 1998 and the EU endorsed the acceptance in June 1998, thereby giving Havana, for the first time, some degree of official standing within the Lomé framework.

Having made this breakthrough, the Cubans moved quickly to strengthen their position during the course of a visit that Castro made to the Dominican Republic in late August 1998 to attend a CariForum summit meeting. Fidel, as usual, stole the show. By the time the conference ended, the CariForum had upgraded Havana to full membership. Accordingly, reported the Associated Press, "Sir Shridath Ramphal, the Caribbean Forum's chief negotiator, said he had notified European Union officials in Brussels, Belgium, that Cuba will join the [Lomé] negotiations. . . . The United States, which maintains an economic embargo against Cuba, has urged Caribbean countries not to admit Cuba to the group."[20] The next obvious step would be to repeat the process (observer status followed fairly quickly by full membership) with CARICOM itself, but by late 1999 this scenario had not unfolded.

The Association of Caribbean States (ACS)

The Association of Caribbean States was first proposed in 1991 by the blue-ribbon West Indian Commission (headed by Shridath Ramphal of

Guyana) that had been established in 1989 to provide CARICOM leaders with ideas regarding future directions for the organization. According to Andrés Serbín, the primary objectives of the ACS were envisaged as follows:

- to maximize regional trade and those economies of scale needed to achieve insertion into the international economic system through trade liberalization;
- to optimize bargaining power with third parties (given the area's post–Cold War decline in strategic importance) through the forging of tightly focused regional alliances based on identification of common (primarily geoeconomic) interests; and
- to move toward various forms of cooperation (and eventual integration) by forging consensus on matters of mutual interest and consolidating a regional identity, based on shared cultural and social traits, that will overcome existing divisions and heterogeneity and benefit the population of the entire region.[21]

The ACS concept was endorsed by CARICOM at its fourteenth summit (Bahamas, July 1993). Subsequently, based upon this commitment, a joint conference of CARICOM and the Group of Three (G3 — Mexico, Venezuela, and Colombia) convened in Trinidad in October 1993 and issued the Port-of-Spain Declaration, making an official call for the creation of the ACS. This pronouncement explicitly designated Cuba as being eligible for membership. The treaty formally launching the organization, with Havana participating as a charter member, was signed on July 24, 1994, in Cartagena, Colombia.[22]

In its broadest sense, the ACS represents another instance of the growing international trend to try to create new centers of economic power by consolidating existing national economies into larger units. As noted, this process can assume various forms ranging from free trade areas to total integration. There is, however, another and much more specific impetus giving rise to the Association of Caribbean States — the emergence of the North American Free Trade Agreement and its possible expansion into other hemispheric markets. The harsh reality is that no single country in the region can match NAFTA's power and resources; individually all are relegated to playing the role of David to the NAFTA Goliath. But collectively the ACS, whose member populations total approximately 202 million people and whose combined GDPs in 1995 (the first full year of existence for the ACS) were roughly $508.4 billion, appears to have some potential to level the playing field somewhat.

Cynics would contend that the odds are slim that the ACS will ever become a truly viable organization. They would point to the fact that prior attempts to promote economic cooperation among the Central American countries have failed rather dismally, the troubled history of the Central American Common Market (CACM) being a case in point.[23] Moreover, it might bode ill that the two main regional groupings within the ACS—the CARICOM nations and the mainland Hispanic states of the Caribbean Basin—have often regarded one another with considerable suspicion and have never displayed much capacity for sustained cooperation. Part, if not much, of this hesitancy can be attributed to cultural/historical factors. In particular, the Latins have been suspicious of the fact that while the CARICOM nations had repudiated Western imperialism in terms of achieving statehood, they continued to maintain close relations with London and enthusiastically embraced the British parliamentary system of government. Such attitudes have been seen by many Hispanics as evidence that the Anglophone countries have not made a complete break with their colonial past and therefore perhaps cannot be trusted fully as partners. On the other hand, the West Indians have frequently been somewhat contemptuous of what they have seen as the Latins' inability or unwillingness to jettison their authoritarian/dictatorial traditions. The negative perceptions on both sides generated by such cognitive filters, along with substantive policy differences, have been major considerations impeding the emergence of more cooperative West Indian–Latin American ties.

Another possible problem confronting the ACS involves the depth of the commitment that some members might have to the organization, with Mexico posing the largest question mark since it already participates in both the ACS and NAFTA. Theoretically such dual membership could allow Mexico to serve as a bridge between the two groups, facilitating the process of collective North-South bargaining by representing the interests of its ACS partners within NAFTA. Equally and perhaps more plausible, however, Mexico may find itself cross-pressured. If indeed Mexico were forced to choose where its primary loyalties lay, skeptics are doubtful that the ACS connection would carry the day. Add to this scenario the fact that other association countries—such as Jamaica and especially Trinidad and Tobago—have expressed interest in joining NAFTA, and the specter of serious fragmentation of the ACS may begin to loom.

Given the mixed picture emerging, Havana has little choice but to be coldly pragmatic in its approach to the Association of Caribbean States. In principle, of course, the ACS has considerable promise, particularly as a vehicle for its members to acquire the collective bargaining power that they desperately need in order to be able to deal effectively with such established Northern economic centers as the EU and the United States/NAFTA. Accordingly it would appear to be in Cuba's best interests to make a concerted effort to bring to bear its influence and its extensive international leadership experience to support the association's development. But Havana must likewise recognize that the ACS, like many of its hemispheric predecessors, may ultimately prove to be little more than a paper organization, a possibility demanding that serious attention be given to alternative contingency planning. Indeed Cuba has already begun to hedge its bets on the association by negotiating bilateral preferential trade agreements with various ACS members; such special arrangements were made with Colombia in September 1995, and negotiations were launched with Trinidad and Tobago in February 1997 after CARICOM had announced that it was tabling Cuba's request for full membership.[24]

A 1990s Balance Sheet

Despite substantial effort and some initial progress with regard to the establishment of the ACS as well as gaining CariForum membership, Havana's hemispheric coalition-building campaign had yet to score any major successes as the 1990s drew to a close. But this situation, while obviously frustrating to the Fidelistas, was not particularly unusual since the process of creating multilateral economic coalitions is normally a complex and time-consuming exercise (as graphically illustrated by the EU and NAFTA experiences). Further complicating the scenario for Havana is the intimidation that Washington has routinely employed to try to deter Latin American and Caribbean governments from cooperating economically with the island.[25] Such obstacles notwithstanding, Havana has persevered and will undoubtedly continue to do so.

CARICOM probably presents the best immediate prospect for a top-of-the-line Cuban coalition-building breakthrough. Specifically, despite the delays that have thus far characterized the process, full membership (perhaps preceded by a short interim period of observer status) appears to be a readily achievable goal. The ACS, however, may prove to have more long-term potential, especially as a collective North-South bargaining unit and as a vehicle for establishing ties to other hemispheric developmental coalitions, such as MERCOSUR and the Andean Group. If these assumptions are correct (which in the ACS case may admittedly be rather optimistic), Havana can in the immediate future be expected to concentrate heavily on consolidating its relationship with CARICOM—but always with an eye on the larger prize of using CARICOM membership as an institutional base for exerting leadership to expand collaboration between the island Caribbean and the Hispanic mainland. Playing such a linkage role effectively should serve to strengthen the ACS significantly and thereby markedly enhance its capacity to serve as a developmental, collective bargaining coalition.

Confronting the Yankee Goliath

Obviously the Cold War's demise radically transformed the basic structure of the global arena and hence the general dynamics of contemporary international affairs, engendering in the process a redefinition of roles and relationships for many of the actors on the global stage. Certainly this has been true for the United States.[26] Washington has, for instance, mended its political fences with such former adversaries as Moscow and Vietnam while simultaneously confronting such complex developments as the displacement of military/security issues by economic concerns as the most dynamic area of contemporary international affairs. What implications, if any, the process of acclimating to a post–Cold War order might have on U.S. policy toward Cuba became a matter of considerable speculation, especially after the 1992 elections as observers awaited the arrival of the first (liberal?) Democrat to occupy the White House in over a decade.

Some observers anticipated a major impact, the basic premise of this viewpoint being that the key impediment to normalized relations had always been Washington's misgivings about Havana's close Cold War ties to the Kremlin. These concerns spanned the spectrum from clearly articulated security-related issues, such as the alleged presence in the late 1970s of Soviet combat troops on the island, to much more imprecise fears that often seemed to be driven by arcane psychological musings rather than a rational calculation of U.S. interests, one example of this paranoid mentality being the idea that the image of the Colossus of the North as a great power was somehow eroded by the presence of a Soviet ally in the Western Hemisphere.

The transition to a post–Cold War order has, of course, rendered such concerns moot; they have no relevance whatsoever to the dynamics of contemporary international affairs. Yet their removal from the U.S.-Cuban equation did not seem to engender any flexibility on Washington's part. Instead, as detailed in the discussion to follow, the Clinton administration engaged in what some have considered a rather devious exercise by raising a whole new set of issues and preconditions that served to block any progress toward normalization. Such behavior has perplexed many

168 | Cuba's Foreign Relations in a Post-Soviet World

people, as is illustrated by an off-the-record comment of a European diplomat stationed in Washington: "The United States talks of a new world order embracing settlement of disputes through diplomacy, full respect for international conventions, unimpeded trade, and the free movement of peoples and ideas across borders. Yet, for no compelling reason that we can see, the United States violates all these principles in its dealings with Cuba. It is not a reassuring performance, and certainly does not reflect the kind of vision and seriousness of purpose one expects of a world leader."[27] Clearly, then, as the comment indicates, the Cold War's demise did not produced the relaxation of tensions anticipated by some optimistic observers. Instead these two old antagonists, which Wayne Smith has colorfully characterized as "the closest of enemies," proceeded to write new chapters in their long history of mutual suspicion and distrust.[28]

The Warped Looking Glass of Normalization

Such things as beauty and reality, we are often told, are to be found in the eye of the beholder, and what ultimately is seen can be strongly influenced by the conceptual lenses through which one views the surrounding world, a phenomenon that psychologists sometimes call selective perception. Thus, as a function of the different assumptions, values, and goals molding the particular looking glass of each group, people may arrive at conclusions very dissimilar, and indeed even polar opposites, about a common problem or issue. Certainly this has been and remains the case with regard to the often Byzantine politics swirling around the question of normalizing U.S.-Cuban relations.

Havana's general stance on normalization has remained fairly stable over the years, although its interest in expending considerable time and energy in pursuing better ties has waxed and waned somewhat. The central pillar of the Cuban perspective has been its unwavering insistence that this question must be addressed on the basis of mutual respect for the principles of sovereignty and nonintervention, which in practical negotiating terms has meant that Havana has been willing, as a prerequisite to normalization, to meet with U.S. representatives in an effort to find solutions to various bilateral issues that one side or the other feels must be resolved in order to move forward. Among the items that it has looked upon as legitimate concerns on Washington's part are compensation for U.S. citizens and corporations whose property in Cuba was expropriated; the quest to assure orderly migration from the island to the mainland; and controlling the problem of drug trafficking. High on the list of Cuban priorities have been the status of the Guantanamo naval base and, most important, the lifting of Washington's economic blockade. What Havana has absolutely refused to accept as a precondition for normalization is anything that it perceives as an attempt on Washington's part to dictate to the Fidelistas what policies they should pursue on the domestic front or what should be the nature of their relations with third parties.

In a general sense, the basic U.S. approach to normalization has also been quite consistent. Washington's standard operating procedure has been to insist upon concessions from the Fidelistas on matters that are not purely or even remotely bilateral in nature as the "down payment" that must be made before there can be any significant discussion of or progress toward better relations. In many instances it would be fair to say that an unstated but nevertheless clear subcontext to these demands has been the desire to put Castro's government and the Revolution in a position where they would be so weakened, so discredited, or so dispirited that they might disintegrate.

While the essence of this agenda has not changed dramatically, tactical shifts have often been made in its implementation. The most common scenario has unfolded as follows: Washington sets forth its preconditions; these are ultimately satisfied, normally due to changing circumstances on the political scene or the operation of intervening variables rather than acquiescence on Havana's part; and at this point the United States lays on the table another set of demands, which serves to recycle the whole process. In short, according to Wayne Smith, one U.S. administration after another has been "moving the goal posts," the result being that there has been no significant, lasting progress toward normalization of relations.

Among Washington's preconditions that were met prior to the Clinton administration were these:

- Havana must remove its armed forces from Africa, particularly from Angola.

  As detailed in chapter 4, the Cuban military had become involved in the Angolan conflict in late 1975 and later, as a result of this deployment, was drawn into a larger struggle that included support for national liberation forces fighting in Namibia. A peace agreement was finally signed in December 1988, which provided, among other things, for Namibian independence and for the withdrawal of all foreign troops from countries that were theaters for the larger conflict (including Angola). Havana, which was a party to the accord, adhered scrupulously to the scheduled plan for a phased withdrawal of forces, its last units leaving Angola in the spring of 1991.

170 | Cuba's Foreign Relations in a Post-Soviet World

- Havana must stop providing support to guerrilla forces and other armed subversive movements in Latin America.

Although such activity was rather high on the Fidelistas' agenda during the 1960s in the course of what some have called the "romantic" or "heroic" period of the Revolution, nothing truly significant had occurred on this front for quite some time. Controversy did erupt in the late 1970s and during the Reagan administration over Washington's accusations that Havana was a major supplier of arms and other forms of military assistance both to Nicaragua's Sandinista guerrillas and to the Salvadoran insurgents. While it is true that there was some Cuban participation, most impartial observers concluded that it was never as extensive or important as the United States claimed and that in any case it ceased rather quickly, probably the main reason being that it had serious potential to complicate Havana's larger normalization strategy.

Beginning in the early 1970s, as we have seen, the goal of improving Cuba's relations with its hemispheric neighbors began to take precedence over extending direct material aid to groups involved in violent power conflicts. In theory, of course, the Fidelistas continued to recognize the legitimacy of armed struggle and defended the principle of proletarian internationalism. But Havana was not inclined to translate such philosophical generalities into concrete policy initiatives, especially any that might involve dispatching Cuban personnel (sending volunteers to advise, fight beside, or provide front-line logistical services to rebel forces) or providing material military aid (arms and related items). Instead, it emphasized that its support would be limited to the moral and/or political variety.

Havana has repeatedly reaffirmed this minimalist stance, one example occurring during an August 1993 visit by Castro to Bolivia, where he stated that while direct assistance to guerrilla movements had been part of the Revolution's policies during its initial phases, Havana now adhered to a noninvolvement stance based on strict respect for the principle of sovereignty and for the democratic political decisions of its hemispheric neighbors.[29] More important than such declarations, however, is the fact that the Fidelistas have not embroiled themselves in such conflicts in any major fashion. The U.S. government itself confirmed in a May 1996 State Department report that Cuba was no longer actively supporting armed struggle in Latin America or any other part of the world.[30]

Cuba Confronts the Post–Cold War Order, 1992 Onward | 171

- Cuba and the USSR must alter their relationship in such a manner as to reduce significantly any Soviet presence in and influence over the island's affairs. In particular, Washington demanded that the tradition of close military cooperation that had long been a central pillar of ties between the two countries had to be abandoned.

  Obviously this issue became moot with the disintegration of the USSR and the Soviet bloc in the late 1980s and early 1990s. The only significant vestige of a Russian military presence beyond that point was an electronic intelligence-gathering station that continued to operate at Cienfuegos on Cuba's southern coast; the station was widely recognized as a legitimate operation necessary to allow Moscow to have an effective capability to monitor various arms control and reduction agreements that it had with the United States.

The fact that all of these traditional prerequisites for normalized relations were met by the late 1980s or early 1990s did not impress or satisfy the United States. Instead, consistent with the moving-goal-posts strategy, a substitute menu was formulated. There was, however, a major new element injected into the equation: while prior preconditions related almost solely to foreign affairs issues, Washington's emphasis now shifted to the domestic arena, where it insisted that various "reforms" had to be instituted. Among the most contentious have been the demands that

- Cuba must dismantle its centrally planned economy, replacing it with a system that basically operates on free market principles.

  The unraveling of its preferential trade agreements with the socialist bloc (along with a preexisting desire to diversify its commercial ties) led Havana to restructure radically the pattern of its international economic relations. Within the context of this process it introduced some major economic changes, two examples being its highly liberalized laws on foreign investment and its willingness (though this has admittedly waxed and waned over the years) to allow limited development of an internal free market where Cubans can launch small-scale operations as private entrepreneurs. In a nutshell, then, what Havana has been pursuing is a policy that appears to many observers to be similar to the Chinese model of a mixed economy.

  But in contrast to its basically positive reaction to Beijing's reforms, Washington has dismissed Cuba's initiatives along the same lines as insignificant and insufficient.

172 | Cuba's Foreign Relations in a Post-Soviet World

- Havana must implement major reductions in its armed forces.

As might be expected, this is a touchy issue from Havana's perspective, for it continues to see the United States as a hostile country, and Washington has been unwilling to provide assurances that it would not take advantage of the situation once Cuba has downsized its military. Such reticence has not resonated well in Havana, especially since Cuba fully understands that the U.S. economic blockade is designed to incite social unrest that would be more difficult to contain if the island's security forces were reduced markedly.

Nevertheless, financial imperatives have led Cuba to reduce its defense budget considerably and to downsize its regular units somewhat.[31] Adding to the equation the fact that Havana no longer receives military aid from Moscow or Eastern Europe strongly suggests that Cuba's force posture has declined in recent years. But again Washington has refused to recognize these developments as significant.

- Havana's human rights performance must meet U.S. standards of acceptability.

Beyond the fact that all governments consider such issues highly sensitive, the situation is complicated in the Cuban-U.S. case by some basic conceptual discrepancies. Western liberal democratic tradition tends to accord top priority to civil or procedural rights (e.g., freedom of speech and religion, legal due process, regularly scheduled multiparty elections) that serve primarily to protect the individual against the government, while the Marxist-Leninist perspective emphasizes the socioeconomic obligations (e.g., housing, jobs, medical care) that the society has to the people as a whole. These philosophical differences almost inevitably produce diametrically opposed responses to situations in which these two sets of rights come into conflict, with communist countries like Cuba seeing nothing particularly wrong with policies and practices that subordinate what they consider the selfish interests of the individual to the exigencies of promoting socioeconomic egalitarianism.

Havana, looking at these competing paradigms as legitimate differences of opinion, has tended to view Washington's uncompromising stance as a political "red herring" that is used as a convenient rationale to justify maintaining its intransigent anti-Cuban policies. Along these lines, the Fidelistas in 1994 released an alleged top secret memo from the U.S. Interests Section in Havana that complained that it was difficult to find evidence of serious,

Cuba Confronts the Post–Cold War Order, 1992 Onward | 173

pervasive patterns of human rights abuses to bolster the State Department's case against the Cuban government.[32]

- Cuba must hold democratic elections within the context of an established multiparty political system. Outside (U.S.?) observers must certify the integrity of the process.

This precondition, which in essence demands a total restructuring of the island's political system to assure that it conforms to a Western liberal model, is absolutely unacceptable to Havana, which sees it as a blatant violation of the nation's sovereignty. Moreover, the Fidelistas argue that the Revolution *is* democratic by virtue of its responsiveness to the basic human needs of the Cuban people, especially those concerning socioeconomic matters. In any case, Havana has stood steadfast behind the nationalistic principle that it will not allow Washington to dictate to it what is politically acceptable.

On a more pragmatic level, the Cubans question the sincerity of Washington's demands: Is the United States genuinely promoting its view of democracy or simply using the whole issue as a ploy in its effort to destroy the Revolution? Certainly there is considerable evidence to support the latter interpretation, for Washington has in various ways indicated that it would reject as illegitimate any election resulting in an endorsement of the current political order or the Castro government. For example, the Helms-Burton law (discussed later in more detail) makes it clear that any election won by Fidel or his brother Raúl would ipso facto be considered undemocratic.[33] Employing these standards, then, would seem to indicate that Washington defines "political reform" in terms of dismantling of the current power structure and removing Fidel from office.

Note with respect to all of these conditions that the United States has offered nothing in terms of assured reciprocity. Washington has not indicated that it would be willing as a good faith measure to open negotiations regarding the status of the Guantanamo naval base, for instance, or to take some steps to begin lifting its economic blockade in response to similar preliminary efforts on Cuba's part to address stated U.S. concerns.[34] Indeed, Washington will not guarantee that normalization will occur even if all its demands are met. Instead, its position has been that its prerequisites must be satisfied before any discussions about improving relations can be undertaken. Representing an opinion of this whole process widely shared among observers, Wayne Smith contends that "these demands were designed as non-starters. . . . The United States does not wish to

174 | Cuba's Foreign Relations in a Post-Soviet World

negotiate [normalization] with Cuba. It simply wants what would amount to Havana's capitulation."[35] Viewing matters against this background of radically different perspectives, it is not surprising that impasse has been the primary characteristic of the normalization process.

Clinton's Cuban Policies

In early 1993 William Robinson published an analysis summarizing what he saw as an emerging consensus within the broad Washington community (which he felt was heavily influenced by Reagan's anti-Sandinista strategy) concerning the most effective way to deal with Havana.[36] Some of his observations outlining the key components of this tacit understanding that proved to be uncannily accurate as predictions about the policies that the incoming the Clinton administration would adopt can be summarized as follows:

- Promoting democracy will displace the traditional themes stressing anticommunism and national security as the preferred rationale for U.S. policy.

- Increased emphasis will be placed on nurturing the emergence of opposition forces within Cuba that represent a viable alternative to the Castro regime.

  But such a scenario carries with it potentially explosive baggage, for it implies that the nucleus of anti-Castro opposition will shift from Miami to the island. The Cuban American National Foundation (CANF) and other well-established, highly influential exile groups almost certainly will strongly oppose any effort in this direction, seeing it as totally incompatible with their desire to control the political-economic dynamics of a post-Castro Cuba.[37] Whether the foreign policy establishment, in the legislative branch or in the executive, has the fortitude to confront the political risks involved remains to be seen.

- The demand for elections in Cuba conducted on Washington's terms (which in many quarters would include U.S. certification that the results are valid) will be nonnegotiable.

- The economic blockade, despite possible posturing suggesting that a gradual lifting might occur in response to Cuban reform measures, will not undergo any truly significant moderation.

  The embargo, says Robinson, "is an essential ingredient of overall policy and will not be lifted. U.S. strategy will seek to undermine Cuba's efforts at reinsertion into the world economy and penetration of capitalist markets. . . . The entire policy will hinge in part on assuring the continuity of Cuba's severe economic crisis and avoiding any possibility of recovery, since the underlying strategy is to convert economic crisis into social discontent, and then to give political expression to that discontent."[38]

The only possible exceptions to this general rule would be modifications seen as enhancing the flow of ideas and other influences that could serve to facilitate U.S. penetration of the island's socio-political arenas.

Keeping this general paradigm in mind, we can now survey some of the highlights of Washington's relations with Cuba during the Clinton administration.

1993 Developments

As promised during the presidential campaign, the Clinton White House became an enthusiastic proponent of the Torricelli Act (also known as the Cuban Democracy Act, or CDA), which was strongly supported by hard-line anti-Castro elements in the Miami exile community and which had been signed into law by President Bush shortly before the November 1992 election. Indeed the new president proclaimed on numerous occasions that the CDA represented the core of his administration's approach to Havana. Yet beyond this rhetoric, there did not seem to be much attention being paid to relations with the island. Basically it was business as usual, with the economic blockade being maintained and the CDA being enforced, although in the latter instance the White House was careful not to push the issue so far as to create serious tensions with other friendly governments, such as Canada and the members of the European Community, which tended to perceive the ban on subsidiary trade in the Torricelli Act as an infringement on their sovereignty. Illegal emigrants from the island still received preferential treatment, being classified as political refugees and therefore receiving automatic asylum in the United States. Radio and TV Martí, the ostensible purpose of which was to provide accurate news and alternative broadcasting for the Cuban people, remained on the air with solid support from the administration, despite the fact that Radio Martí was rightfully criticized as being dominated by and promoting the political agenda of Mas Canosa, leader of the vehemently anti-Castro CANF organization, while TV Martí's operations (which the Cubans effectively jammed) were clearly in violation of agreements and standards governing international telecommunications activity. Finally, Washington

176 | Cuba's Foreign Relations in a Post-Soviet World

continued to portray Castro's government as a major human rights violator, particularly in the United Nations, where it mounted annual campaigns to have Cuba's human rights record condemned.[39]

1994 Developments

In August 1994 the latent tensions that have always lurked in the U.S.-Cuban relationship once more exploded into the open. The catalyst for this development was the growing number of people fleeing the island on often rickety home-made rafts, their primary motivation in most cases being to escape the island's deteriorating economic situation and to make it to the United States, where they knew they would be accepted as political refugees. The surging dimensions of the problem can be seen in the annual figures of the number of rafters reaching U.S. shores: 1988, 59; 1989, 391; 1990, 467; 1991, 2,203; 1992, 2,557; 1993, 3,656; 1994, over 21,000 by September 1.[40]

The Cubans had long felt that the United States was deliberately encouraging such activity as a means to embarrass them. They repeatedly pointed out that every year they provided authorization for a significant number of people to relocate legally but that Washington in effect closed down this avenue by its unwillingness to issue more than a handful of visas to individuals who had Cuban exit permits. This action combined with Washington's practice of providing automatic asylum to Cubans who chose other, illicit routes to leave the country convinced Havana that U.S. officials were simply playing political games with the refugees. The essence of Washington's ploy, said the Fidelistas, was to encourage illegal emigration and thereby create a no-win situation for Havana. When people were leaving, the United States tried to use that fact as evidence to bolster its claim that Castro's government lacked popular support. On the other hand, if Havana tried to prevent such departures, it was accused of police state terrorism. Tiring of this charade, Castro raised the specter of another Mariel exodus.

The term *Mariel* refers to a situation that developed in April 1980. A number of issues, especially U.S. unhappiness over Cuban military involvement in Africa, had contributed to a general deterioration of Havana's relations with the Carter administration. Tensions came to a head when approximately 10,000 Cubans who wanted to leave the country swamped the Peruvian embassy in Havana in the mistaken belief that travel visas were readily available there. Washington and anti-Castro exiles in the United States seized upon this incident to renew their old accusations that the Revolution had created a totalitarian hellhole out of what

Cuba Confronts the Post–Cold War Order, 1992 Onward | 177

had once been a happy, peaceful society. Fidel's reaction was to announce that any exiles in the United States who wanted to take their relatives out of the country could come to the port of Mariel near Havana to "retrieve" them. Thus began a frenzied boatlift that deposited about 125,000 refugees on U.S. shores before it was shut down in October 1980. This chaotic influx had a disruptive impact in South Florida and other popular destinations, especially since it included some hardened criminals and other "undesirables" that Cuba was in effect covertly deporting to an unsuspecting United States.[41] Washington was not amused.

History seemed to be repeating itself when Fidel announced on August 7, 1994 that "this situation cannot continue. Either they [the United States] take serious steps to guard their coasts or we will cease to impede the exit of those who wish to leave the country [via rafts] and we will cease to impede the arrival [by private boats] of those who are seeking their families here."[42] Subsequently Cuban authorities did turn a blind eye toward most rafters, and the number of departures increased dramatically.[43]

The Clinton administration's response was twofold. First, to stem the immediate tide of rafters, the White House announced on August 18 that the United States would no longer provide automatic asylum to illegal Cuban refugees. Instead, the new policy provided that such people would be detained (one site being the U.S. naval base at Guantanamo) while their cases were reviewed and, as was anticipated in most instances, arrangements were made to relocate them to third countries or return them to Cuba.[44]

The president's second move, which was designed at least in part to defuse criticism that he was caving in to Castro and was betraying current as well as future refugees by abandoning the open-door policy, sought to tighten the blockade. A key player in this development was Mas Canosa. He and Florida's governor and a delegation of Miami Cubans had a crucial meeting with President Clinton in the White House on the evening of August 19, 1994. Ann Bardach summarized what transpired: "The president had left his own birthday party to meet with Mas. . . . According to those present, . . . Mas thumped and slapped the table as he spoke, demanding that the president punish Fidel Castro for the refugee crisis. 'You must kick out the last leg of the stool,' he insisted. According to Mas [in a later interview], he had bellowed at Clinton: 'No tengas piedad!'—do not have any pity."[45]

On August 20, the White House announced new sanctions against Cuba that incorporated practically all the measures Mas Canosa had advocated the previous evening. The key provisions, which were designed in particular to restrict even further the flow of dollars to the cash-starved island, were (1) the practice of allowing U.S. nationals to transfer funds to relatives on the island, the maximum annual remittance having previously been set at $1,200 per household, would no longer be permitted; (2) travel to Cuba by those wishing to see relatives and by academics, the two groups who constituted the overwhelming majority of U.S. visitors, was severely restricted, with the White House estimating that the new regulations would reduce the overall travel flow by 90 percent; and (3) most charter flights to the island from Miami, which had been flying almost daily due to the high traffic, were targeted for elimination. Washington calculated that such measures would keep $50 million per year out of Cuba.[46]

Shortly after this foray into confrontationalism, the Clinton administration shifted gears by entering into negotiations with Havana, which resulted on September 9, 1994 in a new immigration accord between the two countries. In its two main provisions, Cuba promised to (and subsequently did) implement measures that would prevent illegal, unsafe departures from the island, such as by rafters, while the United States guaranteed henceforth to admit at least 20,000 Cubans per year in accordance with existing agreements. In addition, in an attempt to clear up some short-term migration problems complicating their relationship, Washington pledged to move quickly to admit the approximately 6,000 Cubans who were on a visa waiting list, and Havana assured the White House that illegal rafters currently being detained at Guantanamo or elsewhere who wished to return to Cuba would be allowed to do so as long as normal diplomatic channels were used to make the arrangements.[47]

1995 Developments

The 1994 elections transformed the U.S. political landscape in many respects by giving the Republican Party control of both houses of Congress for the first time in decades. One consequence with respect to U.S.-Cuban relations was that the leadership of some crucial congressional committees shifted from moderate Democrats to conservative Republicans, who often had a history of virulent hostility toward Havana. Perhaps the most drastic example occurred in the Senate Foreign Relations Committee when the old Cold War warrior Jesse Helms (R, North Carolina) replaced as chair Claiborne Pell (D, Rhode Island), who had publicly stated his belief that the blockade should be lifted.[48] A similar transfer of power took place in the House International Relations Committee, where Lee Hamilton (D, Indiana) passed the gavel to Ben Gilman (R, North Carolina), who would subsequently become a cosponsor of the Helms-Burton bill (discussed later). In the Western Hemisphere Subcommittee of the House International Relations Committee, leadership remained firmly in strong anti-Castro hands as Robert Torricelli (D, New Jersey) was replaced by the equally intransigent Dan Burton (R, Indiana).

The hard-line sentiment that these men represented soon manifested itself in the Helms bill (formally titled the Cuban Liberty and Democratic Solidarity Act of 1995), first introduced in the Senate by its namesake in early February 1995. Essentially the same piece of legislation was subsequently put before the House by Representative Burton. The main provisions of the proposed Helms-Burton bill, which was basically designed to tighten and internationalize the blockade, were:

- Previous U.S. owners of properties nationalized by the Castro government (including people who were Cuban nationals at the time but who subsequently became U.S. citizens) are granted the right to sue (in U.S. courts) any foreign persons or companies that have invested in those holdings.

- Imports into the United States of sugar products from countries that buy Cuban sugar are banned.

- U.S. representatives to international lending institutions such as the World Bank and the IMF are to be instructed to vote against any attempt to grant Havana membership and to reduce Washington's contributions to such organizations by an amount equal to any aid given to Cuba.

- Any citizen of a third country who has participated in the trade or sale of any confiscated U.S. property in Cuba is to be denied entry to the United States.

- The president is instructed to reduce U.S. aid to Russia and other former Soviet states by an amount equal to the value of any military-intelligence assistance that they might provide to Havana.[49]

The Clinton administration did not react favorably to these Congressional initiatives, insisting that existing legislation such as the CDA as well as the general policies being followed were sufficient to protect U.S. interests and to achieve Washington's goals in its relations with Havana. Among its specific objections to the proposed legislation, the White House emphasized that the provisions of the proposed bill concerning property claims could cause disputes with allies and would in any case be difficult to defend against a challenge under international law.[50] Further, the prohibition against the purchase of sugar products would almost certainly be in

180 | Cuba's Foreign Relations in a Post-Soviet World

violation of U.S. obligations under such international accords as the General Agreement on Tariffs and Trade (GATT) and NAFTA. Finally, penalizing Russia and other former Soviet states for their relations with Cuba could impede Washington's ability to promote reform and enhance stability in those countries. It was also pointed out that the Lourdes electronic intelligence-gathering facility that Moscow maintains in Cuba (and for which it pays rent to Havana) is seen by the Russians as integral to the exercise of their rights under the Strategic Arms Reduction Treaty with the United States (START) to monitor compliance with the agreement. Pushing the Kremlin on the Lourdes issue, said Washington, would unnecessarily complicate U.S.-Russian relations and could jeopardize Moscow's ratification of the START II accords. President Clinton summarized the administration's position in a Cable Network News interview: "I support the Cuban Democracy Act, which was passed in 1992 and which we have implemented faithfully. . . . I think we should continue to operate under it. I know of no reason why we need further action."[51]

An indication that the administration, despite its public statements to the contrary, was perhaps starting to lean increasingly toward negotiation rather than confrontation came when, after it held secret talks with Havana that excluded CANF and its allies from the whole process, an expanded migration agreement was concluded in May 1995. Stating that both parties were attempting "to normalize further their migration relationship," the White House announced that the main elements of the new agreement committed the United States to returning to Cuba any illegal immigrants (whether they were intercepted at sea or had made it to U.S. territory, including Guantanamo), where they could, if they wished, apply for legal admission through normal channels, and committed Cuba to refraining from any retaliatory action against such persons returned to the island.[52]

The Helms-Burton bill, having moved smoothly through various committees during the summer despite efforts by moderates to block or at least soften it, was finally approved in essentially its original form by the full House of Representatives on September 21, 1995, by a vote of 294 to 130. On September 20 the administration, via statements sent to Congress by the secretary of state and the Office of Management and Budget, had vigorously restated its objections to the pending legislation and had announced that President Clinton was prepared to veto it if it reached his desk.[53]

Similar misgivings echoed through some quarters of the business community, where Helms-Burton was seen as a Cold War relic with little relevance to the newly emerging international order characterized by free trade and the unfettered movement of capital across the globe. A *Journal of Commerce* editorial typical of such sentiment fumed that the House had "passed an ill-considered bill that aims to dry up foreign investment in Cuba" and that would lead to a "legal free-for-all" of lawsuits regarding expropriated property, which would not "foster peaceful change in Cuba or lead to better U.S./Cuban ties. . . . Other nations, meanwhile, are stepping into the breach and forging closer links, benefitting their own businesses and opening Cuba to democratic influences."[54] This discontent went beyond mere journalistic grumbling. Increasingly, corporate representatives were discreetly lobbying Congress and the White House for an end to the blockade. In August 1995, for example, a business group met with Alexander Watson (Clinton's assistant secretary of state for inter-American affairs) to voice their complaints and were not at all impressed when he tried to mollify them with the standard administration line on the necessity to maintain pressure on Castro's government.[55] In other instances, companies made their positions clear by going to Havana (often in violation of existing U.S. travel restrictions) to discuss future investment and trade prospects with Cuban officials. Indeed, a high-powered delegation of forty-seven chief executive officers, including some from General Motors, Sears Roebuck, Hyatt Hotels, Zenith Electronics, Tandy Corporation (Radio Shack), J.C. Penney, and K-Mart were dining with Fidel on October 6, the very night that Clinton announced some changes in his Cuban policies (detailed later).[56]

The Senate, responding to such external pressures as well as to concerns from within about the wisdom of the bill, passed a watered-down version of Helms-Burton on October 19, 1995, by a margin of 72 to 24. The key modification made by the Senate was to drop Title III, the section authorizing lawsuits, which was the focal point of the administration's objections and its veto threats.[57] At this point, discouraged supporters of the original bill shifted their attention to the next phase of the legislative dance—the conference committee that would attempt to reconcile the differing House and Senate bills—where they hoped to recoup their losses. But parliamentary maneuvering by moderates bogged down the whole process, and nothing significant occurred for the rest of the year.

While the Senate was grappling with Helms-Burton and simultaneously operating against a backdrop of increasing restiveness in corporate quarters, President Clinton shifted once again to the milder side of his good cop–bad cop persona with an apparently conciliatory gesture toward Havana. On October 6, 1995, he announced that he was easing some of

182 | Cuba's Foreign Relations in a Post-Soviet World

the travel and other restrictions designed to stifle any contact that private U.S. citizens might like to establish with the island. For example, he gave U.S. nongovernmental organizations permission to provide material and financial assistance to their Cuban counterparts, broadened the category of people eligible to apply for Treasury Department authorization to travel to Cuba while also lowering some barriers to such trips by Cuban Americans, and indicated his willingness to allow U.S. news organizations to establish permanent bureaus there. These modifications represented somewhat of a retreat from (but certainly not a total abandonment of) the intransigent position on sanctions that he himself had adopted in August 1994.

1996 Developments

The situation blew up in Clinton's face on February 24 when Cuban fighter jets shot down two small aircraft piloted by members of an anti-Castro organization, Brothers to the Rescue (BTTR). Controversy immediately erupted as to whether the BTTR planes, which had already established a clear pattern of international lawlessness by frequently violating Cuba's borders and had brazenly claimed that they intended to continue to do so, were actually inside Cuban airspace when they were destroyed. Havana insisted that they were, adding that they had deliberately ignored warnings from Cuban authorities of the dangers involved.[58] Washington, while conceding that fair notice had been given, rejected Havana's claims about where the incident occurred and was adamant that existing treaties to which Cuba was a party prohibited such action under any circumstances.

Clinton did not wait for such issues to be resolved. Instead, he went first to the UN Security Council and quickly succeeded in getting a resolution passed criticizing Havana's attack on the BTTR aircraft.[59] The most significant initiatives, however, were undertaken unilaterally. On February 26 the White House announced that it was asking Congress to compensate the families of BTTR members who had been killed from frozen Cuban assets controlled by the U.S. government, suspending all charter flights from the United States to the island, expanding the activities of Radio Martí, which broadcasts to Cuba and is considered by Havana to be a provocative propaganda operation, and imposing additional restrictions on visits to and travel within the United States by Cuban officials. In addition, it was prepared to explore a compromise with Congress to facilitate final passage of the Helms-Burton bill. The last item was potentially the most threatening, since the ultimate goal of Helms-Burton, at least as conceived by its creators, was to unleash such severe economic chaos in Cuba that the Castro government and indeed the Revolution itself would be swept away in the ensuing turmoil.

An agreement was indeed quickly reached on the Helms-Burton bill between the White House and congressional conference committee, on February 28, 1996.[60] Each side made some concessions to the other; the main ones were:

White House	Congress
Dropped its previous opposition to Title III, the section allowing lawsuits over expropriated property imposing sanctions on third parties who traffic in such property.	Agreed that Title III would not become effective until August 1, 1996, and then allows the president to suspend implementation at any time for six-month periods if he determines that it is in the national interest to do so. There is no limit on the number of such suspensions.
Accepted various provisions regarding the former Soviet states that could, depending on the nature of economic relations with Cuba, result in reductions of U.S. economic aid.	
	Agreed that the president could under certain conditions nullify reductions in aid related to the operation by former Soviet states of intelligence facilities in Cuba.
Agreed to codification of all existing executive orders related to the imposition of the economic blockade on Cuba, which means that any future modification of the blockade would require congressional approval.	

Although the administration did succeed in getting language inserted into the bill that gave it some flexibility in deciding whether and/or when to implement some measures, it is doubtful that these were major victories, since it was likely that Congress realized that the provisions in question would be challenged by other countries and could well be declared invalid under international law or under various treaties to which the United States is a party.[61] Indeed, if one takes a broad and long-term perspective, it would appear that Clinton gave up much more than he gained, the key item here being the matter of codification of executive orders. In effect, what Clinton almost certainly did by agreeing to codification was to jeopardize seriously his ability (and that of future presidents) to launch initiatives related to improving relations with revolutionary Cuba. From Havana's perspective, the economic blockade has long been the main impediment to mending fences with Washington. Prior to February 28, the White House exercised sole control over this option: the president could

184 | Cuba's Foreign Relations in a Post-Soviet World

forgo better relations by continuing to pursue the blockade, or he could promote normalization by modifying or abandoning it. But such latitude no longer exists, for codification has bestowed a virtual congressional veto over any presidential initiatives concerning the blockade. This action may prove to be Clinton's most enduring and controversial legacy in the complex arena of U.S.-Cuban relations.

This compromise version passed the Senate on March 5, 1996, by a vote of 74 to 22. The House followed suit the next day with a final tally of 336 to 86. President Clinton, despite an increasing crescendo of criticism from various allies and normally friendly governments, made it official by signing Helms-Burton into law on March 12, 1996.

The White House found itself in an increasingly delicate situation with the approach of the August 1, 1996, deadline for deciding whether to implement the highly contentious Title III of the Helms-Burton law. On the home front, the presidential election season was in full swing, with Clinton once again seemingly fixated by the lure of the anti-Castro Cuban vote while in general seeking to move his public image increasingly toward the right on the political spectrum. This campaign strategy demanded that he avoid doing anything that might produce a backlash in the Cuban community or create an opening for the opposition to brand him with the dreaded "L" (for liberal). To postpone the August 1 activation of Title III was potentially risky on both counts. On the other hand, the administration did not want to antagonize further other governments that were vigorously lobbying against any action under Title III and in some cases were even threatening to undertake various kinds of retaliatory measures.

In a move that was clearly designed to avoid confronting the issue directly while simultaneously trying to placate as many interested parties as possible, Clinton announced on July 30, 1996, that he would not postpone implementation of Title III. Hence, as desired by opponents of the Cuban Revolution, Title III was now officially the law of the land. Concurrently, in order to gain time to deal with international opposition to Helms-Burton, the White House stated that it would not allow any lawsuits to be filed under Title III until February 1, 1997.[62] The bottom line in this complex scenario was that Title III was now technically in force, but any action under it was temporarily suspended until February 1 (with an extension of that deadline remaining a possibility).

1997 Developments

Having won a second term rather handily, President Clinton announced on January 3, 1997, that he was indeed extending the suspension of lawsuits under Title III for another six months, citing as his rationale the supposedly more vigorous efforts on the part of U.S. allies and friends to collaborate with Washington in promoting a transition to democracy in Cuba. The implication, in other words, was that other countries, despite their public postures, were becoming increasingly supportive of U.S. policy toward Havana and that such initiatives needed to be rewarded in order to assure even greater future cooperation. To many observers, however, Clinton's explanation appeared either to be naive wishful thinking or, as was more likely, to reflect the hard political reality that many countries (especially the EU nations, Canada, and Mexico) remained adamant in their opposition to Helms-Burton and in their determination to destroy it by whatever means were available (e.g., World Trade Organization or NAFTA proceedings).[63] It would appear that Clinton's extension was essentially motivated by a desire to try to avoid a Helms-Burton confrontation; the president was in effect engaging once again in the waffling tactics for which he had become notorious. Such delays in implementing Title III would become routine, action being regularly taken every six months. Thus, as of late 1999, suspension announcements had been made in July 1997 and in January and July of both 1998 and 1999.

A different story applies with regard to Title IV of the law, which calls for people who buy, invest in, or help to sell U.S. property nationalized by the Fidelistas to be denied entry to the United States. The primary target of such "anti-trafficking" sanctions has been Sherritt Incorporated of Canada, which has become heavily involved in helping to revitalize the Revolution's battered post–Cold war economy. It has been particularly active in the island's nickel mining and oil and gas sectors as well as branching out into agricultural ventures. In the process, it has incurred the wrath of Helms-Burton. Seven members of the board of directors (as well as their spouses and minor children) were informed in 1996 that they could not enter the United States; another four officials were similarly banned in March 1997. Washington charged that the company had "'waltzed in . . . and taken over stolen goods.' [Its] mining operation in Cuba's Moa Bay profits from property confiscated by Fidel Castro's government from [the] New Orleans based Freeport McMoran corporation."[64] The only other firms to have been so censured as of early 1999 were Israel's Groupo B.M. and Mexico's Grupo Domos. The restrictions on Grupo Domos, which had entered a joint venture with the Cuban government to modernize the island's telephone and other communications systems, were later rescinded when the company withdrew from the project.

186 | Cuba's Foreign Relations in a Post-Soviet World

The most important Helms-Burton issue that the Clinton White House confronted during 1997, however, was not the Title III suspensions or specific applications of Title IV but rather the challenge to the entire law being mounted before the World Trade Organization (WTO) by the European Union. The EU had asked the WTO to convene a panel to explore the question of whether Helms-Burton violated international (trade) law, its report being scheduled for April 14, 1997. According to WTO procedures, the protesting party (in this case, the European Union) can withdraw its complaint any time before the panel issues its findings as to whether the dispute merits further consideration. But once this fail-safe point is passed, there is no turning back and the case then goes before the WTO for a final pronouncement. But the United States had announced earlier in the year that it would not take part in such proceedings and would ignore any (adverse) rulings that might ensue, claiming that the WTO lacked jurisdiction over the question because Helms-Burton dealt, according to Washington, with a national security matter rather than a trade question.

Obviously Washington preferred to avoid a situation whereby Helms-Burton would be officially repudiated before the entire international community and the United States would find itself in the highly embarrassing position of undermining the authority and prestige of the WTO, when it had strongly supported creation of the organization. Hence Undersecretary of State Stuart Eizenstat, whom Clinton had appointed as his special envoy for Cuban affairs and who had extensive experience in dealing with European governments, threw himself into an effort to try to arrange some kind of compromise with the EU that would serve to short-circuit the WTO process.

With the April 14 deadline looming menacingly on the horizon, an understanding was finally reached on April 11. The key elements of the agreement were as follows:

- The European Union announced that it would suspend its complaint to the WTO about Helms-Burton while efforts were undertaken with Washington to work out a more comprehensive, permanent accord, the centerpiece of which would be "disciplines" designed to deter foreign investors from dealing in expropriated property. But the EU reserved the right to revive its WTO challenge if this undertaking were not concluded to its satisfaction by October 15, 1997.

- The Clinton administration, on the other hand, promised to continue to delay implementation of Title III of the Helms-Burton law (the lawsuit section) and to seek new legislation from Congress that would also allow the president to waive the law's Title IV travel and visa restrictions.

The ensuing negotiations proved difficult, as most observers had anticipated, and especially from the Europeans' perspective, for they were the ones with the most grievances that needed to be redressed.

Throughout the summer the two sides worked intensely to try to achieve some sort of accommodation. There were key barriers impeding progress:

- The Clinton team wanted sanctions (or disciplines) to be applied retroactively against foreign investors who had acquired or profited from any U.S. property nationalized by the Fidelistas, which in effect would have opened the door to claims and controversies going back to the early 1960s. The Europeans, on the other hand, insisted that enforcement action should be undertaken only against those who violated the agreement's principles after it had been officially ratified. In other words, they wanted immunity for those who might have "trafficked" in the past.

- The EU wanted ironclad assurances that Title III would continue to be waived indefinitely by Clinton and his successors. This request, at least in Washington's eyes, constituted little more than fanciful thinking, for there was no way that Clinton could guarantee the actions of future presidents. Since Title III represented one of the Europeans' most important concerns, this impasse did not sit well with them.

- The Europeans were not at all impressed by or enthusiastic about the administration's commitment to seek legislative authorization for presidential waivers of Title IV, for they knew that Clinton's ability to get the Republican-controlled Congress to agree was questionable at best and in reality probably nonexistent. As such, there seemed to be little likelihood that they would receive any official protection from Title IV. Instead it appeared, as was also the case with Title III, that they would have to continue to rely on the goodwill of the person in the Oval Office to escape any serious Helms-Burton repercussions on this count.

These differences precluded the two parties from meeting their October 15, 1997, target date for an agreement. Nevertheless the EU decided not to carry through on its threat to take the dispute back to the WTO, and the two sides continued their talks. It would be another seven months before

1998 Developments

they would put the matter to rest for good. In the meantime, the Clinton administration was confronted with what had at one time seemed inconceivable—a papal visit to Cuba that had the potential to strengthen Castro's position in his long struggle with the United States.

1998 Developments

After several false starts, it was announced that an agreement had been reached between Havana and the Vatican for a five-day trip to the island by Pope John Paul II beginning on January 21, 1998. Thus the stage was set for one of the most dramatic events of the year—an encounter between the staunchly anticommunist Roman Catholic pontiff, whose 1979 visit to his Polish homeland was widely credited as having played a significant role in helping to bring down its Soviet-style government, and the legendary Fidel Castro, who despite the disintegration of the socialist bloc has never wavered in his commitment to maintaining the Marxist essence of the Cuban Revolution. Clinton officials publicly voiced the optimistic hope that the pope's sojourn would have an influence similar to what had happened in Poland, but privately they worried that it would enhance Fidel's prestige and give added legitimacy to Havana's campaign against the U.S. blockade. Consequently they made it clear before John Paul arrived that the only thing that could improve relations between the countries was implementation by Castro of reforms resulting in a neoliberal economy and a political system modeled on Western democratic lines. In other words, they tried to shift responsibility for continued tensions to Castro in an attempt to defuse an anticipated papal rebuke of U.S. policy.

These fears proved to be well founded. While he did chide the Revolution for its restrictions on religious freedom and generally criticized its human rights record, John Paul's harshest remarks were directed at Washington. In particular, he characterized the U.S. blockade as "oppressive," "unjust," and "ethically unacceptable." Also, in terms similar to those used on other occasions by Fidel, he attacked capitalist neoliberalism as a system that subordinates human beings to blind market forces and generates wealth for the few at the cost of impoverishing the many. Such comments led some observers to conclude that the major winners from the visit were the pope, the Catholic Church in Cuba, Fidel, and the revolutionary government, while the losers were Washington and its anti-Castro allies in the exile community.[65] In reality, however, the impact within the United States of the pope's visit was nil, being limited to a narrow circle of Cuba-watchers who are highly attuned to the nuances of such developments. For the public at large, the story was totally overshadowed by the

Cuba Confronts the Post–Cold War Order, 1992 Onward | 189

Table 6.8. Cuba and Cuban policies: U.S. public opinion polls (in percentages)

Question: End the economic embargo against Cuba?

	Yes	No	
October 1996	32	56	
January 1998	44	46	

Question: Establish diplomatic relations with Cuba?

	Yes	No	Unsure
January 1998	55	30	15

Question: Your opinion of Cuba?

	Favorable	Unfavorable	
March 1996	10	81	
January 1998	23	59	

Source: Compiled from information in "Keep Embargo But Establish Diplomacy Cuba Poll," *Reuters* (January 21, 1998), news item datelined New York provided via the Internet by the CNN Custom News Service.

breaking Lewinsky sex scandal that was enveloping the Clinton White House.

Certainly Havana hoped that John Paul's trip would have a salutary effect on U.S. public opinion, which had been shifting somewhat in Cuba's favor over the past few years. Indeed, as indicated in table 6.8, polls taken just before the papal visit indicated that even though people in the United States did not hold the Cuban Revolution in very high esteem, these attitudes did not translate into enthusiasm for Washington's belligerent policies. Instead, there was clear support for restoring diplomatic ties, while a statistical dead heat reigned with respect to sentiment about the blockade.[66] Some good publicity for the Revolution and against the administration's anti-Cuban posture, reasoned the Fidelistas, should give added momentum to the shift in U.S. public opinion that was already running in their favor, thus bringing added pressure on the Clinton White House to normalize relations.

The uproar over the Lewinsky affair, which erupted just as the pope was arriving in Cuba, shattered all these expectations. The major television networks, from which most people in the United States get their news, had planned intensive coverage of the papal visit. For example, television watchdog Andrew Tyndell predicted that approximately 75 percent of the prime-time newscasts would be devoted to John Paul's trip and to related stories about the Revolution and Washington's relations with it. As part of this all-out effort, he said, "Most U.S. TV networks had sent reporters and

190 | Cuba's Foreign Relations in a Post-Soviet World

producers to Cuba several weeks before the Pope's visit to prepare background pieces which they expected to run during news programs and late night specials all week."[67]

But once the president's sexual exploits with a young intern began to be revealed, the media completely shifted their focus back to Washington. The anchors of the big three television networks were abruptly recalled from Havana to cover the breaking scandal. As a result, the events unfolding in Cuba essentially dropped out of sight as far as the average U.S. citizen was concerned. Television coverage was minimal, and what did appear consisted mostly of superficial sound bites and photo opportunities. The in-depth specials were never aired. Thus was lost a golden opportunity to generate a broad public debate over the future of the long-troubled U.S.-Cuban relationship.

The pope's visit did, however, put some pressure on the Clinton administration to balance its basic vindictiveness toward the Castro government with some humanitarian considerations that would help alleviate the plight of innocent people (on both sides of the Florida Straits) caught in the crossfire. Apparently responding to this sentiment, the White House announced some minor policy adjustments on March 20. Specifically, direct charter flights between Miami and Havana were reinstated, although otherwise tight travel restrictions remained in place, and U.S. citizens with relatives on the island were once again allowed to send them up to $1,200 a year. These were not, of course, new initiatives but simply a return to previous practices that had been discontinued: permission to send cash remittances had been revoked in 1994 after Havana had unleashed the rafters on the United States, and the charters had been grounded in 1996 in retaliation for destruction by the Cuban Air Force of the Brothers to the Rescue planes. In short, Clinton was merely reopening old bridges rather than building new ones.

The argument for even greater flexibility was strengthened approximately a week later, when information began to leak out about a classified Pentagon report prepared for Congress that confirmed what everyone had known for several years: There were no longer any grounds whatsoever for considering Cuba a significant security threat to the United States. Some indication of what the study contained could be deduced from the comments of Marine General Charles Wilhelm, chief of the U.S. Southern Command, who was a major contributor to the study. In a newspaper interview he described the Cuban armed forces as "'dramatically' weakened, cut in half from a peak of 130,000 active personnel a decade ago. He

Cuba Confronts the Post–Cold War Order, 1992 Onward | 191

also noted that Cuba's military equipment is unusable, particularly tactical aircraft like Soviet MiGs."

Today, Wilhelm said, "that armed force has no capability whatsoever to project itself beyond the borders of Cuba, so it's really no threat to anyone around it. As much as 70 percent of the armed forces' effort is involved in their own self-sustainment, in things like agricultural pursuits. . . . It doesn't even begin to resemble the Cuban armed forces that we contemplated in the '80s."[68]

Based on what was known about this forthcoming document as well as well as on other sources, *Miami Herald* analyst Christopher Marquis concluded that a Pentagon consensus about Cuba and U.S. policy toward it was emerging, the main elements of which were:

- Castro is portrayed as a rational leader who does not want to provoke the United States because he fully realizes that such a move could seriously endanger the survival of his government and the Revolution.

- The most immediate potential risk that Cuba poses to U.S. national interests lies in the area of unchecked emigration. But existing agreements between the two countries to assure orderly migration seem to be working, and Havana appears to be fully committed to upholding its commitments under these accords.

- The Defense Department is adamant in not wanting to be drawn into a Cuban civil war or any kind of occupation of the island. Consequently it has serious qualms about any U.S. policy that seeks to provoke economic chaos and/or a popular uprising against the revolutionary government.[69]

The U.S. military was also highly skeptical of charges frequently made by anti-Castro militants in the United States that high-level Cuban officials (perhaps including even Fidel) have been deeply involved in drug trafficking, having found no evidence in their investigations to support such allegations. In any case, the Pentagon's overall position served to undermine the "Cuban security threat thesis" that had for decades been the central pillar of Washington's rationale for its intransigent, uncompromising approach to Castro's revolutionary government.

In late April the administration finally got some good news: the EU had decided not to pursue its complaints against Helms-Burton with the WTO. It was dropping the action entirely, preferring instead to seek a separate negotiated settlement to the dispute. This was, without any

192 | Cuba's Foreign Relations in a Post-Soviet World

doubt, a victory for the Clinton administration and especially for Stuart Eizenstat, the White House's chief representative in the campaign to dissuade the Europeans from carrying through on their threats to force a WTO showdown on the issue. Both parties then agreed to launch an all-out effort to formulate a final solution before Clinton's scheduled May 18, 1998, meeting in England with his European counterparts.

Surprisingly, given the past problems that the two sides had experienced in trying to find some mutually acceptable middle ground, they quickly succeeded this time. On May 18, just hours before the English summit convened, it was announced that a preliminary agreement had been reached. Its main provisions, categorized in terms of whose concerns and demands they addressed, were these:

U.S. Concerns	EU Concerns
A global registry of foreign-owned expropriated properties, which will include countries in addition to Cuba such as Libya and Iran, will be created and any foreign investors (i.e., from the United States or the EU) who subsequently become involved with these properties may be subject to the application of "binding disciplines" or sanctions. The penalties against these subsequent investors will include such things as denial by their governments of loans and loan guarantees, grants, subsidies, and overseas political risk insurance.	The White House will seek from Congress waiver authority with respect to Title IV of the Helms-Burton law, which denies executives of foreign companies that have invested in disputed Cuban property (and their immediate families) entry into the United States.
There will be a blanket ban on all foreign investment in property that is illegally expropriated any time after all EU members approve the overall accord.	Existing European holdings in Cuba will not be subject to the "binding disciplines" normally applied to foreigners who invest in expropriated properties listed on the global register. Instead, only EU investments in Cuba that occur after the agreement goes into force may be subject to sanctions. Moreover, the EU will impose penalties only if the White House succeeds in getting Congress to approve a waiver of Title IV and explicitly agrees to use it to protect EU companies from Helms-Burton.
Every European investment in Cuba will be investigated by the EU to determine whether illegally expropriated property is involved. If so, the investor(s) would become subject to the sanctions mentioned.	The United States pledges that its president will use the waiver authority granted in Helms-Burton to suspend implementation of Title III of the law.

The crucial flaw in this tentative agreement was the fact that Washington's ability to deliver on two key items was extremely questionable, as has been pointed out. First, it was highly unlikely that Clinton would be able to persuade Congress to pass the amendments to the Helms-Burton law necessary to give him waiver authority over Title IV. Second, future presidents, irrespective of any Clinton assurances given to the Europeans, would be completely free under existing U.S. laws to implement Title III if they so desired. Thus from a cynical perspective, one might conclude that all parties involved (especially the EU) knew that the agreement was in reality dead on arrival and were simply using it as a face-saving means to avoid a WTO confrontation that might generate a negative impact on U.S.-European relations considerably greater than the benefits of victory would be.

This neutralization of the potentially damaging implications of Washington's Cuban policies for U.S.-EU relations did not satisfy those who felt that a more fundamental reevaluation of the whole situation was necessary. Consequently, in mid-October a group of prominent people both within and outside the Congress called upon the White House to form a blue-ribbon panel, as President Reagan had done in 1983 to deal with the Central American crisis, empowered to review and make recommendations about U.S. relations with Havana. Among the dignitaries making this request were two former secretaries of state, Henry Kissinger and Lawrence Eagleburger; a former undersecretary of state, William Rogers; a former defense secretary, Frank Carlucci; a former Senate majority leader, Howard Baker, Jr.; and Senator John Warner (R, Virginia) along with fourteen other current members of Congress.

The reaction from anti-Castro quarters was, of course, predictably negative, a main line of criticism being that the proposal was driven by corporate greed rather than by legitimate diplomatic concerns. Three leading hard-liners in the House (Ileana Ros-Lehtinin, R, Florida; Lincoln Diaz-Balart, R, Florida; and Robert Menendez, D, New Jersey) made this argument, charging in a open letter to Clinton that "the idea for this commission came from a group of former members of Congress and high government officials who are now businessmen apparently seeking to subvert the will of the American people and the intent of Congress because of these businessmen's pecuniary interests. We are concerned that some people in the business community care nothing at all about the absolute lack of political freedom, human rights, or independent organized labor in Cuba. We believe that those commercial interests seek to take advantage of the enslaved Cuban people for their financial gain."[70]

Certainly pro-normalization sentiment had been growing in at least some corporate sectors, as illustrated by a March 1998 Mexico-based symposium organized by Alamar Associates for U.S. companies interested in doing business with Cuba: the gathering attracted representatives of more than seventy firms, including such giants as Mobil Oil, Continental Grain, and Bristol-Myers Squibb.[71] The highlight of the conference was a trip to Havana for meetings with such top Cuban officials as Vice President Carlos Lage and Fidel himself. In another case clearly aimed at generating a reservoir of goodwill in anticipation of future commercial opportunities, major U.S. pharmaceutical companies (including Johnson and Johnson, Eli Lilly, and Merck) donated $6 million worth of drugs in 1998 to the Catholic Medical Missions Board for distribution throughout the island. But the suggestion that the commission proposal was the brainchild of some sort of predatory corporate conspiracy hell-bent upon pillaging the island was dismissed by most observers as fanciful hyperbole. The more accurate view saw it as a logical move by mainstream critics who were now looking for a way to resurrect the (aborted) policy debate that they had thought would occur as a result of the pope's visit to Cuba.

The White House, however, was preoccupied with Kenneth Starr's investigation of alleged Clinton misconduct and the growing threat of an impeachment vote in House of Representatives (which did indeed occur in mid-December). Consequently, the White House was not at this point inclined to embark on any venture that might be seen to involve unnecessary political risks. Certainly the Cuban question fell into this category: the anti-Castro passions that had traditionally swirled around the issue had given it the aura of a Pandora's Box that presidents had been loath to open even under the most favorable circumstances. Thus, perhaps not surprisingly, the administration reverted to the conventional, safe line of no concessions to Havana or to those who supported anything that might have the potential to generate some movement toward normalization of relations with Fidel's government.[72]

Proponents of the review commission nevertheless continued to lobby hard for it throughout the rest of the year, hoping that the prestige of those who had authored the original request would tip the balance in their favor. But these yearnings and efforts proved fruitless, for in January 1999 the White House announced that it would not approve the formation of such a board to scrutinize the current state and future directions of the U.S. approach to dealing with revolutionary Cuba.

U.S. Policy Perspectives

One way to look at Clinton's approach to Havana is to see it as having been driven primarily by conventional diplomatic considerations. At the core of this perspective is the idea that Clinton's Cuba policy emerged from a rational decision-making model within which the administration was pursuing (legitimate) national interests utilizing a strategy that had a realistic chance of success while simultaneously minimizing the potential costs and risks of implementation. To what extent do the administration's initiatives seem to have fitted this model?

Certainly an argument can be made that White House policy making with regard to Havana was heavily influenced by a clearly perceived set of interests from which flowed a coherent menu of goals. In some instances these interests and goals were consistent with key elements of overall U.S. global strategy, such as the frequently stated commitment to the promotion worldwide of Western-style political democracies and free-market economies. Other considerations were much more Cuba-specific, such as driving Castro from power and assuring that U.S. nationals are compensated for property expropriated by the revolutionary government.

Controversy has raged over the "legitimacy" of some of Washington's aims, in particular its obsession with eliminating Fidel and his brother Raúl from the political equation through such ploys as the previously mentioned Helms-Burton provisions that any election won by them is unacceptable. The policy's defenders insist that attaching such preconditions to Cuban political activity is absolutely necessary to assure the emergence of a genuine and stable democracy on the island. But many critics see such stipulations as a thinly disguised and totally unconscionable exercise in vintage Yankee arrogance, raising once again the sorry specter of the imperialistic Colossus of the North violating Cuban sovereignty by attempting to impose its political (and economic) will on the island. Indeed, say the most cynical observers, such behavior proves that the old Platt Amendment mentality is still very much alive and thriving within the Washington Beltway.

A strong case could be made that any policy incorporating such provisions would represent egregious abuse of human rights on Washington's part, for it has long been recognized in the international community that self-determination is a fundamental liberty that must be universally respected. Clearly Helms-Burton violates this basic principle, proclaiming in unambiguous terms its desire to place restrictions on the freedom of the Cuban people to decide who will govern them. Further inflaming the situation is the hypocrisy involved, with Washington simultaneously insisting that the Fidelistas clean up their human rights performance and seeking to enforce a U.S. law with provisions that contain blatant human rights transgressions.

While such debates are both necessary and useful, they become largely moot when attention shifts to the question of the success potential of the administration's policies. Here, aside from some pockets of optimism (or wishful thinking?) within the Beltway and in Miami, there appears to be broad consensus that Washington's prospects for achieving its Cuban goals are minimal. Certainly the historical record is hardly encouraging: nine U.S. presidents, many of them much tougher and more intransigent than Clinton, have tried in one way or another to destroy the Cuban Revolution, and all have failed. Admittedly there may have been a novel window of opportunity in the early 1990s when the Revolution's economy unraveled as the Soviet bloc disintegrated and Havana seemed especially vulnerable to external pressure, but that opening seemed to have disappeared as the decade drew to a close. All indicators suggest that the island has ridden out the worst of its destabilization, with its economy registering healthy growth rates (heavily driven by foreign investment and tourism) of 2.5 percent in 1995, 7.8 percent in 1996, and 2.5 percent again in 1997. Thus Washington's hopes for a cataclysmic crisis that would serve as the catalyst for the Revolution's demise appear to have been in vain; Cuba has adjusted to the post–Cold War international economic order.

Compounding these problems for Clinton were the diplomatic costs, especially in the form of serious tensions with traditional allies, associated with his Cuban policies. Speaking in general terms, there appears to be little international enthusiasm for continued confrontation with Havana. Instead, the majority view unquestionably supports reconciliation. Moreover, in some instances governments have gone beyond merely expressing disagreement with U.S. policy and have taken countermeasures against what they consider outrageous infringements by Washington on their rights and interests.

International opinion as expressed in the United Nations has been somewhat mixed with regard to various U.S.-Cuban disputes. On the one hand, members have until recently supported Washington's contention that Havana has a flawed human rights record demanding UN attention. Beginning in 1991 the United States regularly submitted a resolution to the United Nations Human Rights Commission accusing Cuba of violations and requesting UN action to investigate and remedy the situation. Washington prevailed for seven consecutive years before finally suffering a setback in 1998. The breakdown of votes over the past few sessions has been as follows:

	In favor	Opposed	Abstaining
1994	24	20	9
1995	22	8	23
1996	20	5	28
1997	19	10	24
1998	16	19	18

For the most part, then, Washington's viewpoint has prevailed on this issue, although the large number of abstentions since 1994 suggests that many governments do not consider this quarrel to be a crucial issue and hence are not willing to expend their political capital by taking sides.[73]

The situation changes dramatically, however, with respect to the U.S. economic blockade. In a role reversal that sees Havana annually proposing resolutions calling on the General Assembly to condemn this policy, recent votes have gone as follows:

	In favor	Opposed	Abstaining
1993	88	4	57
1994	101	2	48
1995	117	3	38
1996	137	3	25
1997	143	3	17
1998	157	2	12

Israel was the only country that consistently joined the United States in casting negative ballots in the 1994–98 tallies, but its sincerity would seem to be somewhat suspect since it has maintained rather vigorous trade relations with the island and allows its nationals to invest there. (Israeli firms were reported in 1995 to be second only to Mexican companies with regard to financial involvement in the Cuban textile industry.)[74]

This pattern to a great extent repeats itself when attention shifts to the European Union (EU), an organization in which one finds Washington's most important and most long-standing allies. Although EU countries shared many of the Clinton administration's concerns about human rights issues in Cuba, this common ground was often overshadowed by the divisiveness engendered by the question of the blockade. Not only have many European governments disagreed in principle with this policy, but even more disconcerting is what they have often viewed as unacceptable and

198 | Cuba's Foreign Relations in a Post-Soviet World

even illegal efforts on Washington's part to force them to abide by (and therefore in effect become a party to) various blockade actions.

A blatant example of such behavior, say the Europeans, are certain provisions of the 1992 Torricelli law prohibiting foreign (European) subsidiaries of U.S. companies from trading with or investing in Cuba. Such a ban, in the opinion of many Europeans and others, violates international laws and customary legal norms that proscribe states from engaging in exercises of extraterritoriality. Basically what this means (in lay terms) is that a government cannot attempt to expand enforcement of its laws into the jurisdiction of other states. The critics' basic arguments go as follows:

> The subsidiaries in question are "subjects" of the legal codes of the countries within which they are located because they have been chartered (i.e., have been made legal entities with rights and obligations) by their hosts. Therefore the operations of these companies are governed solely by the laws of their host nation (and, of course, relevant international law). If the host nation allows trade with and investment in Cuba, Washington cannot prevent foreign subsidiaries of U.S. companies from doing so. In other words, U.S. laws that prohibit such activities cannot be applied outside of the United States to legal entities (the subsidiaries) that are not under its jurisdiction. To try to behave in such an "extraterritorial" fashion is not permitted.

Based on this interpretation of international law, the EC and some other governments went beyond mere criticism and actually launched counter-offensives against the CDA. For example, the *New York Times* reported in November 1993 (approximately one year after the Torricelli bill had been signed into law) that "Canada has issued an order to block compliance with the extraterritorial claims of the Cuban Democracy Act, and has protested a provision barring any vessel that enters Cuba from unloading freight in U.S. ports for 180 days after departing Cuba. Along with other countries, Britain has made it an offense to comply with extraterritorial provisions of the law."[75]

The EU (and others) see the Helms-Burton law as even more arrogant and intrusive than the CDA, insisting that some of its stipulations violate existing U.S. international commitments. Consequently, as explained, the EU initiated action to bring the legislation before the WTO in an attempt to get the Helms-Burton law nullified as a violation of WTO provisions in particular and international law in general, although it later abandoned this effort after a separate agreement was reached with the Clinton administration. Russia, which was specifically targeted for possible Helms-Burton sanctions, likewise voiced through its parliament its consternation about what it perceived to be an illegitimate, ill-advised attempt by Washington to dictate foreign policy to Moscow.

Closer to home, the Western Hemisphere, once a bulwark of support for the U.S. hard line against Cuba, has for all practical purposes abandoned Washington on this issue. Not only have all hemispheric nations reestablished diplomatic relations with Havana, but many have developed vigorous networks of trade, investment, and economic cooperation with the island that they are seeking to expand. Some countries, of course, never embraced the U.S. blockade, Canada and Mexico being the leading examples. Currently, despite the fact that both are partners with the United States in NAFTA and therefore have major economic interests at stake in their relationship with Washington, they have maintained their independent stands on the Cuban question. They continue to serve as major hemispheric sources of trade and investment for Havana and have not seemed inclined to change the basic thrust of their Cuban policies even if confronted with the specter of U.S. retribution.[76] Both governments have attacked Helms-Burton as an egregious breach of the NAFTA accords and have threatened to try to get its most objectionable sections (which basically means Titles III and IV) voided by invoking NAFTA's appeal process.[77]

Such defiance has tended to become the rule rather than the exception in recent years. For instance, members of CARICOM have been unusually vociferous in their criticism of the CDA, Helms-Burton, and Washington's blockade schemes in general, insisting that they will pursue whatever Cuban policies they wish. Perhaps the most vivid illustration of such sentiment came when Eugenia Charles, the leader of Dominica who had previously been one of the Caribbean's most fervent supporters of the Reagan administration's intransigent anti-Castroism, said in February 1993, "I don't think that the embargo should continue—they should let people trade with Cuba if they want to."[78] She reiterated this position the following month, declaring that Dominica would trade with Havana as long as it remained profitable to do so and that "the U.S. must realize that we [in the CARICOM region] are independent countries and in the same way that they choose their friends we must be allowed to choose ours. . . . If they haven't realized that the Cold War is over, we have."[79] Subsequently, despite the Clinton administration's obvious unhappiness with the idea and crude threats of economic reprisals from some elements in Congress, the CARICOM countries established a joint commission with Havana

(December 1993) to promote trade and economic cooperation.[80] In a similar vein, Chile broke ranks with Washington in April 1995 by reestablishing full diplomatic relations with Havana after a hiatus of more than twenty years. This action was taken even though Santiago was fully aware of Washington's disapproval and the possibility of future retaliation, as was implied in the comment of one State Department official that normalization "won't make things easier" with regard to Chile's ambition to become NAFTA's fourth member.[81]

Taking into account all these considerations, the Clinton administration's approach to its relations with revolutionary Cuba would appear to be sorely lacking in the attributes normally associated with rational decision making and high-quality diplomacy. Specifically, its policies exhibit these serious flaws:

- They have lacked broad consensus, both domestically and also within the global community as a whole, regarding the legitimate U.S. interests involved.
- Their prospects for attaining their goals, according to most impartial observers as well as the historical record, have been deemed to be minimal even according to the most optimistic calculations and virtually nonexistent by most.
- Finally, the political costs involved in terms of their negative impact in other sectors of Washington's foreign affairs (with respect to Canada and the European Union) have been significant.

In other words, as has so often been the case in the past, the approach adopted by the Clinton White House for dealing with Havana displayed traits characteristic of a formula for frustration and failure rather than success.

A second major body of opinion regarding the essential nature of Clinton's Cuban policies has seen them as being driven primarily by domestic political expediency. This scenario has emphasized such often interrelated factors as catering to the narrow concerns of domestic interest groups, the perceived potential impact of international initiatives on reelection prospects, or making foreign policy concessions within the context of a quid pro quo relationship with legislators.

President Clinton's performance in dealing with U.S.-Cuban relations exhibited a characteristic many deem to be common to his presidency: a tendency to sacrifice leadership on the altar of electoral and political expediency. His operational code of decision making often seemed to be dominated by excessive sensitivity to shifts in the political winds, the main

Cuba Confronts the Post–Cold War Order, 1992 Onward | 201

concern apparently being to avoid controversy whenever possible and to take whatever action was seen as most greatly enhancing his political fortunes. This propensity produced a situation on the Cuban front whereby Clinton, while occasionally indicating some willingness to moderate his stance toward Havana, usually aligned himself with those advocating the maintenance and even the intensification of an uncompromising, intransigent position.

During the 1992 presidential campaign, for example, Clinton often appeared willing to mortgage future policy in return for perceived short-term electoral advantage. The key Cuba-related episode here was the alliance that he forged with Jorge Mas Canosa, leader of the Cuban American National Foundation and the most powerful of Miami's anti-Castro figures, in the hope that such a move would allow him to carry Florida and its twenty-five electoral votes (the fourth largest bloc of all fifty states). Clinton's embrace of Mas Canosa and CANF came in an April 1992 speech in Miami, where in effect he portrayed the Bush administration as being soft on Castro because of its misgivings about the Cuban Democracy Act, which had been languishing in Congress for more than a year. By proclaiming his enthusiasm for the proposed legislation, which he described as a "big opportunity to put the hammer down on Fidel Castro and Cuba," Clinton forced the Bush White House to support it actively.[82] Financially this ploy paid Clinton major dividends: his campaign committee shortly thereafter received contributions totaling approximately $500,000 from CANF loyalists and other anti-Castro Cubans. Ultimately, however, this strategy did not produce the anticipated results. Clinton lost Florida, receiving in the process only 18 percent of the Dade County (Miami area) Cuban vote.[83]

The new administration quickly learned that the policy ambitions of CANF and its allies went far beyond the scope of the CDA or any other single piece of legislation. That rude awakening came in late January 1993, when it became known that Cuban-born Mario Baeza was its leading candidate for nomination to serve as assistant secretary of state for inter-American affairs. Baeza, who had no real history of cooperative links to the anti-Castro Cuban community and was generally considered by outside observers to be a moderate on relations with Havana, was totally unacceptable to CANF. In the uproar that ensued, Mas Canosa, Congressman Robert Torricelli (D, New Jersey), and others charged, among other things, that Baeza was soft on Castro and hence not fit to occupy a central policy-making position in hemispheric affairs. Despite the fact that there was strong support for Baeza from other sectors, the White House quietly abandoned him and never formally sent forward his nomination. Obviously the Miami hard-liners were delighted with the outcome, but others were quite dismayed at what was widely interpreted as an abdication of policy responsibility on the part of the White House.[84]

Charges that Clinton's proclivity to intertwine too tightly (re)election considerations and foreign policy surfaced once again in October 1995 as the presidential campaign season began to heat up. As described in the section on "1995 Developments," the White House decided to implement various modifications in the Cuban blockade that would provide more opportunities for travel to and exchanges with the island. Whether this move represented a genuine policy initiative, in effect recognizing the legitimacy of calls coming from various quarters for more tolerance toward and even rapprochement with Havana, was a matter of considerable conjecture. Many who supported the president's actions in principle had serious reservations about his true motives. In particular, they doubted that he was honestly trying to lay the groundwork for improved relations and instead suspected that it was nothing more than crass electoral considerations that were once again driving him to play the Cuban card. Typical of this skepticism were the following comments by Yvette Collymore: "But even as Clinton announced the easing of restrictions, administration officials insisted that the underlying embargo will be tightened, reportedly by hiring more officials to oversee the embargo's strict implementation. . . . Clinton may definitely be weighing his [1996 campaign] fortunes. In the 1992 election against former president George Bush, the Democrat narrowly won the state of New Jersey and narrowly lost Florida [both states have large Cuban communities]. By announcing that the embargo would be strictly implemented even as he loosens some restrictions, Clinton may be trying to play both sides of the political field."[85] In early 1996, however, he would revert to a more conventional and, in the eyes of many Cuban Americans, a more politically correct intransigent stance by embracing what many foreign affairs analysts felt was a deeply flawed "deal" that made not only Helms-Burton but also all previous executive orders concerning the Cuban economic blockade the law of the land. Whether it was good policy or not, Clinton in the 1996 election did carry Florida with unprecedented and crucial support from the state's traditionally pro-Republican Cuban voters.

Finally, the most unflattering view of the Clinton administration has looked upon its Cuban policies as essentially an exercise in amateurism. The "amateur hour" characterization has portrayed the administration and especially the president as having little interest or expertise in foreign affairs, thus suggesting that serious policy initiatives (via the above diplomacy model) have seldom been launched and that crises have often been mishandled.

Bill Clinton came to the White House with little background in foreign affairs. Instead, the political sword he wielded was forged in the crucible of domestic politics. Consequently, according to this line of analysis, his inclination was to become so engrossed in and enthused about internal problems such as health care that foreign policy issues tended to be relegated to a subordinate position on his list of priorities (with some obvious exceptions like the Bosnian conflict, the confrontations with Iraq, and relations with other great powers). This phenomenon was not, of course, unique to Clinton; most people enter the Oval Office due mainly to their zest for and their mastery of the domestic rather than the international arena. Indeed, of all the post–World War II presidents, it is probably fair to say that only Nixon assumed office with a primarily international perspective on its role (with Eisenhower and Bush also having fairly extensive experience in overseas affairs). Clinton was somewhat unusual, however, in the sense that unlike most of his modern predecessors, he did not appear to develop a greater affinity for foreign affairs the longer he was in power. Instead, he maintained an almost pristine domestic affairs orientation to his leadership duties, usually turning his attention to the international scene only when events forced him to do so.

One can adopt such a hands-off approach to certain policy areas as long as responsibility for them is delegated to experienced, highly competent subordinates, but it is questionable that Clinton did so with regard to Cuban affairs. The Mario Baeza incident discussed illustrates his willingness to allow domestic political considerations to overshadow a potential nominee's qualifications when appointing advisors whose sphere of responsibility included relations with Havana. Most impartial observers felt that Baeza would be an excellent assistant secretary of state for inter-American affairs: he enjoyed strong support from high-level State Department professionals, was experienced in hemispheric matters, and had a strong background in international economics (which would appear to be a crucial qualification, given the increasing prominence of such considerations in U.S.–Latin American relations). Nevertheless Clinton abandoned him, sacrificing professionalism in the face of strong CANF opposition.

The August 1996 appointment of Stuart Eizenstat as Clinton's "Special Representative for Promotion of Democracy in Cuba" likewise raised some questions about the degree of (Cuba-related) professionalism involved. Eizenstat's main public service credentials revolved around his tenure as an advisor to President Carter on domestic affairs, his three years as U.S. envoy to the European Union, and his position as undersecretary of commerce for international trade under Clinton. While his EU background undoubtedly represented an asset with respect to trying to defuse European anger generated by the Helms-Burton law, Eizenstat's expertise in Latin American and Cuban relations was somewhat limited, his only major foray into this field having been in helping to relocate Cuban refugees who came to the United States via the 1980 Mariel exodus (a sojourn during which he developed strong, sympathetic ties with the anti-Castro exile community).

In dealing with Havana, then, the Clinton presidency seems to have suffered from a scarcity of interest and experience in its upper levels. One should not, therefore, be particularly surprised that the administration's Cuban policies tended to be reactive rather than proactive (which is a polite way of saying that leadership, imagination, and initiative have been sorely lacking) and that political expediency often trumped more professional considerations. Such is often the nature of foreign policy making when done by neophytes rather than professionals.

These policy perspectives all tended to lead to the same general conclusion: anyone in Cuba or the United States who hoped to see some moderation of Washington's stance toward Havana had to be somewhat skeptical about the prospects of seeing any significant initiatives from the Clinton administration in its waning years that might help to breach the ramparts of suspicion and hostility built up during four decades of confrontation. Such a course of action would require the diplomatic dimension to be preeminent in Clinton's approach to U.S.-Cuban relations. But there was little to suggest that such a reorientation would be forthcoming, especially given the White House's apparent reluctance to expend the considerable political capital that would be necessary to overcome the resistance of highly influential counterrevolutionary elements in the exile community and the Helms-Torricelli-Burton clique on Capitol Hill.

The foundation for this pessimistic proposition was firmly in place even before the presidency was engulfed by the Lewinsky firestorm and the impeachment vote that it produced, creating a situation in which Clinton became a severely crippled lame duck whose overwhelming imperative was simply to complete his second term. Tinkering with the existing policy toward the Fidelistas was unlikely to contribute anything significant to this endeavor and indeed could entail considerable risks by providing the president's critics with an opportunity to pillory him by capitalizing on the intense anti-Castro passions that have always swirled around the Cuban question in some U.S. quarters. In short, self-interest as defined by callous cost-benefit calculations had produced an equation that seemed to relegate Havana to the political back burner as the Clinton White House approached its final months.

However, as chronicled in the concluding chapter that follows, some countervailing forces within the United States that were inclined toward at least some degree of normalized relations began to make their presence felt as the Washington-Havana stalemate confronted the dawn of a new century. Consequently, despite a history of shattered expectations, those favoring a relaxation of tensions still had some grounds for hope.

7

Conclusion

The End of a Road Less Traveled?

In this exploration of revolutionary Cuba's often audacious forays into the complex and sometimes even dangerous arena of international politics, I have relied heavily on several basic themes to try to bring some coherence to a complex subject that many people, especially those outside the fairly small fraternity of professional Cuba-watchers, may find rather esoteric and perhaps even intimidating. The three key threads utilized here, introduced in the opening chapter and woven together throughout, have involved emphasis on:

- The unique nature of the role that Havana has often assumed on the world stage, employing Robert Frost's imagery of the "road less traveled" as the metaphor for this particular dimension of the Fidelistas' approach to foreign affairs.

  In developing this proposition, special attention has been devoted to highlighting those elements of the Fidelistas' international profile that have differed markedly from the patterns exhibited by most of their hemispheric neighbors. Among the Revolution's most distinctive traits have been its close (yet not always trusting) ties to the socialist bloc, its ability to establish itself as a significant player and ultimately as a leader within the Third World community, and of course its almost legendary status as the Latin American regime most successful in both infuriating and frustrating the United States during the latter half of the twentieth century.

- The concept of counterdependency politics as the overarching principle that has motivated and molded much of Havana's behavior toward other actors in the global arena over the course of the Revolution.

The primary concern of this policy perspective, which is deeply rooted in the island's strong nationalistic tradition, has been to assure that Cuban sovereignty is truly *effective* rather than merely formal in nature. In other words, the Fidelistas have been driven by desire to create and defend conditions in which Cuba can control its own destiny to the greatest extent possible, as opposed to existing as some sort of stereotypical banana republic that has only the trappings of independence (e.g., diplomatic recognition by other states, membership in the UN and other international organizations) while in reality its affairs are dominated by some outside power(s).

In short, then, just as the Containment Doctrine can be said to have provided Washington with a "grand strategy" during the Cold War years, so also can counterdependency politics be seen serving a similar foreign policy function for the Cuban Revolution.

- The tumultuous Cuban-U.S. relationship, which from Havana's perspective has produced the greatest threats to the Revolution's effective sovereignty and therefore has in effect functioned as the touchstone for many of the Fidelistas' counterdependency initiatives that have taken them down foreign policy paths that few, if any, other Latin American countries have been willing to explore.

Having followed the long-term evolution of these themes and having analyzed in depth their many nuances, a few final brush strokes concerning their current status and future relevance are now needed to complete this portrait. Specifically, two interrelated issues must be addressed. To what extent can the three themes that we have pursued still be considered key elements or traits of Havana's foreign policy? And what are the prospects that they will continue, at least in the foreseeable future, to be the touchstones around which the Revolution's international relations revolve? The latter consideration is the more important, of course, for it may be able to provide some insights into the broad outlines of Havana's future role on the global stage.

Recognize, however, that like weather or stock market predictions, such political forecasting can be a highly uncertain endeavor—especially in the often volatile area of foreign affairs, where situations and the policies designed to deal with them can change rapidly. The clearest Cold War example of this phenomenon was the Soviet Union's climactic disintegration as a superpower, which few observers foresaw with any great accuracy, and the radical reconfiguration that ensued in the general ebb and

208 | Cuba's Foreign Relations in a Post-Soviet World

flow of relations among states. The currents that swirl through the Cuban scene may likewise prove to be rather unpredictable, the most obvious unknown being the trauma that may occur when Fidel Castro no longer leads the country where he has so long been the dominant political influence. Nevertheless, after surveying some of the most recent developments on Havana's global horizons and despite the pitfalls involved, an effort to project at least the likely broad contours of its approach to the new millennium would seem appropriate as a closing note to one of the most remarkable twentieth-century dramas in Latin America.

Cuba and the General Global Community

As is the case with many other developing nations, the backdrop against which Havana's post–Cold War international relations have played out has increasingly taken on an economic coloration. In other words, the links that have long existed between foreign policy concerns and the island's developmental dynamics have in recent years tended to become even more important. Consequently the general state of the country's economic health may sometimes be used as a rough barometer for gauging its situation in the global arena (especially with respect to developmental coalition building and related activities) and indeed may in certain instances represent an important variable influencing whether certain overseas initiatives are undertaken, a hypothetical scenario being that recessionary pressures might lead Cuba to explore more vigorously the prospects for normalization of its U.S. relations.

A brief survey of the economic landscape indicates that things went rather well for Havana in 1999. The government's initial target in terms of annual GDP expansion was 2.5 percent (compared to the somewhat meager 1.2 percent increase recorded in 1998). But first-half performance data proved to be much better than anticipated, the growth rate at that point being 6.1 percent. Admittedly, said Cuban government officials, it was not likely that such momentum could be maintained over the remaining six months, but they did feel that it was reasonable to raise their projection for the whole year to at least 4.0 percent.[1]

The main engines driving this recovery seemed to be the sugar and tourism sectors, with solid six-month productivity gains also being registered in the industrial (+5 percent) and agricultural (+6 percent) areas. The sugar harvest was up approximately 18.1 percent (from a revolution-era low of 3.2 million tons in 1998 to about 3.78 million tons), while the increase in gross tourist revenues was estimated at approximately 20 percent.[2] These trends clearly reaffirm the emergence of tourism as revolutionary Cuba's most lucrative business. The sector does, however, exhibit one glaring financial weakness—expert observers have suggested that only about 66–70 cents of every tourist dollar actually stay in the country (primarily because there is a large foreign presence in the airline and hotel services where visitors usually make their largest expenditures). Assuming that these calculations are correct, Havana's net share of the approximately $2.1 billion that tourists were projected to spend on Cuban vacations in 1999 would be roughly $1.39–$1.47 billion.

This positive economic news, which suggests that Havana's efforts on the international stage to establish or strengthen developmental links were paying solid dividends in 1999, was offset somewhat on the political side of the foreign relations equation by tensions emerging with some governments over human rights questions. The catalyst for this friction was legislation approved by the National Assembly in February 1999, titled the "Law for the Protection of the National Independence and Economy of Cuba," which Havana said was necessary to counter continuing U.S. efforts to destroy the Revolution. Under these new regulations the courts could impose jail terms of up to twenty years on those who were convicted of collaborating with Washington and its blockade policy by supplying information that could be used by U.S. authorities to impose Helms-Burton sanctions on foreign companies investing in Cuba; by distributing or possessing subversive literature produced by the U.S. government; or by participating in meetings or demonstrations designed to promote or facilitate Washington's attempts to sabotage the country's economy or to undermine its government. Other provisions involved sanctions for dissident journalists who circulate damaging material through the foreign media, especially outlets in the United States.[3] Shortly after this law was passed, in what was seen abroad as a gesture by Havana to demonstrate that it did indeed intend to be tough in dealing with such issues, four prominent dissidents who had been arrested twenty-two months earlier on other sedition charges were quickly tried and sentenced to jail terms ranging up to five years.

Many governments, especially in Latin America and elsewhere in the developing world, accepted Havana's contention that such actions represented legitimate self-defense in the face of escalating U.S. hostility, but the response from the industrialized bloc was not always so sympathetic. One glaring example was Canada, which by the late 1990s had emerged as one of Cuba's most important economic associates in the entire global community. To show its displeasure, Ottawa announced in March 1999 that it

210 | Cuba's Foreign Relations in a Post-Soviet World

was undertaking a comprehensive review of its relations with Havana. Most observers did not expect this initiative to produce any radical policy reversals, but it nevertheless provided a ready means for Canadian officials (such as Prime Minister Jean Chrétien and others) to fire some rhetorical warning shots across Havana's bow. Madrid, which had been acting as one of Cuba's main advocates within the European Union, was likewise unhappy, announcing that a long-planned May 1999 state visit to the island by Spain's king and queen would now be postponed.[4]

It was within the context of the annual UN Human Rights Commission battle, however, that Havana's critics scored their most significant coup. As usual, a draft resolution criticizing Cuba's record was submitted to the group (the main sponsors being the Czech Republic and Poland). In 1998 Havana had achieved a major diplomatic breakthrough when for the first time it succeeded in defeating such a motion (see chapter 6). But in 1999 that victory was reversed by a razor-thin margin of one vote. The voting breakdown was as follows:

Supporting the resolution (21)	Opposing the resolution (20)	Abstaining (12)
Argentina	Bhutan	Bangladesh
Austria	Cape Verde	Botswana
Canada	China	Colombia
Chile	Congo	El Salvador
Czech Republic	Cuba	Guatemala
Ecuador	Congo Republic	Liberia
France	India	Madagascar
Germany	Indonesia	Mauritius
Ireland	Mexico	Mozambique
Italy	Niger	Nepal
Japan	Pakistan	Philippines
Latvia	Peru	Senegal
Luxembourg	Qatar	
Morocco	Russia	
Norway	Rwanda	
Poland	South Africa	
Korea	Sri Lanka	
Romania	Sudan	
United Kingdom	Tunisia	
United States	Venezuela	
Uruguay		

Note that all eight members of the commission from the European Union as well as such major Cuban trading partners as Canada and Japan weighed in against Havana, thus interjecting discordant notes into what had over recent years often been rather amiable bilateral relations.[5]

The contradictory picture of the situation on Cuba's international front resulting from these apparently mixed messages (i.e., economic progress versus political setbacks) was further complicated in June 1999 when Havana announced that it was replacing Roberto Robaina as its foreign minister. His successor, appointed despite a lack of formal diplomatic experience, was thirty-four-year-old Felipe Pérez Roque, one of Fidel's closest associates, who for the past decade had served as Castro's chief of staff. Practically all outside observers were caught off guard by this development, for it was widely felt that Robaina had been performing effectively. He had, for instance, received especially high marks with regard to mobilizing international opposition to the Helms-Burton law and the U.S. economic blockade. Also during his watch, significant progress was made in terms of diversifying the island's political and economic ties with the Western world; one recent illustration was the normalization of relations with such long-time antagonists as Guatemala and the Dominican Republic. Indeed, given Robaina's successful record and the solid position he appeared to have within the Revolution's inner leadership circles, it was widely speculated that he might eventually emerge as Fidel's political heir (the two other names most frequently mentioned were Ricardo Alarcón and Carlos Lage; see chapter 1).

No detailed official explanation for this move was provided by the government. The announcement in *Granma*, the Communist Party publication considered to be the official state newspaper, contained only vague criticism of Robaina, saying that Castro decided on the change "taking into account the current complexity of the tense international situation, its growing importance for the future of our country and of the world and the need for deeper, more rigorous, more systematic and more demanding work in this area."[6] The conventional wisdom among Cuba-watchers generally focused on two reasons for the shift: Fidel had abandoned the more moderate Robaina as a signal that Cuba was poised to adopt a harder line in foreign affairs, especially toward the United States; and/or Robaina was in effect being held responsible for the increased tensions in Cuba's international relations resulting from human rights criticisms. Some opinion in Havana, however, leaned toward a more personalistic rather than policy-oriented explanation. The basic problem, according to this perspective, was that the Robaina-Alarcón relationship was not especially close or cooperative, thus creating between two of his closest advisors a difficult situation that Castro ultimately had to resolve. If this perspective is accurate, the outcome might seen to bode rather well for Alarcón's leadership prospects.

One major achievement in 1999 in Cuba's hemispheric relations was its increasingly cordial ties with Venezuela, the catalyst for this development being the dramatic emergence of Hugo Chávez on the political scene. For decades the reins of power in Caracas had been controlled by the country's two centrist parties, Democratic Action (moderate liberal) and COPEI (moderate conservative). But popular discontent with this situation grew during the 1990s, fueled by anger over growing governmental corruption and erosion of the oil-rich nation's living standards. This tinderbox produced an abortive coup in 1992 led by Chávez, at that point a fairly obscure lieutenant colonel in the paratroopers. Subsequently Chávez would resort to more conventional tactics, creating a coalition of smaller leftist and national parties called the Patriotic Pole, which he led to a decisive victory in Venezuela's December 1998 presidential election.

Chávez was inaugurated in February 1999, with Castro prominent among the dignitaries in attendance. The two leaders quickly cemented a close working relationship. Fidel, for example, deliberately seemed to assume an unusually low public profile at an April 1999 ACS meeting in the Dominican Republic, thereby allowing Chávez to move into the spotlight and enhance his credentials as a rising star on the hemispheric stage. Such fraternal gestures were reciprocated in mid-1999 when Venezuela announced that it was negotiating several major oil agreements with Cuba, at least some of which it hoped would be ready to sign at the upcoming November 1999 Ibero-American Summit conference in Havana. Although the draft proposals were not explained in detail, they seemed to revolve around two key ideas. First, an arrangement essentially amounting to barter would be established whereby Caracas would provide long-term guarantees to supply the island with oil under preferential terms and would accept payment in the form of commodity exports rather than scarce hard currency.[7] Second, Venezuela would be permitted to launch petroleum exploration projects in Cuba and would also be given the opportunity to invest in refinery operations there (particularly the 76,000-barrel-per-day facility at Cienfuegos built by the Soviets, which had been lying idle because its Russian technology needed upgrading to modern, commercially competitive standards). Chávez fully realized, of course, that such economic cooperation involves a real risk of antagonizing Washington and running afoul of U.S. blockade legislation (Helms-Burton), but he did not seem to be deterred by such considerations. This willingness to

Conclusion: The End of a Road Less Traveled? | 213

test the limits of U.S. tolerance was probably reinforced by indications that Washington's hard line was facing some vigorous domestic challenges (to be discussed).

Cuba and the United States

There were no major developments in the U.S.-Cuban relationship as the twentieth century moved through its final year; neither government seemed inclined to launch any dramatic or even mildly imaginative initiatives that might be seen as having some potential to moderate the diplomatic chill between them. Such reticence on the Fidelistas' part was rooted in their conviction that the current impasse was the inevitable consequence of Washington's intransigence, exemplified by the Torricelli and Helms-Burton laws, and Washington therefore had to assume responsibility for making the first significant move. As long as such a gesture was not forthcoming, Havana was content to give top foreign affairs priority to expanding the success that its counterdependency campaign had experienced with respect to enhancing its political space (via normalization of bilateral relations) and to pursuing opportunities for developmental coalition building.

The situation in the United States was proving to be much more complicated, for it became clear as the year progressed that there were different and in some cases contradictory currents flowing in some key political circles. The starkest example of such emerging fault lines could be found in the contrasting positions taken by the policy-making establishment and some elements within the business community.

At the official level of state-to-state dealings there was little in the way of progress toward normalization. There had been some sentiment in Washington favoring a comprehensive reassessment of U.S. policy toward the Revolution, as noted in chapter 6. This idea, which emerged in late 1998 and had the support of a wide range of influential figures both within and outside the government, generally resonated well in Havana, with enthusiastic optimism emerging in some quarters that a breakthrough might be looming on the northern horizon.[8] But early in the new year the Clinton administration announced that it would not agree to the formation of such a review board, with Secretary of State Madeleine Albright reasserting the standard White House position: "Although we do not support the establishment of the panel at this time, we will work with them [its congressional proponents] towards establishing a democratic transition in Cuba."[9] However, apparently in an effort to avoid overly antagonizing those forces in Congress and elsewhere that were open to a more moderate approach in dealing with Havana, the president suggested various modifications in the existing blockade, for example:

- easing restrictions on the sale of food and medicines to Cuba by allowing certain entities in Cuba having no official connections or status (e.g., private farmers, independent businesses, and nongovernmental organizations) to make such purchases;

- streamlining Treasury Department licensing procedures for U.S. citizens who are qualified to travel to the island, with eligibility requirements becoming somewhat less restrictive;

- allowing any person in the United States (not just Cuban Americans, as was previously the case) to donate up to $1,200 per year to individuals and nonprofit humanitarian organizations in Cuba.

This package of changes officially went into effect on May 10, 1999.[10] Such moves did not particularly impress Havana, which tended to dismiss the whole exercise as a public relations stunt designed to appease blockade opponents both in the United States and in the larger international community.[11] Fidel's indignant reaction, characterizing the new rules as a "fraud," the real purpose of which was to increase the destabilization pressure on the Revolution, set the overall tone of the Cuban response. Havana was especially suspicious of Washington's emphasis on promoting contacts with and providing moral and material support to elements inside the country that were totally separate from the government (e.g., private entrepreneurs, members of NGOs), seeing this preference for operating through unofficial channels as a tactic geared to undermine the regime by opening up the island's civil society to penetration by antirevolutionary forces such as CANF and by facilitating cooperation between domestic subversives and their U.S. allies or sponsors.[12]

It appeared that problockade, antinormalization sentiment would remain well entrenched in any future U.S. administration, since both leading contenders for the 2000 presidential nominations—Governor George W. Bush of Texas on the Republican side and for the Democrats Vice President Al Gore—announced that they intended to maintain the existing confrontational policy. Bush, considered by many as 1999 came to a close to be the likely winner, seemed to be especially receptive to the entreaties of counterrevolutionaries. For instance, ignoring the fact that one of his main foreign policy consultants—George Schultz, who had served as President Ronald Reagan's secretary of state—had strongly endorsed the idea of creating a bipartisan review commission to reexamine policy toward Havana, Bush apparently preferred to rely instead, when Cuban matters were involved, on the hard-line advice of Congressman Lincoln Diaz-Balart (R, Florida), a leader among the vehement anti-Castro elements in Miami.[13] This stance could to some extent be understood in personal as well as political terms, for Bush's brother Jeb, elected Florida's governor in 1998, has extremely close ties with CANF. Gore, while perhaps not as emotionally committed to the issue as Bush, nevertheless seemed determined to follow Clinton's strategy of flaunting an anti-Fidelista position as a means of generating electoral and financial support in South Florida.

The policy-making equation had shifted significantly, however, in the sense that the Oval Office no longer wields the trump cards with regard to relations with Cuba. Such power now resides on Capitol Hill due to Clinton's acceptance of the provision in the Helms-Burton bill that gave Congress control over the U.S. blockade. Consequently no president, current or future, can significantly modify or end that policy via an executive order (as was possible prior to Helms-Burton). Instead, any future change would require a favorable vote in both the House and the Senate. To achieve such an outcome would not be easy, for the mode of operation in Congress is such that the scales tend to be heavily weighted in favor of members seeking to wield negative power (i.e., those who wish to block legislation from being enacted). In other words, it is much easier for opponents of a proposal to kill it than it is for supporters to guide it through the labyrinth of obstacles that must be navigated in order to emerge with a new law of the land.

Thus if change is to come, new centers of influence would have to emerge within the U.S. body politic that could mount a viable challenge on Capitol Hill to the stranglehold long exercised over policies toward Cuba by well-entrenched hard-line interest groups. There have, of course, always been some elements that have supported normalization with Havana, the main traditional strongholds of such sentiment having been various progressive organizations and the academic community, but such activists have never been able to exert much leverage. To be blunt, Washington has simply ignored them.

In the post–Cold War period, however, some new and rather surprising advocates of rapprochement have appeared on the scene, with three groups possessing perhaps the greatest impact potential:

- Moderate (and often second-generation) elements within the Cuban community, who can see nothing to be gained by continuing to fight the old battles under the banner of CANF or its allies.

Certainly a development that strengthened the position of this camp was the death on November 23, 1997, of Jorge Mas Canosa—the founder and highly effective leader of CANF. Indeed, some observers felt that the backlash against Helms-Burton both overseas and within the United States (e.g., among exiles unhappy with the hardships that the law created for their families and friends on the island) had somewhat eroded CANF's near stranglehold over Washington's Cuban policies even before Mas Canosa passed from the scene. In any case, no matter what one felt about CANF's evolving fortunes prior to his demise, almost everyone agreed that Mas Canosa was irreplaceable and that the organization's political influence would suffer accordingly.

- Conservatives who believe that "constructive engagement" poses a greater threat to Castro's political future than does ongoing confrontation and blockade. One of the earliest post–Cold War examples of a high-profile attempt to tout this new approach to the general public occurred on right-wing luminary John McLaughlin's television program on January 8, 1993, which saw the host rejecting a hard line (including support for the CDA advocated by some of his guests) and arguing instead for normalization.[14]

- Sectors of the U.S. corporate community have become increasingly skeptical about the wisdom of continued confrontation when measured against potential business opportunities. This position, suggests Donna Rich Kaplowitz, is not based on altruism or a sudden flowering of ideological tolerance in corporate boardrooms. Rather, using the Torricelli law as an example, she notes that "U.S. corporations have quietly and consistently registered their opposition to the CDA for reasons of simple economics. CDA will force U.S. corporations to lose market shares to their competitors."[15] Thus the Fidelistas have found themselves in the paradoxical position of being informally allied to segments of the gringo capitalist class that they have long reviled, underscoring the axiom that business, like politics, can make strange bedfellows.[16]

In purely quantitative terms, Cuba's prospects as a market or trading partner cannot match those of nations like the PRC or Vietnam (two former Cold War antagonists with which the United States has normalized relations despite their continued aversion to Western-style political and economic models). But within the Caribbean Basin, traditionally the center for U.S. economic activity in Latin America, the island has a number of assets operating in its

Conclusion: The End of a Road Less Traveled? | 217

favor. Its population, for example, is among the larger ones in the region. Moreover, its people in general have a fairly high degree of education, and in some sectors, notably health services and biotechnology, their expertise reaches world-class levels.

Undoubtedly there are important segments of the U.S. business community who think that the island has considerable commercial potential, for despite the blockade, numerous firms have discreetly established contact with Cuban authorities to explore the possibility of future trade and investment arrangements. The British magazine *Economist* reported, for example, the total number of visits to the island by representatives of interested U.S. companies over a three-year period to have been approximately 500 in 1994, 1,300 in 1995, and 1,500 in 1996.[17]

Reinforcing this interest have been surveys such as that issued by Political Risks Services in April 1995, which ranked Cuba among the top thirty nations in the world with the fewest investment/trade risks for international companies, and a one-week series of stories from Havana by CNN's program *Moneyline* (April 1995) presenting a generally favorable picture of recent economic reforms and other related actions undertaken by the Cuban government while simultaneously voicing cautious criticism of the U.S. blockade policy.[18]

Individually these new power centers may not be sufficiently influential to effect a policy change, the business community being a possible exception. But their cumulative impact when combined with existing progressive forces could tip the scales in favor of normalization and thereby render the symbolic barrier represented by the Florida Straits as obsolete as the Berlin Wall.

Certainly 1999 saw corporate interests becoming increasingly assertive in their efforts to make some progress toward breaking the impasse in U.S.-Cuban relations.[19] Figuratively leading the charge were representatives from the agricultural and pharmaceutical sectors, while the travel industry watched with great anticipation for any signal that a resumption of business with the Pearl of the Antilles, once the flagship of Caribbean tourism, might be possible.

Ironically, farm interests that were often based in conservative Republican strongholds of the midwestern heartland formed the vanguard in attempting to pressure Congress into taking a more flexible position on trade with Cuba. In early August 1999, seeing the island as a potentially lucrative customer for U.S. corn, wheat, rice, animal feeds, fertilizers, and

218 | Cuba's Foreign Relations in a Post-Soviet World

the like, they mounted a major lobbying campaign and succeeded in convincing the U.S. Senate to include in an agricultural bill an amendment sponsored by Senators John Ashcroft (R, Missouri) and Charles Hagel (R, Nebraska) that would have allowed exporters to acquire one-year licenses for basically unrestricted sales of medical and farm products to Havana. Despite strong opposition from Senator Jesse Helms (R, North Carolina) and anti-Castro Cuban groups, the Ashcroft-Hagel proposal was accepted by an overwhelming vote of 70–28. José Cardenas, the director of CANF's Washington office, reacted bitterly: "This is something that has absolutely been pushed onto the radar screen by the ag lobby groups. They've been playing this for all it's worth, that Mr. and Mrs. Family Farmer are being pushed off their farms."[20] Ultimately opposition from leaders in the House of Representatives would force Congress to remove the amendment before the final version of the bill was passed in late September 1999, but its supporters vowed to continue the fight for legislation to ease the trade sanctions on Cuba.

At about the same time that business interests were increasing their congressional lobbying activity against the U.S. blockade, the AFL-CIO likewise weighed in with its own opposition by announcing on August 4, 1999, that its Executive Council had passed a resolution endorsing efforts under way in Congress to lift restrictions on the sale of food and medicines to the island. This was in many respects a dramatic and unexpected gesture, for the organization had a long history of generally championing Washington's anticommunist crusades overseas, and it had been especially supportive in Latin America. During the Cold War, for example, it had provided training and other forms of assistance throughout the hemisphere to efforts designed to "immunize" workers against appeals from radical left-wing quarters. It went even further in Chile during the early 1970s, directly allying itself with various Nixon administration conspiracies to mobilize Chilean truckers' unions against Salvador Allende's Marxist government. Given this tradition, it should come as little surprise that Fidel Castro's revolution had long been stamped with the AFL-CIO's seal of disapproval. Nevertheless it was now willing to abandon that confrontational stance, although it strove in the process to avoid publicity as much as possible in order to minimize the risk that anti-Castro representatives on Capitol Hill might retaliate by trying to reduce the more than $20 million in federal funds that the organization had routinely been receiving for its overseas projects.

Officials at the state level also began to add to the chorus of dissent, a breakthrough coming in late October 1999 when Republican Governor

George Ryan of Illinois made an official visit to the island accompanied by a forty-five-member delegation that included not only governmental personnel but also representatives of such major Illinois businesses as the giant agro-corporation Archer Daniels Midland.[21] This was the first time since Castro had come to power that a U.S. governor had made such a trip. In a burst of candor Ryan initially described his excursion as a "trade mission," although he later switched to the less controversial label of "a humanitarian visit" involving delivery of more than $1 million of various donated supplies.

Drug companies, on the other hand, have been unabashedly forthright in indicating that their desire for improved relations is driven by commercial considerations. Capitalizing on this sentiment, Peter Nathan made arrangements for the first U.S. trade fair in revolutionary Cuba to take place in late January 2000. The exposition was scheduled to be open to practically all sectors of the U.S. health care community, with major pharmaceutical firms expected to be there in force, given Cuba's richly deserved reputation in the field for highly innovative world-class research. Nathan, who had organized such conventions in many parts of the world, extended invitations to more than 5,000 U.S. companies making everything from conventional medicines to ambulances and heart pacemakers. Perhaps even more intriguing than the prospects of the event itself was the apparent change in some official attitudes toward it. Nathan said he received absolutely no help or encouragement in 1996 when he first asked the U.S. government for permission to stage such an exhibit. By mid-1999 the situation had changed to the point where, he reported, "officials from the several departments that manage the trade embargo against Cuba 'can't do enough for me. They've been incredibly helpful.' Officials even suggested that the veteran trade fair organizer expand his list of U.S. companies hoping to do business with the Cuban government."[22]

In essence, then, it would appear that some circles within the administration were finally beginning to recognize that there was considerable and growing pent-up demand for more contact with the island from the highly influential business community and that this should not be ignored. Thus they seem to have become increasingly willing to hedge their bets by interjecting some flexibility into their position in the ongoing domestic debate over relations with Havana.

As the twentieth century came to an end, it remained to be seen whether all this activity would serve as the catalyst for some significant progress in normalizing relations between Havana and Washington. Certainly the historical record did not lend itself to much optimism, for one U.S. administration after another had proven unwilling to make its peace with Fidel and his revolution. As noted, the rationale for such intransigence had varied over time, spanning a continuum that included such dimensions as ideological aversion, perceived security threats, and domestic political opposition. Also, operating at a more primal level was the traditional U.S. assumption that its status as the Colossus of the North conferred upon it intrinsic hegemonic prerogatives in the Caribbean Basin. This mind-set, say its critics, has generated an arrogance that has rendered Washington psychologically incapable of compromising with those it considers upstarts who refuse to accept their (secondary) place in this order. Without any doubt whatsoever, the Cuban Revolution has stood at the apex of this "demonology of insubordination" ever since it burst upon the scene in 1959. All of these considerations have combined over the years to create an atmosphere within which the United States has not really explored any option toward Cuba other than unrelenting hostility. And despite the lack of indications that this strategy would achieve its basic goal of bringing the Fidelistas to heel, Washington seemed determined to continue to pursue it into the next millennium.

In particular, as noted, it appeared that such sentiment would remain popular in either a Bush or a Gore White House. Assuming this to be the case seems to lead to the conclusion that any major normalization initiative following the 2000 election would have to come from Congress. Clearly there now seemed to be considerable legislative support for a more cordial posture, as illustrated by the drama of the Ashcroft-Hagel amendment. But the fate of that initiative also drove home the harsh reality that a dedicated congressional minority can and often does succeed in frustrating the will of the majority. Consequently, despite the fact that a climate more conducive to normalization seemed to be emerging, the voices of moderation could well fall victim in the end to the intrigues of domestic politics swirling though Washington's corridors of power.

In any case, regardless of what might happen on its U.S. front, the larger question confronting the Cuban Revolution is whether it can continue to play a unique role on the international stage in a post–Cold War world.

Surveying the Contours of the Road Ahead

Assuming that nothing will occur in the foreseeable future that will radically alter Cuba's social landscape, it seems reasonable to suggest that

Conclusion: The End of a Road Less Traveled? |

counterdependency politics will remain a key component of Havana's foreign policies. Such nationalistic aspirations to maximize the country's effective sovereignty are an integral element of the Fidelista ethos and have greatly influenced the Revolution's international agenda from the beginning; they are likewise deeply embedded in the larger society's political culture. This sentiment traces its roots to the earliest days of the independence struggle, and its resonance continues today, generating within many sectors of the population a firm commitment to assuring that the island is not subjected to the indignities of such spiritual descendants of the Platt Amendment as the Helms-Burton provisions seeking to dictate to the Cubans what is "acceptable" political behavior on their part.

The picture becomes much murkier, however, once one moves beyond the general (and fairly safe) observation that counterdependency politics will in all likelihood continue to be a central conceptual pillar of Havana's overall international strategy. Specifically, it is difficult to project with any great confidence how these concerns might manifest themselves in terms of specific actions and initiatives. Nevertheless there are some broad policy outlines that can probably be expected to emerge or to be pursued even more vigorously than has been the case.

Certainly it can be anticipated that the counterdependency motif will function as an impetus for ongoing and perhaps even greater efforts on Cuba's part to involve itself in developmental coalition-building activities in the Western Hemisphere. Attention at the more practical level will, of course, focus on organizations like CARICOM, the ACS, and perhaps MERCOSUR. But while these initiatives move forward (sometimes very gingerly), there appears to be a larger philosophical debate emerging about the basic thrust that hemispheric economic cooperation should adopt, and Havana clearly wants to exert some major influence on its outcome. Essentially the issue involves two competing integration paradigms, which for our purposes can be called Neo-PanAmericanism and Neo-Bolivarianism. These schools of thought can be summarized as follows:

- Neo-PanAmericanism refers to the notion that a comprehensive process of commercial and financial integration should be implemented, which in effect would represent a contemporary economic manifestation of the classical Pan-American ideal of hemispheric cooperation in dealing with political and security questions. The Organization of American States was the institutional vehicle that was created in 1948 to facilitate and orchestrate this more traditional view of collaboration. Like its predecessor, Neo-PanAmericanism implies participation by and, at least from Washington's perspective, a leadership role for United States.

In the context of the early twenty-first century, the Free Trade Area of the Americas project embraced by both the Bush and the Clinton administrations has been widely seen throughout the hemisphere as the organizational framework within which Washington hopes to put into place its revitalized, retooled version of Pan-Americanism.

- Neo-Bolivarianism represents the Hispanic (and Anglophone Caribbean) alternative to the foregoing scenario, which is often considered seriously flawed by its susceptibility to U.S. domination. The key idea here is that any contemporary developmental cooperation schemes launched by hemispheric states should be modeled along the lines of Simón Bolívar's vision of a politically unified Latin America that would be clearly separate from and independent of the colossus to its north.

As such, the Neo-Bolivarian approach to economic cooperation in the hemisphere rejects, at least for the time being, any significant involvement in the process on Washington's part. Instead it sees the whole enterprise unfolding under Latin American rather than U.S. leadership, the ultimate goal being to achieve a level of integration that would put the hemispheric community (defined as South America and the Caribbean Basin countries) in a position where its pooled economic power would, to a great extent, be sufficient to counterbalance that of the United States.

It appears to me that Cuba hopes to function as a catalyst for the development of Neo-Bolivarianism and as a facilitator of progress toward achieving its integrative agenda. In particular, the Fidelistas seem inclined to try to assume a vanguard role in any such movement by building on their Revolution's long history of dogged defiance of the United States as well as on their more recent successes in strengthening their political and economic ties with a wide range of Latin American and Caribbean countries.

Among the various Neo-Bolivarian options that Havana could explore, it seemed as of late 1999 to be especially attracted to the idea of serving as a broker for greater cooperation between the fledgling ACS and the better established MERCOSUR group.[23] While any progress along these lines would certainly be welcomed by the Fidelistas, midwifing a significant merger of the two organizations would obviously represent a triumph of unprecedented proportions for Cuba's post–Cold War policy of develop-

Conclusion: The End of a Road Less Traveled? | 223

mental coalition building. Admittedly this prospect does not appear to be on the immediate horizon, but the fact that Havana seems to be in the process of giving it a greater degree of visibility suggests that such initiatives are becoming higher priority items on its hemispheric agenda.

It is unlikely, however, that this growing activism in hemispheric affairs, rooted in Cuba's tradition of counterdependency politics, will reflect the special mystique that characterized the Revolution's international role for most of its history. Instead it would appear that the high drama that the Fidelistas generated for so many years in pursuing their road less traveled has largely come to an end. No longer can Havana's foreign policy be expected to fit the charismatic mold (involving such remarkable feats as winning wars in Africa, implementing ambitious foreign aid programs, and striding boldly across the world stage as the leader of the nonaligned bloc) that led Jorge Domínguez and others to rank Cuba as unique among the actors to emerge on the international scene in the latter half of the twentieth century. This special status was very much a product of the Cold War, during which the Fidelistas capitalized astutely on the opportunities provided to develop and implement the dual-track strategy discussed in chapter 4. But such globe-trotting audacity on Havana's part now seems, like many other things, to have been a casualty of the Soviets' demise.

Such developments do not by any stretch of the imagination mean that revolutionary Cuba is going to fade into obscurity. As long as Fidel's legacy continues to exert an influence, Cuba is not going to become just another small sun-drenched island, its significance on the world scene limited to its tourist clientele. But it is also fair to say that Havana's profile at the highest and broadest levels of international affairs is not likely to be as prominent as it was during the halcyon days of the 1970s and early 1980s. Instead the most probable venue for Cuba to continue its tradition of activism and leadership is in the more limited confines of hemispheric affairs. Thus, as almost certainly had to happen sometime, the global road that Cuba successfully blazed during the Cold War seems to have come to an end.

One important dimension of Havana's contemporary international image undoubtedly will remain: it will retain its near-legendary status as the Latin American David defying the Yankee Goliath. Indeed, it appears that such will be the case whether any normalization of U.S.-Cuban relations occurs or not.

Turning first to a no-rapprochement scenario, the key consideration is that Havana has already met the challenge of making the changes in both its domestic and foreign policies necessary to assure that the Revolution

224 | Cuba's Foreign Relations in a Post-Soviet World

will survive in the post–Cold War world. As noted, the international adjustments have involved diversifying the island's political relations and radically restructuring its economic ties, thereby avoiding the isolation that Washington assumed was inevitable and would ultimately cause the Fidelistas' edifice to crumble. By making this often agonizing transition, Cuba has firmly established itself as a viable member of the twenty-first century's new world order and has thus proven that it can withstand Washington's hostility even under the worst circumstances. A continuation of its confrontational relationship with the United States into the new millennium would therefore probably not pose a mortal threat to the Revolution. Consequently, if no major relaxation of tensions between the two countries occurs, Havana can be expected in the years ahead to continue to be a successful practitioner of counterdependency politics and thereby to write additional chapters in its long history of frustrating the Yankee Goliath's aspirations.

On the other hand, it is possible that any normalization of relations that may occur will take place more on Cuban than on U.S. terms. For instance, it is inconceivable to any but the most incorrigible anti-Castro elements in the United States that a settlement could occur on the basis of the Helms-Burton provisions calling for virtual political suicide on the part of the Revolution. A more likely script would see Washington gradually backing away from its hard-line position of demanding unacceptable concessions from Havana and instead beginning to make some pragmatic compromises that would serve as incremental stepping stones moving the two governments toward a reconciliation.

When looking in late 1999 at how this stage has been set, Cuba's foreign policy seems to deserve some credit for having positioned Havana effectively. In the first place, although the island's economic security certainly is not as great today as when it was a CMEA member, Havana has nevertheless implemented counterdependency reorientations in the post–Cold War era that are functioning to make it less vulnerable to U.S. economic warfare than many observers had expected it would be. This does not mean that the impact of Washington's hostility has been neutralized, for that is hardly the case. Cuba continues to confront the harsh reality of a serious recession that has been aggravated by U.S. efforts to capitalize on the situation in the hope that Castro's government will thereby be seriously destabilized and eventually driven from power.

Obviously this Doomsday prophecy has not been fulfilled, and few impartial analysts view it as a concept with any future. Thus, Havana has created conditions in which, because there is no compelling economic

Conclusion: The End of a Road Less Traveled? | 225

need for it to make major concessions to Washington in order to improve the bilateral relationship, responsibility for making normalization initiatives in effect rests with the United States. In short, Cuba can wait and see what Washington is willing to do to ease the situation.

Second, Havana's counterdependency achievements have also served to enhance its already considerable political and diplomatic credentials in the hemispheric as well as in the larger international community, thereby further undermining the position of those in the United States who argue for a hard-line policy of Cuban exceptionalism. The basic idea here is that it is rather difficult to portray Havana as a special case—a "rogue government"—requiring abnormally harsh treatment when practically all other countries in the Western Hemisphere and elsewhere (among them Washington's closest traditional allies) maintain conventional diplomatic relations with Cuba, many are expanding their trade and commercial ties to the island, and some are establishing cooperative developmental coalitions with it.

Obviously such a climate is less hospitable to those elements in the United States that have heretofore tended to dominate the policy-making process with regard to the Revolution—particularly CANF and its allies in Congress. Thus there may be greater opportunities in coming years than there have been in some time for those open to some concessions on Washington's part to begin to exert a significant influence in the domestic debate that has long raged over the normalization of U.S.-Cuban relations.

Should the process actually unfold in this manner, the island's reputation as a giant-killer would soar. In effect, it would finally have won the battle to have its sovereignty and legitimacy officially recognized by the United States. Indeed practically all Cuban nationalists, Fidelista or otherwise, would probably agree that pulling off such a coup would more than compensate for the risks taken and the sacrifices made along the way.

Notes

1. Prelude: Setting the Cuban Stage

1. This section is based mainly on material from "General Information on Cuba" (downloaded from the Internet at www.brunel.ac.uk/depts/chaplncy/cuba1.htm).

2. The pre-1990 material on the Cuban economy and the Revolution's social development is drawn (to a great extent verbatim) from H. Michael Erisman, "The Odyssey of Revolution in Cuba," in Anthony Payne and Paul Sutton (eds.), *Modern Caribbean Politics* (Baltimore: Johns Hopkins University Press, 1993), 220–25.

3. The specific growth figures can be found in Max Azicri, *Cuba: Politics, Economics, and Society* (London: Pinter Publishers, 1988), 140, and Juan del Aguila, *Cuba: Dilemmas of a Revolution,* rev. ed. (Boulder, Colo.: Westview Press, 1988), 107.

4. Information taken from "Economic Integration Imperative for Latin America," *Granma Weekly Review,* February 12, 1984, 9.

5. For additional information, see del Aguila, *Cuba: Dilemmas,* 148.

6. Specific figures for the 1980–84 period can be found ibid., 108, and in Andrew Zimbalist, "Introduction," in Andrew Zimbalist (ed.), *Cuban Political Economy: Controversies in Cubanology* (Boulder, Colo.: Westview Press, 1988), 2.

7. These figures come from del Aguila, *Cuba: Dilemmas,* 203.

8. Azicri, *Cuba: Politics,* 145–46.

9. The longitudinal data are provided by Claes Brundenius, *Revolutionary Cuba: The Challenge of Growth with Equity* (Boulder, Colo.: Westview Press, 1984), 73, 113.

10. Quoted ibid., 110.

11. For more details regarding the PQLI, see Morris D. Morris, *Measuring Conditions of the World's Poor: The Physical Quality of Life Index* (New York: Pergamon Press, 1979). Criticisms of the PQLI were voiced almost immediately following the 1979 publication of Morris's book. See, for example, David A. Larson and Walton T. Wilford, "The Physical Quality of Life Index: A Useful Indicator?" *World Development* 7, no. 6 (June 1979): 581–84.

12. The 1984 rating, which is typical of Cuba's high PQLI scores during the 1970s and 1980s, was published in Charles W. Kegley, Jr., and Eugene R. Wittkopf, *World Politics: Trends and Transformations,* 3d ed. (New York: St. Martin's Press, 1989), 112.

228 | Notes to Pages 9–22

13. Most of the material in this section on the Cuban economy is drawn from Central Intelligence Agency, *1996 World Factbook* (downloaded from the Internet at www.odci.gov/cia/publications/nsolo/factbook/cuba.htm#Economy).

14. Looking at a cross section of Latin American and Caribbean nations produces the following 1995 per capita GDPs (in 1990 U.S. dollars, with the countries ranked from the higher to the lower figures): Barbados = 6,573; Argentina = 5,983; Chile = 3,259; Brazil = 2,969; Colombia = 1,720; Jamaica = 1,709; Guatemala = 915; and Bolivia = 903. Data downloaded from the Internet website of the InterAmerican Development Bank at www.1adb.org/database iadb.org/int/basicrep.

15. Some of the material in this section presenting a capsule profile of Cuba's history is drawn from "General Information on Cuba" (see note 1) and from "Brief History of Cuba" (downloaded from the Internet at www.fiu.edu/~fcf/histcuba.html).

16. This biographical section is based on material drawn from Carlos Ripoll, "José Martí" (downloaded from the Internet at www.fiu.edu/~fcf/jmarti.html), and from "The Five Pillars of Phi Iota Alpha" (downloaded from the Internet at www.oswego.edu/~fia/HISTORY/pillars.htm#MARTI).

17. During this period the U.S. government instituted various measures, including abrogation of the Platt Amendment (May 1934), in an unsuccessful effort to help Batista quiet popular unrest on the island.

18. This biographical sketch is based on material drawn from "Fidel Castro" (downloaded from the Internet at www.idbsu.edu/surveyrc/staff/jaynes/marxism/bios/castro.htm).

19. This biographical sketch is based on material drawn from "Ernesto Guevara Lynch de la Cerna" (downloaded from the Internet at artemis.centrum.is/~baro/krissi/rage/che/che.htm).

20. See the following historical studies by Louis A. Perez, Jr., for excellent analyses of the Cuban nationalist tradition and the island's volatile relations with the United States: *Cuba between Empires, 1878–1902* (Pittsburgh: University of Pittsburgh Press, 1982); *Cuba and the United States: Ties of Singular Intimacy* (Athens: University of Georgia Press, 1990); and *Cuba: Between Reform and Revolution* (New York: Oxford University Press, 1995).

2. Cuban Foreign Policy and Counterdependency Politics

1. This list is derived from Jennie K. Lincoln, "Introduction to Latin American Foreign Policy: Global and Regional Dimensions," in Elizabeth Ferris and Jennie Lincoln (eds.), *Latin American Foreign Policies: Global and Regional Dimensions* (Boulder, Colo.: Westview Press, 1981), 3–18; Elizabeth G. Ferris, "Toward a Theory for the Comparative Analysis of Latin American Foreign Policy," in Ferris and Lincoln, *Latin American Foreign Policies*, 239–57; and Alberto van Klaveren, "The Analysis of Latin American Foreign Policies: Theoretical Perspectives," in Heraldo Muñoz and Joseph S. Tulchin (eds.), *Latin American Nations in World*

Politics (Boulder, Colo.: Westview Press, 1984), 1–21. Among the best-known general surveys of international relations theory are James N. Rosenau (ed.), *International Politics and Foreign Policy,* rev. ed. (New York: Free Press, 1969), and James E. Dougherty and Robert L. Pfaltzgraff, Jr., *Contending Theories of International Relations: A Comprehensive Survey,* 2d ed. (New York: Harper and Row, 1981).

2. For example, elements of the Fidelista personalismo approach could be incorporated into either the surrogate/superclient or realist perspectives. Likewise, one can find certain compatibilities between the realist and surrogate/superclient schools.

3. Although Realists see this Hobbesian struggle for power as the essence of the political process and therefore concede that the possibility of violent conflict always hangs over the global stage, they likewise contend that their approach to international affairs engenders the most viable (although admittedly not foolproof) formula for maintaining peace. Their basic argument is that since the inevitable internal logic of their scenario mitigates against any one actor always having the capacity to dominate everyone else — because an attempt by any state to increase its power significantly will constitute a possible threat to the security of others and will trigger compensatory countermoves — a delicate but nevertheless viable long-term equilibrium is prone to emerge based on a dynamic balance of power.

The classic presentation of the Realist school can be found in Hans Morgenthau, *Politics among Nations: The Struggle for Power and Peace,* 4th ed. (New York: Alfred A. Knopf, 1967).

4. Detailed discussions of the early ideological clashes between the Cubans and the Soviets can be found in Jacques Levesque, *The USSR and the Cuban Revolution* (New York: Praeger Special Series, 1978), and K. S. Karol, *Guerrillas in Power: The Course of the Cuban Revolution* (New York: Hill and Wang, 1970). See chapter 3 of this work for a more extended discussion of the evolving Cuban-Soviet relationship, including these ideological and policy disputes.

5. For a more detailed presentation of this characterization of Cuban policy as a combination of core ideological principles and pragmatism/opportunism, see Nelson Valdés, "Cuba and Angola: The Politics of Principles and Opportunism," paper presented at the conference on the Role of Cuba in World Affairs, University of Pittsburgh, November 15–17, 1977.

6. Such "missionary" activity, as is the case with most endeavors, can take various forms. The most benevolent involves peaceful proselytizing and persuasion, as that by the early Christian apostles. But at the other end of the continuum one can find coercion and sometimes brutality on a grand scale, as illustrated by the crusades unleashed by medieval Catholic Europe against the Moslem world and by the violence used routinely by the Spaniards to convert the indigenous peoples they found in the Western Hemisphere.

7. The practical grounds for caution were simple — Havana did not want to

230 | Notes to Pages 28–36

provide Washington a ready excuse to take retaliatory action that could threaten the Revolution's survival. The Fidelistas' theoretical/ideological rationale is more complex and nuanced but ultimately boils down to the proposition that outsiders, no matter how friendly, should not play a leading role in other people's revolutions, for this would undermine the authenticity of the whole process and thereby contribute to its ultimate failure.

8. This checklist is taken from John T. Rourke, *International Politics on the World Stage,* 5th ed. (Guilford, Conn.: Dushkin Publishing Group, 1995), 133–42. For a good general discussion of the Great Man approach that includes references to many specialized studies, see Frederic S. Pearson and J. Martin Rochester, *International Relations: The Global Condition in the Late Twentieth Century,* 3d ed. (New York: McGraw-Hill, 1992), 185–91.

9. Carlos Alberto Montaner, *Fidel Castro and the Cuban Revolution: Age, Position, Character, Destiny, Personality, and Ambition* (New Brunswick, N.J.: Transaction Publishers, 1989). For my review of the book, see *Studies in Comparative Economics* (Summer 1993).

10. Some good examples of analyses that address the issue of institutionalization are Max Azicri, *Cuba: Politics, Economics, and Society* (London: Pinter Press, 1988); Jorge I. Domínguez, "Revolutionary Politics: The New Demands for Orderliness," in Jorge I. Domínguez (ed.), *Cuba: Internal and International Affairs* (Beverly Hills, Calif.: Sage Publishing, 1982); and Archibald R. M. Ritter, "The Organs of People's Power and the Communist Party: The Nature of Cuban Democracy," in Sandor Halebsky and John M. Kirk (eds.), *Cuba: Twenty-Five Years of Revolution, 1959–1984* (New York: Praeger Publishers, 1985).

11. These three entities are discussed in Marifeli Pérez-Stable, *The Cuban Revolution: Origins, Course, and Legacy* (New York: Oxford University Press, 1993), chap. 3.

12. The part of the following section dealing with the Surrogate Thesis is an abbreviated version of material that first appeared in H. Michael Erisman, *Cuba's International Relations: The Anatomy of a Nationalistic Foreign Policy* (Boulder, Colo.: Westview Press, 1985), 3–4, now out of print.

13. See David Ronfeldt, *Superclients and Superpowers: Cuba/Soviet Union and Iran/United States* (Santa Monica, Calif.: Rand Corporation, 1978).

14. Edward González, "Complexities of Cuban Foreign Policy," *Problems of Communism* 26 (November–December 1977): 2.

15. Moynihan's phrase is quoted in "Castro's Globetrotting Gurkhas," *Time,* February 23, 1976, 25.

16. González, "Complexities," 2–3.

17. Anthony Payne, "Giants and Pygmies in the Caribbean," *World Today,* August 1980, 293.

18. This and the following section on the key elements of a counterdependency-oriented foreign policy are based on material that first appeared in H. Michael Erisman, *Pursuing Postdependency Politics: South-South Relations in the Carib-*

Notes to Pages 36–41 | 231

bean (Boulder, Colo.: Lynne Rienner Publishers, 1992), here updated and revised to maximize its utility in analyzing Cuba's international relations.

19. Works representative of or related to these three schools are John A. Hobson, *Imperialism: A Study* (Ann Arbor: University of Michigan Press, 1965); Vladimir I. Lenin, "Imperialism: The Highest Stage of Capitalism," in Robert C. Tucker (ed.), *The Lenin Anthology* (New York: W. W. Norton, 1975); Kwame Nkrumah, *Neo-Colonialism: The Last Stage of Imperialism* (New York: International Publishing Company, 1965); and Raul Prebisch, *Towards a Dynamic Development Policy for Latin America* (New York: United Nations, 1963).

20. James N. Rosenau, "Pre-Theories and Theories of Foreign Policy," in R. Barry Farrell (ed.), *Approaches to Comparative and International Politics* (Evanston, Ill.: Northwestern University Press, 1966), 65. For more detail regarding the concept and the dynamics of penetrated systems, see pp. 60–71.

21. Dependency theorists contend that a pivotal factor often driving those composing the comprador class into such an alliance is their desire to preserve a national socioeconomic status quo characterized by extreme patterns of maldistribution within which they have traditionally occupied a privileged position. To assure that they can continue to reap the substantial benefits involved, they are willing to accept a dependency relationship in order to acquire external allies who have a vested interest in protecting the comprador class and the social order that has spawned it.

22. These interests that the United States wanted to nurture and protect were heavily economic in nature. The political hegemony that Washington increasingly exercised over Cuba, as exemplified by the Platt Amendment, helped to create an environment in which U.S. entrepreneurs were readily able to secure valuable business concessions and able to expand drastically their position in the island's economy. This process can be illustrated by data drawn from Marvin D. Bernstein, *Foreign Investment in Latin America* (New York: Alfred A. Knopf, 1966), 147–48, which shows U.S. private investment in Cuba growing from a rather modest $50 million in 1896 to $265 million in 1915. A similar pattern can be seen with respect to commerce. U.S. export sales to the island, which enjoyed highly preferential treatment as a result of the Reciprocal Trade Agreement of 1903, increased approximately 641 percent in the fairly short period covering 1897 ($27 million in exports) to 1914 ($200 million, making Cuba at that point the world's sixth largest customer for Yankee goods and services).

23. Excellent examples or summaries of the Latin American school of dependency studies can be found in Andre Gunder Frank, *Development and Underdevelopment in Latin America* (New York: Monthly Review Press, 1968); Fernando Cardoso and Enzo Faletto, *Dependency and Development in Latin America* (Berkeley: University of California Press, 1979); Ronald Chilcote and Joel Edelstein (eds.), *Latin America: The Struggle with Dependency and Beyond* (New York: John Wiley and Sons, 1974): and Heraldo Muñoz (ed.), *From Dependency to Development* (Boulder, Colo.: Westview Press, 1981).

232 | Notes to Pages 41–44

24. Ronald Chilcote, "Dependency: A Critical Review of the Literature," *Latin American Perspectives* 1, no. 1 (1974): 4. Another well-known definition of dependency given in the same article (p. 4) is that of Teotonio dos Santos: "By dependence we mean a situation in which the economy of certain countries is conditioned by the development and expansion of another economy to which the former is subjected. The relation of inter-dependence between two or more economies, and between these and world trade, assumes the form of dependence when some countries (the dominant ones) can expand and be self-sustaining, while other countries (the dependent ones) can do this only as a reflection of that expansion, which can have either a positive or negative effect on their immediate development."

25. James A. Caporaso, "Introduction to the Special Issue of *International Organization* on Dependence and Dependency in the Global System," *International Organization* 32, no. 1 (Winter 1978): 1, 2.

26. Some dependency theorists have made provision for exceptions to the rule of stark center-periphery dichotomies by introducing the notion of "dependent development," which revolves around the idea that under certain circumstances a dependent LDC may experience a degree of industrialization and other forms of modernization allowing it to rise well above Third World norms. Such nations are often called NICs (newly industrializing countries). But recognize, caution the dependendistas, that such development is occurring within the context of an ongoing dependency relationship. Thus the fundamentals have not changed: the basic contours of unequal power are unaltered, economic progress in the periphery is still conditioned by its linkages with the center, and the primary beneficiaries continue to be metropolitan interests along with their comprador allies. For more detail regarding this line of analysis, see Fernando Henrique Cardoso, "Associated-Dependent Development: Theoretical and Practical Implications," in Alfred Stepan (ed.), *Authoritarian Brazil* (New Haven: Yale University Press, 1973), and Cardoso and Faletto, *Dependency and Development*.

27. William Appleton Williams, *The Tragedy of American Diplomacy* (New York: Dell Publishing Company, 1962), 47–48.

28. William Demas, *Consolidating Our Independence: The Major Challenge for the West Indies*, Distinguished Lecture Series, Institute of International Relations (University of the West Indies, Republic of Trinidad and Tobago, 1986), 23.

29. The great European colonial powers, especially England, fully appreciated and were masters at capitalizing upon the imperialistic opportunities that such isolation presented, using divide-and-conquer tactics with devastating effectiveness to help build and maintain their far-flung empires. Likewise, disunity and isolation in the face of the U.S. government's policy of westward expansionism contributed significantly to the tragic fate of the indigenous North American nations.

30. Bengt Sundelius, "Coping with Structural Security Threats," in Otmar Höll (ed.), *Small States in Europe and Dependence* (Boulder, Colo.: Westview Press, 1983), 295.

Notes to Pages 45–50 | 233

31. For more information regarding the extremely varied field of game theory, see such representative contributions as Thomas Schelling, *The Strategy of Conflict* (New York: Oxford University Press, 1960); Martin Shubik, *Games for Society, Business, and War: Towards a Theory of Gaming* (New York: Elsevier Press, 1975); Steven H. Brams, *Game Theory and Politics* (New York: Free Press, 1975); and Glenn H. Snyder and Paul Diesing, *Conflict among Nations: Bargaining, Decision-Making, and System Structure in International Crises* (Princeton, N.J.: Princeton University Press, 1977).

32. Caporaso, "Introduction to the Special Issue," 4.

33. John Ravenhill, *Collective Clientelism: The Lomé Conventions and North-South Relations* (New York: Columbia University Press, 1985), 8.

34. This concept of "strategic dependency" is similar to the superclient thesis discussed earlier in this chapter.

35. NAFTA membership often represents such a temptation to Latin American governments, who are cross-pressured between the realization that solidarity on their part is needed to be able to deal effectively with Washington's efforts to unify the hemisphere economically under its leadership or control and the lure of being among the first to gain privileged access to the combined markets and financial and technological resources of one of the world's greatest centers of economic power (i.e., the United States and Canada).

36. Lomé provides a mechanism whereby a long list of former European colonies known as the ACP (Africa/Caribbean/Pacific) Group negotiate with the European Community to establish a formal accord that regulates economic relations between the two parties. These Lomé agreements have provided ACP members with preferential trade access to EC markets as well as with various types of developmental aid programs. The first Lomé Convention was signed in 1975, and it has subsequently been renegotiated every five years. The 1990 version covered a ten-year span, as opposed to the five-year agreements that had previously been the norm. It is unclear at the time of writing whether a Lomé V pact will be forthcoming in 2000. Certainly there is some reluctance within the EU ranks to continue the arrangement, one key reason being the relative deprioritizing of North-South relations as the EU devotes increasing attention to its ties with former Soviet bloc countries.

For information about the Lomé process, see Ravenhill, *Collective Clientelism,* and Ellen Frey-Wouters, *The European Community and the Third World: The Lomé Convention and Its Impact,* Praeger Special Studies (New York: Praeger Publishers, 1980).

3. In the Shadow of the Superpowers, 1959–1972

1. The first agrarian reform law was promulgated in May 1959 and resulted in transferring approximately 44 percent of Cuban farmland to state ownership while 56 percent remained in private hands. A second agrarian reform law in October 1963 increased state ownership to 63 percent. The fact that U.S.-owned properties (especially sugar plantations) were affected by these nationalization

234 | Notes to Pages 50–54

campaigns contributed significantly to the deterioration in relations between Washington and the new revolutionary government in Havana. For a good summary of these agrarian reform laws, see Medea Benjamin, Joseph Collins, and Michael Scott, "The Agrarian Revolution," in Philip Brenner et al. (eds.), *The Cuba Reader: The Making of a Revolutionary Society* (New York: Grove Press, 1989), 89–101.

2. The literature that incorporates a hegemonic conception of the U.S. approach to Latin American affairs is extensive. This line of analysis is developed in James Petras, Michael Erisman, and Charles Mills, "The Monroe Doctrine and U.S. Hegemony in Latin America," in James Petras (ed.), *Latin America: From Dependence to Revolution* (New York: John Wiley and Sons, 1973), 231–72.

3. For more information on the historical evolution of this concept, see Frederick Merk, *Manifest Destiny and Mission in American History: A Reinterpretation* (New York: Vintage Books, 1963).

4. Two of the most famous pieces advocating this approach to international affairs, which ultimately became known as the Containment Doctrine, were George Kennan's pivotal "Mr. X" article and National Security Council Report 68. See X [George Kennan], "The Sources of Soviet Conduct," *Foreign Affairs* 25 (July 1947): 566–82; and "NSC-68, A Report to the National Security Council: United States Objectives and Programs for National Security" (mimeographed, April 14, 1950, Washington, D.C.). Kennan wrote his article under the pseudonym "X" because he was a State Department official at the time (specializing in Russian and Soviet affairs) and therefore preferred to remain anonymous. NSC-68, which was not declassified and made public until more than twenty years after it was written, is one of the seminal documents of the Cold War. For an excellent brief discussion of it, see James A. Nathan and James K. Oliver, *United States Foreign Policy and World Order* (Boston: Little, Brown, 1976), 126–36.

5. Anti-Americanism, which clearly is part of Cuba's political culture and certainly has been a central feature of the Revolution's policy repertoire, is more nuanced than most people in the United States realize. Its primary focus is Washington's tradition of hegemonic behavior, which means in effect that the target of its wrath is the U.S. government's policies toward the island. Otherwise, Cubans remain extremely friendly toward the American people, as anyone who has visited the island can readily attest, and find many aspects of U.S. culture highly attractive.

6. Such disputes are not unusual when nationalization occurs. Typically the owners want compensation based on the "fair market value" of their property. In other words, they want to be paid on the basis of whatever they (or a friendly appraiser, which in some cases might be their home government) say the holdings would bring if sold on the open free market. Those doing the nationalizing often prefer some sort of "discount formula." For example, they may offer compensation based on existing tax-assessed value, which might be low if corruption (i.e., bribing officials) or other factors allowed the owners to undervalue their assets in order to escape local taxes. In other cases, reimbursement may be calculated by

Notes to Pages 54–61 | 235

deducting from the property's current value the "excess" or "illegal" profits (as determined by the nationalizing government) that the prior owners allegedly received. It was such disagreements that paralyzed the compensation negotiations between revolutionary Cuba and the United States.

7. Quoted in Morris H. Morley, *Imperial State and Revolution: The United States and Cuba, 1952–1986* (New York: Cambridge University Press, 1987), 64.

8. It should be noted that Moscow's commitment to buy Cuban sugar at world market prices was not a windfall for Havana because traditionally, due to special arrangements with importing nations, sugar-exporting countries have been able to get above-market prices. As such, Havana was in a sense giving the USSR a discount by selling its sugar at market prices. The Kremlin did, of course, reciprocate in the petroleum area.

9. The importance of the U.S. sugar market to the Cuban economy as a whole can be readily understood when one considers that during the period 1949–58, exports generated approximately 36 percent of the island's gross national product; about 84 percent of Cuba's exports consisted of sugar and its by-products (e.g., rum); and the United States normally purchased over 50 percent of those sugar exports.

10. Jorge Domínguez, *Cuba: Order and Revolution* (Cambridge, Mass.: Belknap Press of Harvard University Press, 1978), 146.

11. Not only was the United States in the process of establishing a comprehensive embargo on its trade with Cuba, but it was also bringing pressure to bear on other countries (especially in the Western Hemisphere and Europe) to do likewise. For example, in September 1960 Washington announced, via the Mutual Security Appropriations Act, that henceforth any country providing military or economic assistance to Cuba would be excluded from all U.S. foreign aid programs. For details on this and other efforts to "persuade" third parties to join the embargo, see Morley, *Imperial State,* 121–26. Ultimately these efforts to isolate Cuba economically would generally succeed in the Western Hemisphere (the two main holdouts being Mexico and Canada), but they would fare poorly in Western Europe.

12. Some of the assassination plots considered seem rather bizarre, one example being the suggestion to use contaminated cigars to poison Castro. But what many would see as the most controversial move taken by the CIA in its efforts to kill Castro was the alliance that the agency forged with the Mafia (whose highly lucrative gambling and prostitution operations in Havana had been eliminated by the revolutionary government). In essence, what the CIA was doing was subcontracting the actual "hit" to the Mafia. Among the major mob figures involved in these plans were John Roselli, Sam Giancana, and Santos Trafficante. The last two individuals were later alleged by many critics of the Warren Commission Report to be involved in the assassination of President John F. Kennedy.

13. The United States used some economic incentives to mobilize this support, making it plain that participation in a $500 million Latin American economic aid program that Congress had recently passed would be limited to those countries

236 | Notes to Pages 61–66

that were willing to support Washington's anti-Castro agenda. The final vote on the San José Declaration was unanimous because Cuba walked out of the conference in protest against the proposed document.

14. See the section in chapter 2 on "Cuban Foreign Policy as a Revolutionary Crusade" for additional information about the principle of proletarian internationalism and its role in Havana's foreign policy.

15. Historical information about the international brigades can be found in Verle Johnson, *Legions of Babel: The International Brigades in the Spanish Civil War* (University Park: Pennsylvania State University Press, 1968), and R. Dan Richardson, *Comintern Army: The International Brigades and the Spanish Civil War* (Lexington: University Press of Kentucky, 1982). One of the most famous fictionalized treatments of the subject is Ernest Hemingway's novel *A Farewell to Arms*. Note that the island's close cultural-historical links with both Spain and Hemingway would probably serve to make most progressive Cubans (like Castro) highly familiar with and sympathetic to the internationalist ethos symbolized by the Spanish brigades.

16. For one of the most comprehensive pieces of reportage on the guerrilla phenomenon that swept Latin America in the 1960s, see Richard Gott, *Guerrilla Movements in Latin America* (New York: Anchor Books, Doubleday and Company, 1972). The operations summarized here are discussed on pp. 13–16.

17. See Robert D. Tomasek, "Caribbean Exile Invasions: A Special Regional Type of Conflict," *Orbis* 17 (Winter 1974): 1354–82 on foreign-supported exile invasions as a well-established practice in Caribbean intraregional politics. For more detailed information on the Caribbean Legion, see Charles D. Ameringer, *The Democratic Left in Exile* (Miami, Fla.: University of Miami Press, 1974), 59–110.

18. See Gordon Connell-Smith, *The Inter-American System* (London: Oxford University Press, 1966), 250–53, for more information regarding the resolution and the Punta del Este conference.

19. An extremely detailed examination of the blockade can be found in Michael Krinsky and David Golove (eds.), *United States Economic Measures against Cuba: Proceedings in the United Nations and International Law Issues* (Northampton, Mass.: Aletheia Press, 1993).

20. Canada, which was not a member of the OAS at this time, joined Mexico in refusing to participate in the U.S.-sponsored blockade of Cuba. For approximately a decade, Ottawa and Mexico City were the only two members of the hemispheric community that were willing to defy Washington on the Cuban question. For an excellent analytical review of Canada's evolving policy toward revolutionary Cuba, see John M. Kirk and Peter McKenna, *Canada-Cuba Relations: The Other Good Neighbor Policy* (Gainesville: University Press of Florida, 1997).

21. Quoted from "The Duty of a Revolutionary Is to Make the Revolution: The Second Declaration of Havana," in Martin Kenner and James Petras (eds.), *Fidel Castro Speaks* (New York: Grove Press, 1969), 105.

Notes to Pages 69–77 | 237

22. In addition to the medium-range missiles that were nuclear-capable, Juan O. Tamayo reported in the *Miami Herald* that Cuba also had received approximately 100 tactical nuclear weapons for battlefield use from the USSR; see "A Nuclear Secret in '62 Missile Crisis," *Miami Herald,* May 3, 1998 (downloaded from the *Herald*'s webpage dealing with Cuban news). These weapons were operational at the time of the Missile Crisis and thus available for use had the United States decided to take military action against the island. Apparently the CIA and U.S. policy makers were unaware of this development. Therefore, assuming that the technological capability of the Cuban armed forces to inflict mass casualties was negligible to nonexistent, they plunged blindly into what was a dangerous situation. For additional information on these weapons and the Missile Crisis in general, see Aleksandr Fursenko and Timothy Naftali, *"One Hell of a Gamble": Khrushchev, Castro, and Kennedy, 1958–1964* (New York: W. W. Norton, 1997).

23. The Cuban Missile Crisis generated a cottage industry of books and other studies. A representative sample follows (in chronological order): Robert F. Kennedy, *Thirteen Days: A Memoir of the Cuban Missile Crisis* (New York: W. W. Norton, 1969); Graham T. Allison, *Essence of Decision* (Boston: Little, Brown, 1971); Herbert S. Dinerstein, *The Making of a Missile Crisis, October 1962* (Baltimore: Johns Hopkins University Press, 1976); and James G. Blight et al., *Cuba on the Brink: Castro, the Missile Crisis, and the Soviet Collapse* (New York: Bantam Books, 1993).

24. William LeoGrande, "Cuban-Soviet Relations and Cuban Policy in Africa," paper presented at the 1979 conference of the International Studies Association, Toronto, Canada, 4–5.

25. See W. Raymond Duncan, "Cuba," in Harold E. Davis and Larman C. Wilson (eds.), *Latin American Foreign Policies: An Analysis* (Baltimore: Johns Hopkins University Press, 1975), 166–69.

26. The Kremlin was never willing to guarantee Cuba's security via some type of formal, official agreement, such as a mutual defense treaty that would have assured a response by Soviet forces to a third-party attack on the island. Consequently, contrary to popular belief, Havana was never a full-fledged military ally of the USSR; Cuba never became a member of the Warsaw Pact (the Russian equivalent of the NATO alliance), nor did it ever conclude a bilateral defense agreement with Moscow. Instead, the USSR limited its commitment to nonbinding (and often imprecise) declarations of support and to providing admittedly substantial amounts of military assistance (equipment and training).

27. Levesque, *USSR and the Cuban Revolution,* 121.

28. Regis Debray, *Revolution in the Revolution?* (New York: Grove Press, 1967).

29. LeoGrande, "Cuban-Soviet Relations," 6.

30. Mongolia was the first developing country to become a full member of CMEA, with Vietnam achieving such status in 1978.

31. González, "Complexities," 4.

238 | Notes to Pages 79–84

4. Beyond the Superpowers

1. The diversification gambit mentioned here is discussed in some detail in chapter 2. Like diversification, the concept of developmental coalition building, at least as used here, is fairly straightforward. Basically it involves the establishment of formal multilateral economic arrangements whereby a developing country is extended various advantages. Trade preferences are probably the most common benefit provided, although the equation might also include financial credits, grants, investment prerogatives, and/or technical assistance. These special relations should be fully institutionalized by being incorporated into an official, long-term agreement (i.e., a multilateral treaty) and operating under the aegis of an administrative structure (e.g., a commission or secretariat) that is fully empowered to oversee and coordinate implementation of the accords. In short, such coalition building entails some movement on the part of a developing country toward economic integration with a clearly defined (and limited) set of partners. Among the most frequent first steps taken is membership in a free trade agreement or a common market. Some examples, at least on the North-South plane, would be Mexico's membership in NAFTA and, of course, Cuba's involvement in the now-defunct CMEA.

2. Cuba enjoyed special status with regard to Soviet security aid when compared to Moscow's allies who were members of the Warsaw Pact. Normally the Eastern European states were expected to reimburse the Kremlin (at least in part) for the equipment and other types of military assistance that they received. Cuba, on the other hand, paid nothing; arms, logistical supplies, training, and advisory services were all provided free of charge by the USSR.

3. Quoted in Frieda M. Silvert, "The Cuban Problematic," in Martin Weinstein (ed.), *Revolutionary Cuba in the World Arena* (Philadelphia: Institute for the Study of Human Issues, 1979), 23.

4. Jorge Domínguez, "Cuban Foreign Policy," *Foreign Affairs* 57 (Fall 1978): 83.

5. Chile's policy of normalized relations with Havana did not survive the Allende government. It was destroyed by a U.S.-supported military coup on September 11, 1973. One of the first moves made by the new ruling junta was to sever all existing ties with Cuba.

6. The English-speaking Caribbean nation with which Cuba had the most cordial dealings throughout most of the 1970s was Jamaica, following Michael Manley's election as prime minister in 1972. Although a democratic socialist rather than a full-fledged Marxist, Manley nevertheless displayed growing admiration for the Cuban socioeconomic model (particularly following his 1976 reelection landslide) as well as interjecting an increasingly militant nonaligned coloration into his foreign policy. Havana responded enthusiastically, extending substantial moral and material support to what it perceived to be Kingston's progressive proclivities. During an October 1977 Jamaican state visit, for example,

Notes to Pages 84–88 | 239

Castro seized every available opportunity to stress his government's eagerness to extend developmental aid, promising buses for Cuban-built schools, tractors for sugar cooperatives, prefabricated housing for construction workers, and doctors, teachers, and technicians wherever they were needed.

7. Remember that while these countries were the first in the Western Hemisphere to break ranks with Washington on the question of isolating Cuba, Mexico and Canada had never supported the U.S. blockade policy and had instead maintained diplomatic and economic relations with Castro's government from its inception.

8. More information and analyses regarding Cuba's involvement in such IGOs can be found in Steven Reed, "Participation in Multinational Organizations and Programs in the Hemisphere," in Cole Blasier and Carmelo Mesa-Lago (eds.), *Cuba in the World* (Pittsburgh: University of Pittsburgh Press, 1979), 297–312.

9. This move by the OAS put pressure on the United States to moderate its economic blockade of Cuba. Washington did so on August 21, 1975, by announcing that it would no longer deny foreign aid to countries engaged in transporting trade goods to Cuba and that it would henceforth allow ships involved in such activity into U.S. ports. Also, Washington said it would now allow overseas subsidiaries of U.S. companies to trade with Cuba, as long as the items involved were not produced in the United States

10. Washington's cynical attitude toward this often controversial relationship was immortalized by President Franklin Roosevelt when, in response to a critical question as to why the United States was willing to support brutal, corrupt dictators such as Anastasio Somoza in Nicaragua, FDR quipped that Somoza "may be a son of a bitch, but at least he's our son of a bitch."

11. For more details regarding these alliances, see U.S. Department of State, Special Report no. 90, "Cuba's Renewed Support for Violence in Latin America" (December 14, 1981), 5–8, 10–11. Jorge I. Domínguez, *To Make a World Safe for Revolution* (Cambridge, Mass.: Harvard University Press, 1989), provides in chapter 5, "Support for Revolutionary Movements," an in-depth analysis of the motivations behind and the nature of Fidelista radicalism during this period.

12. An excellent study of the rise and demise of the New Jewel Revolution can be found in Tony Thorndike, *Grenada: Politics, Economics, and Society* (London: Frances Pinter Publishers, 1985).

13. These figures and others relating to Cuba's foreign assistance programs can found in H. Michael Erisman, "Cuban Development Aid: South-South Diversification and Counterdependency Politics," in H. Michael Erisman and John M. Kirk (eds.), *Cuban Foreign Policy Confronts a New International Order* (Boulder, Colo.: Lynn Rienner Publishers, 1991), 153–54.

14. Domínguez, *Make a World Safe*, 176–77, provides the following set of figures and sources for the peak number of Cuban military advisors in Nicaragua: 200 (1984), Fidel Castro; 300–400 (1987), a Cuban military officer who defected to the United States; and 3,000 (1985), U.S. government.

240 | Notes to Pages 89–95

15. This Ortega figure comes from William Ratliff, "Fidel Castro's Crusade in the Caribbean Basin," in Georges Fauriol and Eva Loser (eds.), *Cuba: The International Dimension* (New Brunswick, N.J.: Transaction Publishers, 1990), 80.

16. Washington warmly welcomed the triumph of Chamorro's ideologically moderate and pro-Western coalition, hailing it as a landmark achievement for the democratic principles that the Reagan Doctrine was supposedly promoting. Others took a more cynical view of the administration's fondness for democracy, pointing out that it had refused to accept as legitimate the Sandinistas' overwhelming victory in the 1984 national elections, which were certified as open and absolutely fair by the large contingent of international observers on hand. Instead, the Reaganites continued to characterize Daniel Ortega's regime as a totalitarian dictatorship and to support the Contra war against it. Obviously it was the outcome of Nicaraguan elections rather than their democratic nature that determined Washington's attitude toward the country's government. Such duplicity, it might be noted, was nothing new; the Nixon White House had behaved in an almost identical fashion toward the Chilean democratic 1970 election that produced Salvadore Allende's socialist government.

17. Among the moderate/conservative candidates who prevailed in the late 1970s or early 1980s were Milton Cato in St. Vincent (December 1979), Kennedy Simmonds in St. Kitts–Nevis (February 1980), Eugenia Charles in Dominica (July 1980), George Chambers in Trinidad and Tobago (November 1981), John Compton in St. Lucia (May 1982), and Lynden Pindling in the Bahamas (June 1982).

18. The main regional organization encompassing the English-speaking Caribbean is CARICOM (the Caribbean Community and Common Market), which at this point had thirteen members. The only CARICOM governments that refused to support the Grenada invasion and were forthright in publicly chastising the Reagan administration for its involvement were Guyana and Trinidad and Tobago. At the opposite end of the spectrum, Jamaica, Barbados, Dominica, St. Vincent and the Grenadines, St. Lucia, and Antigua all directly participated in some way in the assault.

19. Domínguez, *Make a World Safe*, p. 239.

20. Census data indicate that blacks constitute 11 percent of Cuba's population, a figure comparable to that of the United States. But when the 51 percent of the islanders who are classified as mulattos are added to the equation, a heavily African-oriented demographic portrait emerges.

21. Wolf Grabendorff, "Cuba's Involvement in Africa: An Interpretation of Objectives, Reactions, and Limitations," *Journal of Interamerican Studies and World Affairs* 22, no. 1 (February 1980): 24.

22. No consensus emerged on when the first Cuban troops arrived in Angola. The U.S. government, anxious to create the impression that Cuba was the first outside country to send combat units to Angola, suggested that the first Fidelista units arrived sometime before August 1975 (prior to the first South African de-

Notes to Pages 95–103 | 241

ployment), while Havana insisted upon an early November timetable. The prevailing opinion seems to be that there was a small Cuban presence in October, then the major buildup began in early November in response to the offensive unleashed by the South African army.

23. UNITA became a major beneficiary of the Reagan Doctrine during the 1980s. The MPLA government—along with Nicaragua's Sandinistas and Afghanistan's Soviet-supported regime—became a priority target for the Reagan administration, and UNITA was the instrument Washington chose for its destruction. The large amount of subsequent U.S. aid that flowed into UNITA's coffers was a major factor in sustaining its challenges to the central government in Luanda.

24. The close Cuban-Soviet cooperation in fighting the Somalian invasion did not extend to the Eritrean situation. With the Somalis defeated, Haile Mariam's government turned its full attention to the insurgents in Eritrea, with whom it refused to negotiate or compromise. Moscow pressured Havana to use its troops already in the country to help put down the rebellion. The Fidelistas refused, however, partly because they did not want to offend pro-Cuban Third World governments that were friendly toward the Eritrean cause and also because involvement would have tarnished their anti-imperialist credentials seriously, since they had previously characterized the Eritrean struggle as a legitimate war of national liberation. In any case, Havana's stubborn independence here was often cited as evidence of the invalidity of the Surrogate Thesis.

25. The following discussion of Cuba's developmental aid programs draws heavily upon material previously published in Erisman, "Cuban Development Aid." Some sections from this chapter in Erisman and Kirk, *Cuban Foreign Policy,* are incorporated verbatim here.

26. These figures come from Julie M. Feinsilver, "Cuba as a World Medical Power: The Politics of Symbolism," *Latin American Research Review* 24, no. 2 (1989): 12, 15.

27. See table 9.1 in Erisman, "Cuban Development Aid," 153–54, for data covering the entire global deployment of Cuban developmental aid personnel.

28. Donna Rich, "Cuban Internationalism: A Humanitarian Foreign Policy," in Brenner et al., *Cuba Reader,* 407, reported that in 1985 there were twenty-four such schools serving at least 300 foreign students each. The Cuban government covered all the expenses for food, lodging, education, medical care, pocket money, and travel. Havana also assumed all the costs involved in providing instructors from the students' home countries to offer courses dealing with their nation's language, history, geography, and culture.

29. A detailed discussion of the power struggle within the Nonaligned Movement between Cuba and its detractors can be found in Erisman, *Cuba's International Relations,* 80–87.

30. William LeoGrande, "The Dilemmas of Cuban Policy in the Third World," draft manuscript, 1981, 8.

242 | Notes to Pages 104–8

31. Members of the Movement of Nonaligned Nations voted 56 to 9 (with 26 others abstaining or absent) in favor of the resolution condemning the Kremlin's intervention in Afghanistan. Twenty-two other developing nations not in the movement joined the anti-Soviet majority, bringing the Third World total to 78 for censure, 9 against, and 28 abstaining or absent. The overall UN vote on the resolution was 104 in favor, 18 against, 18 abstaining, and 12 absent.

32. Basically the Fidelistas argued that they had voted against the resolution not because they approved of the Kremlin's actions but rather because they wanted to demonstrate their opposition to what they saw as attempts on Washington's part to advance its Cold War agenda by inflaming and exploiting the crisis.

5. Engulfed by the Maelstrom

1. Such comments were repeatedly made to me by prominent Cubans in both academic and governmental circles during a visit to Havana in June 1990. The consensus among them was that the challenge would be met, although there was considerable disagreement regarding the best way to do so. In the United States, on the other hand, the prevailing sentiment (especially in the mass media) seemed to be that Castro's days in power were numbered and that the Revolution would not survive much longer.

2. Writing in the Latin American Studies Association journal, Nelson P. Valdés, "Cuba Today: Thoughts after a Recent Visit," *LASA Forum* 15, no. 3 (fall 1984), provided some idea of Cuba's premier development status when he noted that "the Overseas Development Council created a Physical Quality of Life Index (PQLI) to measure and rank life expectancy, infant mortality, and literacy. Cuba ranked above all underdeveloped countries on all three variables. A study by David A. Brodsky and Dani Rodrik disclosed that Cuba had the highest welfare score of 133 Third World countries" (22).

3. Similar to the market economy concept of gross national product (GNP), gross social product was a measure of general economic productivity used by CMEA members to gauge the overall performance of their centrally planned command economies.

4. Domínguez, *Make a World Safe*, 91–92. The performance gap between Cuba and its hemispheric neighbors was illustrated by Valdés in "Cuba Today," when he reported that "the overall [Cuban economic] growth rate 1981 to 1983 went up 22.6 percent while Latin America had a negative rate of 2.8 percent" (22).

5. A note on Cuban economic data: I do not claim that the economic data presented in the tables for this and subsequent chapters are absolutely accurate in terms of specific figures (e.g., the amount of Cuban exports to a particular country or region in a particular year). Indeed, as one surveys the data sources—such as Cuban government statistics, the International Monetary Fund, Cuba's trading partners—one finds considerable variation in the numbers. This phenomenon may arise from the use of different currency exchange rates, different reporting procedures, or different categorization formulas. Although no guarantee is made re-

Notes to Pages 108–15 | 243

garding the precise accuracy of the individual figures, an effort has been made here to use such data with the primary goal of uncovering long-term patterns in Cuban trade and economic activity.

6. It should be noted that such preferential deals are not unusual in the sugar trade. The United States, the European Union, and others have often had such agreements with their Third World suppliers. Indeed, it is estimated that in the early 1980s only one-fifth of all international sugar transactions occurred at "world market prices."

7. Domínguez, *Make a World Safe,* 90.

8. John T. Rourke, *International Politics on the World Stage,* 6th ed. (Guilford, Conn.: Dushkin–McGraw-Hill, 1997), 39.

9. Not all elements in the USSR were so charitable. The *Moscow News,* for example, was one of the most vociferous sources of Soviet criticism of Cuba, castigating Castro for his reluctance to embrace the concepts of glasnost and perestroika and serving as one of the main forums for those who wanted the USSR to distance itself from its Caribbean ally, if not sever practically all relations. Such virulent anti-Cuban attitudes probably contributed significantly to Havana's announcement in August 1989 that it was prohibiting the *Moscow News* (along with another Russian magazine called *Sputnik*) from being circulated in Cuba.

10. This material comes from the chronology section of "America and the World, 1991/92," *Foreign Affairs* 71, no. 1 (1992): 200–207.

11. See, for example, Andrew Zimbalist, "Teetering on the Brink: Cuba's Current Economic and Political Crisis," *Journal of Latin American Studies* 24 (May 1992): 407–18, and his "Dateline Cuba: Hanging on in Havana," *Foreign Policy* 92 (Fall 1993): 151–67.

12. For a good journalistic snapshot of the Revolution's response to this economic state of emergency (which the government called the "special period in peacetime"), see "Crisis—The Special Period in Peacetime," chap. 8 in Marc Frank, *Cuba Looks to the Year 2000* (New York: International Publishers, 1993), 137–57.

13. Zimbalist, "Dateline Cuba," 154.

14. These figures are drawn from Carlos Alzugaray, "Cuban Security in the Post Cold War World: Old and New Challenges and Opportunities," paper presented at the International Symposium on "Cuba in the International System" held in Ottawa, Canada, September 1993, 20, and Teresa Gutierrez, "Cuba: Revolution at Crossroads," news article provided by *NY Transfer News Collective* via electronic mail (August 9, 1993), 1.

15. From Andrew Zimbalist, "Cuba, Castro, Clinton, and Canosa," in Archibald Ritter and John M. Kirk (eds.), *Cuba in the International System: Normalization and Integration* (New York: St. Martin's Press, 1995), 24.

16. Most observers would pinpoint as the flashpoint of the crisis the announcement in August 1982 by the Mexican government (the Third World's second-largest debtor nation behind Brazil) that it stood on the verge of involuntary de-

244 | Notes to Pages 115–22

fault because it did not have the funds to make its next loan repayment. For a more detailed analysis of Castro's proposals to resolve the problem, see H. Michael Erisman, "Cuban Foreign Policy and the Latin American Debt Crisis," in Carmelo Mesa-Lago (ed.), *Cuban Studies 18* (Pittsburgh: University of Pittsburgh Press, 1988), 3–18.

17. Even the Latin Americans, who often were prone to succumb to U.S. pressure in such situations, were solidly behind Havana in this instance, as evidenced by the fact that in May 1989 the Latin American–Caribbean caucus in the UN chose Cuba as its consensus nominee to fill the hemispheric slot in the Security Council being vacated by Brazil.

18. Tourist information is taken from María Dolores Espino, "Tourism in Cuba: A Development Strategy for the 1990s?" in Jorge Pérez-López (ed.), *Cuban Studies 23* (Pittsburgh: University of Pittsburgh Press, 1993), 58; *CubaINFO 5*, no. 5 (April 12, 1993): 6; and "Castro Says Tourism Taking Off Impressively," Reuters news item, Havana, January 31, 1994 (provided via electronic mail).

19. The raw dollar figures used to calculate these percentages were not adjusted for inflation. Had they been recalibrated, the percentage increases would be less. It is, however, extremely unlikely that such a modification would alter the overall pattern.

20. Some sources, such as the International Monetary Fund (IMF), have presented figures that appear to place Venezuela consistently in the company of these three leading sources of Cuban imports. Such statistics can be somewhat misleading, however, because they do not necessarily represent Venezuelan exports in the purest sense of the term. As described later in chapter 5, in order to save on shipping costs, arrangements were often made whereby Caracas provided the actual oil involved in Soviet or Russian sales to Cuba, and Moscow reciprocated by supplying petroleum to Venezuela's European customers; Caracas has not, therefore, been exporting to Cuba oil that it has actually sold to Havana but rather has been servicing Soviet or Russian sales. But organizations such as the IMF have included the value of this petroleum in their calculations of Cuba's imports from Venezuela, thus artificially inflating the total. The figures for Venezuela in table 5.9 are UN data that do not include the value of oil involved in such swaps.

21. "Peru Suspends Trade with Cuba," *CubaINFO 2*, no. 12 (July 19, 1990): 4–5.

22. Reported in *Update on Cuba*, September 17, 1990, 8. In this article, special attention is given to the recommendation by the Colombian government on June 25 that Colombian exporters should suspend all transactions with Cuba because Havana had recently announced that it could not for the time being make any payments on its trade debt to Colombia.

23. *CubaINFO 4*, no. 7 (June 23, 1992): 6.

24. *CubaINFO 4*, no. 8 (July 21, 1992): 6, and "Carlos Lage Visits Brazil, Colombia, Venezuela," *CubaINFO 6*, no. 3 (February 18, 1994): 7.

25. Joint ventures and other forms of cooperation between Cuban enterprises

Notes to Pages 122–29 | 245

and foreign investors were authorized by Decree Law No. 50 of February 1982. Regarding joint ventures, which were the centerpiece of the legislation, Havana restricted foreign partners to a maximum of 49 percent ownership. As such, the dependency-sensitive Cubans were assured ultimate control over the operations.

26. See "Debt-for-Equity Swaps with Mexico," *CubaINFO* 5, no. 1 (January 15, 1993): 5

27. Zimbalist, "Dateline Cuba," 159. See also H. Michael Erisman, "Cuba's Evolving CARICOM Connection," in Ritter and Kirk, *Cuba in the International System*, 135–36, for information regarding the incident that occurred in July–August 1993 when several members of Congress (led by Robert Torricelli, chair of the House Foreign Affairs Subcommittee on Western Hemisphere Affairs) sent letters to CARICOM leaders threatening to deny their countries any future trade concessions if CARICOM did not abandon its plans to develop closer economic ties with Cuba. The CARICOM leaders refused to bow to such blackmail.

28. The CDA is popularly known as the Torricelli Law because its main sponsor and promoter in the U.S. Congress was Representative Robert Torricelli, a Democrat from New Jersey.

29. As a corollary to these normalization efforts, Havana had made it quite plain that it now had no interest in or intention of promoting armed revolutionary struggle in Latin America. In theory, of course, the Fidelistas still recognized the legitimacy of armed struggle and the principle of proletarian internationalism, but at this point Havana was not inclined to translate these concepts into main pillars of its foreign policy.

30. Donna Rich Kaplowitz, "U.S. Subsidiary Trade with Cuba: Before and After the Cuba Democracy Act," in Ritter and Kirk, *Cuba in the International System*, 249.

31. Overviews and analyses of evolving Cuban-CARICOM relations can be found in John Walton Cotman, "Cuba and the CARICOM States: The Last Decade," in Donna Rich Kaplowitz (ed.), *Cuba's Ties to a Changing World* (Boulder, Colo.: Lynne Rienner Publishers, 1993), 145–64, and H. Michael Erisman, "Evolving Cuban/CARICOM Relations: A Comparative Cost-Benefit Analysis," in Louis A. Perez, Jr. (ed.), *Cuban Studies 25* (Pittsburgh: University of Pittsburgh Press, 1995), 207–27.

32. Quoted in Cotman, "Cuba and the CARICOM States," 146.

33. For details, see *CubaINFO* 3, no. 12 (August 2, 1991): 4; *CubaINFO* 4, no. 6 (May 18, 1992): 4; and Cotman, "Cuba and the CARICOM States," 146–47.

34. Multidestination tourism quickly emerged as one example of such collaboration where the prospects for mutual benefits appeared to be considerable. The basic idea here calls for Cuba and its CARICOM neighbors to "share tourists" (and the money they spend) by cooperating in putting together packages whereby visitors are moved from one island to another over the course of their vacations rather than following the tradition of spending all their time in one country.

35. CARICOM had ten observers in 1992, three of which were sovereign His-

246 | Notes to Pages 130–34

panic states—the Dominican Republic, Mexico, and Venezuela. The other seven were Anguilla, Bermuda, the Cayman Islands, Haiti, the Netherlands Antilles, Puerto Rico, and Suriname.

36. These developments are discussed in *CubaINFO* 4, no. 8 (July 21, 1992): 4; *Caribbean Contact,* July–August 1992, 10; and "CARICOM Considers Closer Trade Relations with Cuba," a synopsis of Inter Press Service reports provided via electronic mail by PeaceNet (April 2, 1993).

37. The trade information comes from "Cozying up to the Caribbean," a summary of news reports from the Cuban newspaper *Granma* that was provided via electronic mail from Havana by the Grupo de Video Joven (April 26, 1993).

38. For information about the Lomé process, see Ravenhill, *Collective Clientelism,* and Frey-Wouters, *The European Community and the Third World.* As noted earlier, the 1990 version differed from its predecessors in that it was agreed that it would run for ten years.

39. For a more detailed analysis of this subject using a variation of the counter-dependency concept used here, see Erisman, *Pursuing Postdependency Politics.*

40. For a more pessimistic analysis of Cuba's prospects for trade with Mexico at this point, see Ernest H. Preeg, *Cuba and the New Caribbean Economic Order* (Washington: Center for Strategic and International Studies, 1993), 65–66.

41. "With Foreign Investment Up, Cuban Debt Market Grows," *CubaINFO* 5, no. 15 (November 24, 1993): 8.

42. See Eduardo Molina, "Cuba: Foreign Businesses Cash in on Efforts to Attract Investors," Inter Press Service news item provided via electronic mail (November 8, 1992), and "Cuban-Mexican Textile Joint Venture," *CubaINFO* 4, no. 13 (November 13, 1992): 7.

43. See "$1.5 Billion from Mexican Company to Revamp Cuban Telephone System," *CubaINFO* 6, no. 9 (July 1, 1994): 9.

44. "Heads of Mexico, Colombia, Venezuela Tell Castro They Can't Give Aid to Cuba," *Wall Street Journal,* October 24, 1991, 13.

45. For a concise general overview of evolving Cuban-Brazilian relations, see Luiz L. Vasconcelos, "The Limits and Possibilities of Cuban-Brazilian Relations," in Rich Kaplowitz, *Cuba's Ties to a Changing World,* 183–98.

46. The figures for Cuban export earnings do not include revenues received from Brazilian tourists to the island. In 1990, for example, it is estimated that Brazilian tourists spent $15 million in Cuba. Obviously, combining such tourist revenues with regular export earnings makes the overall trade picture with Brazil even more positive from Havana's perspective.

47. For example, the 1992 CIA handbook on Cuban trade statistics (covering 1985–91) does not contain any Chilean entries.

48. Vasconcelos, "Limits and Possibilities," 189.

49. "Carlos Lage Visits Brazil, Colombia, Venezuela," *CubaINFO* 6, no. 3 (February 18, 1994): 7.

50. It was announced in January 1994 that the government of the Argentinean province of La Pampa was, with Buenos Aires' authorization, making an initial

Notes to Pages 134–39 | 247

purchase of 100,000 doses of a Cuban anti-meningitis vaccine to deal with an outbreak of the disease. At an estimated cost of $7–8 a dose, the potential revenue involved was fairly insubstantial. Information provided via electronic mail by Radio Havana Cuba (January 19, 1994).

51. Material in this section was provided by John M. Kirk. His text was edited but is basically unchanged. See Kirk and McKenna, *Canada-Cuba Relations.*

52. A variety of Canadian mining companies became active on the island in the 1990s, with Alberta-based Sherritt International Incorporated being by far the most important due to its multifaceted operations, which involved nickel and cobalt mining in the eastern provinces, drilling for oil and gas in the center, and launching oil enhancement and biotechnological activities in the west. Another Canadian company, Joutel Resources, rather easily raised $4 million from European investors who were attracted by Havana's generous exploration and development concessions of 1.2 million acres (which made Joutel the largest foreign landholder in Cuba). The company's CEO was quoted as observing that some 25–30 percent of the company's shares were in U.S. hands, due in no small degree to "the potential for high yields in the company's Cuban prospecting." For details, see "Canadian Mining Concern to Sign Joint Venture Contract," *CubaINFO* 5, no. 9 (July 16, 1993): 9.

53. Commenting on the value of this agreement, Sherritt's chairman Ian Delaney noted: "The Moa and Fort Saskatchewan facilities are uniquely compatible and the Cuban reserves of nickel and cobalt are superb. Our past relationships in Cuba have been very satisfactory. We believe that this new partnership will set a new style of business in Cuba." See "Canada and Cuba to Join in Nickel and Cobalt Production," *CubaINFO* 6, no. 9 (July 1, 1994): 8.

54. To give some idea of the steady growth of Canadian tourism to Cuba, there were approximately 21,000 Canadian visitors in 1980, 40,000 in 1985, 74,000 in 1990, and 130,000 in 1993. To put the 1993 figure in a U.S. context, it would be equivalent to having over a million American tourists traveling to the island annually.

55. Some estimates put Cuba's hard currency debt as high as $8 billion (U.S.) as of 1990; see, for example, *Update on Cuba,* September 17, 1990, 9, which cites as its source the *Journal of Commerce,* August 7, 1990. Generally, however, the figure most commonly used by outside observers was $6 billion.

56. These figures come from Gillian Gunn, "Cuba's Search for Alternatives," *Current History* (February 1992): 60, and Radio Havana Cuba, text of broadcast provided by PeaceNet via electronic mail (December 27, 1994).

57. William Ratliff, "Cuban Foreign Policy toward Far East and Southeast Asia," in Fauriol and Loser, *Cuba: The International Dimension,* 223, reported that between 1975 and 1983 Cuba's imports from China averaged 2.7 percent of its overall imports, while the comparable figure for exports was 3.7 percent. In the case of Japan, its share of Cuba's total trade peaked at 12.4 percent in 1974, declined to 3.5 percent in 1978, then slid further to 1.3 percent in 1983.

58. Reported in *Update on Cuba,* October 10, 1990, 6.

248 | Notes to Pages 143–48

6. Cuba Confronts the Post–Cold War Order

1. Hans Vogel, "Small States' Efforts in International Relations: Enlarging the Scope," in Otmar Holl (ed.), *Small States in Europe and Dependence* (Boulder, Colo.: Westview Press, 1983), 54–59.

2. A good summary of this perspective can be found in Donald E. Schulz, *The United States and Cuba: From a Strategy of Conflict to Constructive Engagement* (Carlisle, Pa.: Strategic Studies Institute, U.S. Army War College, 1993).

3. For information on the emergence of such sentiment among Cuban-American entrepreneurs and the U.S. business community in general, see "Cuban-American Business Group Rejects U.S. Trade Ban," Reuters news report (February 23, 1994) from Havana, provided via the Internet by the Cuba-L list, and "U.S. Big Business Express Interest in the Cuban Market," transcript of Radio Havana Cuba broadcast (December 24, 1994), provided via the Internet. The latter report mentions that those within the U.S. business community who are calling on Congress to normalize relations and thereby to open up trade and investment opportunities include Lee Iaccoca (former CEO of Chrysler) and officials of the Radisson hotel chain.

4. Nelson Valdés, "The United States and Cuba: The Time for New Thinking," manuscript provided electronically via the Internet (March 5, 1993), and David Bernell, "The Curious Case of Cuba in American Foreign Policy," *Journal of Interamerican Studies and World Affairs* 36, no. 2 (summer 1994): 65–69. Even U.S. Assistant Secretary of State for Inter-American Affairs Alexander Watson suggested in the course of comments regarding the question of readmitting Havana to the OAS that Cuba and communism no longer pose a security threat to the Western Hemisphere, as reported in "Alexander Watson Speaks on Cuba's Readmission to OAS," *CubaINFO* 6, no. 2 (January 28, 1994): 1.

5. These data are drawn from "Cuban Economy Grows but Money Remains Tight," *Caribbean Week,* August 31–September 13, 1996, 64; "Economic Report: Recovery Continues and Sugar Harvest Reaches 99 Percent of Target," *Cuba-INFO* 8, no. 10 (August 1, 1996): 7–8; and Cuban Ministry of Economy and Planning, "Cuba, Economic Report, 1996" (document procured from Cuban government sources via the Internet).

6. These figures come from a Reuters news story (May 26, 1998) titled "Cuba Says Recovery Continues Despite Sugar Decline," downloaded from the CNN Internet website. The 1998 projections would be undermined by droughts and hurricanes that devastated the island later in the year.

7. The basic rule of thumb seems to be that it takes some time to process the Cuban trade data to determine exactly where particular pieces of information (temporarily warehoused in the category "Other") belong in the overall classification scheme. Thus over time, the data logged as Other shrink to more reasonable proportions, as is illustrated by the tables in chapter 5 dealing with statistics from

Notes to Pages 148–60 | 249

the 1980s, where Other normally represents only about 1 percent of the total and never exceeds 6 percent (as opposed to the 20 and 30 percent shares that often appear in the 1990s tables).

8. I have referred in previous chapters to the special arrangement allowing Cuba to buy large amounts of Soviet oil on highly favorable terms (at low prices with payment in rubles) and then sell on the open market whatever was left over after its domestic demands had been met. This sweetheart deal generated large amounts of hard currency that Havana could then use to underwrite its purchase of goods and services from industrialized nations such as Japan.

9. This material is based on a summary of Joseph M. Perry, Louis A. Woods, and Jeffery W. Steagall, "Hemispheric Trade Alignments and the Trade Options for Post-Transition Cuba," paper presented at the Third Annual Meeting of the Association for the Study of the Cuban Economy, Florida International University, Miami, August 12–14, 1993, 3–4 (document downloaded from the Lanic Internet website at www.lanic.utexas.edu/la/cb/cuba/asce/cuba3/perry1.html).

10. CARICOM is a regional organization composed primarily of former British colonies. Its members (1999) are Jamaica, Trinidad and Tobago, Barbados, Guyana, the Bahamas, Grenada, Dominica, St. Lucia, St. Vincent and the Grenadines, Antigua and Barbuda, Belize, St. Kitts–Nevis, Montserrat (the only nonindependent territory in the organization), Suriname, and Haiti (the country most recently granted admission).

11. The twenty-five full members of the ACS are Colombia, Costa Rica, Cuba, the Dominican Republic, El Salvador, Guatemala, Honduras, Nicaragua, Panama, Mexico, and Venezuela plus fourteen of the fifteen CARICOM countries (Montserrat, a member of CARICOM, is not included because it is not independent).

12. For details about Cuba's entry to ALADI, see the Inter Press Service's story "Trade-Cuba: Admission to ALADI Boosts Ties with Region," dateline Havana, November 9, 1998 (downloaded from CNN's Internet website). See also "Cuba New Member of Latin Trading Bloc," *CubaINFO* 10, no. 15 (November 16, 1998): 5. Havana's entry was officially validated in mid-August 1999 after a study concluded that the island's economy was sufficiently open to allow it to be incorporated into a free-market system such as ALADI; see *CubaINFO* 11, no. 10 (August 4, 1999): 7.

13. The quote, which is from the SELA charter, comes from G. Pope Atkins, *Latin America in the International System,* 2d ed., rev. and updated (Boulder, Colo.: Westview Press, 1989), 200. See pp. 199–200 for a summary of SELA's formation and operations.

14. The treaty creating LAFTA was negotiated in 1960 and ratified in 1961 by seven countries—Argentina, Brazil, Chile, Peru, Paraguay, Mexico, and Uruguay. Subsequently Colombia, Ecuador, Venezuela, and Bolivia became members. Its primary goal was to establish a free trade area among its members within twelve years (by 1973), although this target was later extended to 1980. Failure to meet

250 | Notes to Pages 160–65

this deadline along with other shortcomings disillusioned participants, who in 1980 replaced it with ALADI. Cuba became ALADI's twelfth full member in November 1998.

15. Since CARICOM was a driving force behind the establishment of the Lomé framework, its members are automatically covered by any compact reached.

16. See "Caribbean Community Rebuffs Cuba Petition," Associated Press wire report (August 8, 1996) from Georgetown, Guyana, provided via the Internet by the Cuba-L list.

17. See "In Brief" section of *CubaINFO* 9, no. 3 (February 27, 1997): 9. Cuban membership was not rejected outright; the decision instead was to delay action for the time being.

18. It is not certain at the time of writing that a Lomé V pact will be forthcoming in 2000 when the current agreement expires. Certainly there has been some reluctance within the EU ranks to continue the arrangement, one key reason being the relative deprioritizing of North-South relations as the EU devotes increasing attention to its ties with former Soviet bloc countries. The prevailing opinion among observers seems to be that there will be a Lomé renewal but with terms that are likely to be considerably less favorable to the ACP states than was previously the case.

19. "Trade-Cuba: Havana to Dodge U.S. Blockade via CARICOM Membership," an Inter Press Service report, dateline Havana, April 1, 1998 (downloaded from CNN's Internet website).

20. "Cuba to Join EU-Caribbean Talks," an Associated Press report, dateline Bridgetown, Barbados, August 27, 1998 (downloaded from the *Washington Post*'s Internet website). See also "Castro Continues Diplomatic Initiative in Santo Domingo," *CUBAInfo* 10, no. 12 (September 10, 1998): 6.

21. Andrés Serbín, "Towards an Association of Caribbean States: Raising Some Awkward Questions," *Journal of Interamerican Studies and World Affairs* 36, no. 4 (winter 1994): 64.

22. General information regarding the ACS and Cuban involvement in it can be found in "CARICOM Summit," *CubaINFO* 5, no. 14 (November 5, 1993): 7, and "Cuba to Join New Caribbean Trade Group," *CubaINFO* 6, no. 5 (April 8, 1994): 7. See also Warwick Scales, "Clinton, CARICOM, and the Caribbean," published in the *Washington Report on the Hemisphere* and provided via electronic mail on May 3, 1994. For news reports regarding the signing of the treaty establishing the ACS, see *Caribbean Week* 5, no. 22 (August 6–19, 1994): 1–2, and *Granma International* (English ed.) 29, no. 30 (July 27, 1994): 15.

23. Perry et al., "Hemispheric Trade Alignments," 6, notes that the CACM was established in 1960 with the ultimate goal of creating a Central American free trade zone. The war that broke out in 1969 between Honduras and El Salvador (popularly known as the "Soccer War") effectively paralyzed the whole process, with the CACM henceforth existing only as a paper organization. The warfare and severe political instability that characterized the region in the 1980s further com-

Notes to Pages 165–73 | 251

plicated the situation. Efforts were made in the early 1990s to reinvigorate the CACM, but progress has been limited.

24. The Colombian agreement is reported in Charles W. Thurston, "Cuba Builds Ties Despite U.S. Ban," a December 4, 1995 news item from the *NewsHound* electronic news service of the *San Jose Mercury News* (California), provided via the Internet by the Cuba-L list. The negotiations with Trinidad and Tobago are reported in "In Brief," *CubaINFO* 9, no. 3 (February 27, 1997): 9.

25. An example of such intimidation with regard to the CARICOM countries is detailed in Michael Erisman, "Evolving Cuban-CARICOM Relations: A Comparative Cost/Benefit Analysis," *New West Indian Guide* 69, nos. 1–2 (1995): 51–53.

26. This section on U.S.-Cuban relations is a revised and updated version of material I wrote that was published as "US-Cuban Relations: Moving Beyond the Cold War to a New International Order?" in Ransford W. Palmer (ed.), *The Repositioning of US-Caribbean Relations in the New World Order* (Westport, Conn.: Praeger Publishers, 1997), 51–81. Reprinted by permission of the editor, copyright 1997 by Ransford W. Palmer.

27. Quoted in Wayne S. Smith, "Cuba after the Cold War: What Should U.S. Policy Be?" *International Policy Report* (Washington: Center for International Policy, March 1993), 6.

28. Smith uses this characterization in the title of his book *The Closest of Enemies: A Personal and Diplomatic History of U.S.-Cuban Relations since 1957* (New York: W. W. Norton, 1987). This is a fascinating account that revolves around Smith's direct experiences as a U.S. diplomat specializing in Cuban affairs who was there during the early years of the Revolution and who later served as head of the U.S. Interests Section in Havana from 1979 to 1982. The book should be considered required reading for anyone interested in relations between Washington and revolutionary Cuba.

29. See "Castro Supports Democracies" (August 11, 1993), news story by the *NY Transfer News Collective* provided via the Internet.

30. See "State Department Releases 1995 Terrorism Report," *CubaINFO* 8, no. 7 (May 23, 1996): 5–6.

31. A Voice of America broadcast reported on March 22, 1994, that Cuba was cutting its defense budget by approximately 50 percent. Dr. Jaime Suchlicki, a Cuban specialist at the University of Miami, was quoted as follows: "The bulk of the cuts, it seems, are going to be coming from the Air Force and the Navy. The Army will be cut somewhat, but not substantially. This is naturally the result of the crisis that Cuba is undergoing economically and the fact that Russia is not providing Cuba with the weapons and the support it was providing in the past." Transcript provided by the *Voice of America* via the Internet.

32. This document, titled "Update on the Cuban Refugee Program," was addressed to the U.S. Secretary of State, the CIA, and the Immigration and Naturalization Service from the U.S. Interests Section in Havana (January 1994, Reference

252 | Notes to Pages 173–77

#H/18422/693-4). It was published in *CUBA Informs You,* a publication of the Cuban Embassy in Ottawa, Canada (March 4, 1994).

33. See Sections 205(a) and 206 of the Cuban Liberty and Democratic Solidarity (LIBERTAD) Act of 1996, popularly known as the Helms-Burton law, where it is clearly stated that neither an interim transition administration that would prepare the island for democratic elections nor a (supposedly) democratically elected government can include either Fidel or Raúl Castro. In short, even if Cubans adhere to all of the requirements in the act designed to assure that elections are fair, Washington will not consider the country to be truly democratic and hence worthy of normalized, friendly relations with the United States if the voters' choice is Fidel or Raúl.

Looking beyond such legislative arrogance, the Cubans can point to various hemispheric precedents to support their contention that the U.S. commitment is not to democratic elections as such but only to elections that produce results that are consistent with or that further its hegemonic pretensions in the region. Two key examples are the Allende case in Chile (early 1970s) and Sandinista Nicaragua. In the latter instance, numerous international observer teams certified that the 1984 elections won by the incumbent Sandinistas were fair and democratic, but Washington continued to characterize the Nicaraguan government as "totalitarian" and to pursue policies aimed at overthrowing it.

34. This was the position of the Executive Branch even before the Helms-Burton law became effective in March 1996. Because Helms-Burton codified all the executive orders relevant to the blockade into law, the president no longer has the power to lift all or some of these measures within the context of normalization negotiations. Instead, congressional authorization is now necessary before any modifications can be made.

35. Wayne S. Smith, "U.S.-Cuban Relations: The View from Washington," in Erisman and Kirk, *Cuban Foreign Policy,* 88.

36. William I. Robinson, "Consensus in Washington on New Cuba Policy?" *NotiSur* 3, no. 8 (February 23, 1993), text provided via the Internet by the Cuba-L list.

37. For a summary of these plans and ambitions, see Schulz, *United States and Cuba,* 21–22.

38. Robinson, "Consensus in Washington." 4.

39. The U.S. State Department publishes an annual report containing its analysis of the human rights situation in Cuba. Normally the report is published in February for the previous year (e.g., the 1994 report was published in February 1995). Copies can be obtained from the State Department's Public Affairs Office.

40. These figures are presented in *CubaINFO* 6, no. 11 (September 1, 1994): 6. The entire issue is devoted to a chronology and summary of the rafter crisis.

41. For more information about Mariel and U.S.-Cuban migration issues in general, see Felix Roberto Masud-Piloto, *With Open Arms: Cuban Migration to the United States* (Totowa, N.J.: Rowman and Littlefield, 1988), and Kenneth N.

Skoug, Jr., *The United States and Cuba under Reagan and Shultz: A Foreign Service Officer Reports* (Westport, Conn.: Praeger Publishers, 1996).

42. Quoted in "Castro Threatens a Second Mariel," Associated Press news item (August 7, 1994) provided by the *NY Transfer News Collective* via the Internet.

43. The following data from *CubaINFO* 6, no. 11 (September 1, 1994), regarding Cuban refugee arrivals in the United States are illustrative of the heavy traffic in August 1994: August 21, 1,293; August 22, 2,548; August 23, 3,253; August 24, 3,096; August 25, 1,679; August 30, 1,582; and August 31, 2,044. Beyond these figures were a significant number of people who were assumed to have been lost at sea.

44. For details, see "Press Conference by the President—August 19, 1994," White House, Office of the Press Secretary, Washington, D.C., transcript downloaded from the White House's Internet website, and "Dire Straits," *Time,* August 29, 1994, 28–32.

45. Quoted in Ann Louise Bardach, "Mas Canosa: Mobster and Megalomaniac, Part 1: Our Man in Miami," *New Republic,* October 3, 1994, 1, transcript provided via the Internet.

46. For a much more detailed explanation of the U.S. position and the rationale behind it, see "Press Briefing by Secretary of Defense William Perry, Attorney General Janet Reno, Under Secretary of State for Political Affairs Peter Tarnoff, and Commissioner of the INS Doris Meissner—August 24, 1994," White House, Office of the Press Secretary, Washington, D.C., transcript downloaded from the White House's Internet website.

47. For more details, see "Statement by the Press Secretary—September 9, 1994," White House, Office of the Press Secretary, Washington, D.C., transcript downloaded from the White House's Internet website; "Good Cop, Bad Cop," *Time,* September 12, 1994, 48–49; and "US, Cuba Reach Immigration Accord, Exodus Halts," *CubaINFO* 6, no. 12 (September 22, 1994): 1–6.

48. Claiborne Pell, "Time to Overhaul United States Policy toward Cuba," *Congressional Record—Senate* (January 5, 1995), transcript provided via the Internet.

49. Summarized from information provided in "Helms Legislation Targets Cuba, Foreign Investors," *CubaINFO* 7, no. 3 (February 23, 1995): 2.

50. Perhaps the most detailed statement of the administration's position can be found in Alexander Watson (assistant secretary of state for inter-American affairs), "United States Policy toward Cuba—Testimony before the Western Hemisphere Subcommittee of the House Committee on International Relations, 16 March 1995," U.S. Department of State, Bureau for Inter-American Affairs, Washington, D.C., transcript downloaded from the Department of State's Internet website. See also "Watson Testifies on Helms-Burton Cuba Legislation," *CubaINFO* 7, no. 5 (April 6, 1995): 3–4.

51. Quoted in "Clinton on Helms-Burton Bill and Overall Cuba Policy," *CubaINFO* 7, no. 6 (April 27, 1995): 5.

254 | Notes to Pages 180–83

52. The full text of the agreement as well as reaction to it, including information about the protest resignations of the State Department's two top Cuba desk officers, can be found in *CubaINFO* 7, no. 7 (May 18, 1995): 1–8. Copies of the agreement can also be obtained from the White House Internet website at www2.whitehouse.gov.

53. See Executive Office of the President, Office of Management and Budget, "Statement of Administration Policy, H.R. 927 [Helms/Burton Bill]" (September 20, 1995), and Secretary of State, "Letter Sent to the Speaker of the House of Representatives" (September 20, 1995). Documents provided by the Cuba-L list via the Internet.

54. Editorial, "Confronting Castro," *Journal of Commerce.* Reprinted in the *San Jose Mercury News,* September 27, 1995. Text provided by the Cuba-L list via the Internet.

55. Details about this meeting can be found in "Businesses Press to End Cuban Embargo, U.S. Is Challenged to Justify Keeping Havana a 'Special Case,'" *New York Times,* August 27, 1995 (text provided via the Internet by the Cuba-L list). Such lobbying was applauded and encouraged in an editorial titled "Helpful Corporate Pressure on Cuba," *New York Times,* September 4, 1995 (text provided via the Internet by the Cuba-L list).

56. For details, see Michael McGuire, "Freer Cuba Travel Raises Trade Hope," *Chicago Tribune,* October 13, 1995 (text provided via the Internet by the Cuba-L list), and "47 CEOs Dine with Castro after Same-Day White House Briefing," *CubaINFO* 7, no. 13 (October 12, 1995): 6.

57. The Senate also eliminated another controversial portion of the proposed bill that would have denied U.S. visas to any person (and the family of any person) who "trafficked" in the expropriated property of U.S. (i.e., Cuban-American) citizens. Like Title III, this provision was designed to intimidate foreigners who might otherwise be inclined to invest in Cuba.

58. For a good summary of the incident and Washington's initial response, see Tom Weiner, "U.S. Takes Cuban Air Action to U.N. Security Council," *New York Times,* February 26, 1996 (text provided via the Internet).

59. Washington did not get everything it wanted from the Security Council. The original U.S. draft resolution called for condemnation of the attack as an illegitimate use of force in violation of international law and a threat to international order. The language in the final version was less harsh, stating only that the council "strongly deplored" the incident. In the often arcane world of diplomatic semantics, this shift in emphasis was significant since it suggested that the United Nations was unlikely to be interested in considering any additional, more severe sanctions.

60. For a summary of the provisions of the compromise bill, see U.S. Information Agency, "Congress Nears Passage of Stronger Cuba Sanctions," March 5, 1996 (text downloaded from the USIA's Internet website).

61. Canada, for example, immediately reaffirmed its previously announced

Notes to Pages 183–94 | 255

intention to challenge Title III as a violation of the NAFTA treaty if Helms-Burton did indeed become U.S. law.

62. On August 24, 1996, Clinton appointed Undersecretary of Commerce for International Trade Stuart Eizenstat to serve as the administration's "Special Representative for Promotion of Democracy in Cuba," his main responsibility being to try to defuse international opposition to the Helms-Burton law in general and Title III in particular.

63. For details, see "Title III Waiver Satisfies Few," *CubaINFO* 9, no. 1 (January 15, 1997): 4–5.

64. "State Department Slaps Sherritt Again," *CubaINFO* 9, no. 4 (March 20, 1997): 2.

65. A good example of this line of analysis can be found in Wayne Smith, "The Pope's Visit to Cuba: Who Won, Who Lost?" *CubaINFO* 10, no. 2 (January 29, 1998): 11–12.

66. Although the percentages given indicate a slight advantage for the pro-blockade position in 1998, the margin of error in such polls is usually 2–4 percentage points (depending on the size of the sample and how closely it mirrors the country's overall demographics). This means that any of the figures given could be off by 2–4 points. Consequently no definitive conclusions can be reached regarding the 1998 results because, in contrast to their 1996 counterparts, they do not "beat the spread."

67. This quote as well as additional material regarding television and press coverage of the papal visit can be found in "Politics-U.S.: Sex, Lies Trump Pope, Castro for U.S. Media," Inter Press Service news report, dateline Washington, D.C., January 23, 1998 (downloaded from CNN's Custom News Service website on the Internet).

68. Christopher Marquis, "Pentagon Calls Cuban Armed Forces Weak," *Miami Herald,* March 29, 1998 (downloaded from the *Herald*'s Internet website).

69. Marquis, "Pentagon Calls."

70. Quoted in "Republican Senators, Former U.S. Officials Ask Clinton for Cuba Policy Review," *CUBAInfo* 10, no. 14 (October 26, 1998): 2.

71. Corporate disenchantment with the Cuban blockade contributed significantly to the creation in April 1997 of a coalition called USA Engage, to oppose unilateral trade/investment sanctions (including those against such countries as Iran and Libya). Organized and led by the National Foreign Trade Council, the group quickly attracted over 400 companies as members supporting its basic belief that economic embargoes do not in most cases represent a rational approach to foreign affairs, since they seldom achieve their larger policy goals but cost the United States billions of dollars in commercial opportunities and thousands of jobs.

72. An earlier incident demonstrating this mind-set had occurred in September, when Washington refused to issue Alamar Associates the documents necessary for a trip to Havana that it was planning as part of a U.S.-Cuban business seminar

256 | Notes to Pages 194–200

essentially identical to one it had organized without any complications six months earlier (March 1998), thereby in effect obliterating much of the project's attraction. For details, see "Clinton Administration Withdraws Approval for Cuban Business Summit," *CUBAInfo* 10, no. 12 (September 10, 1998): 4–5.

73. The voting data were drawn from "U.N. Commission Approves Resolution Criticizing Cuba," *CubaINFO* 8, no. 6 (May 2, 1996): 7; "U.S. Wins Cuba Vote," *CubaINFO* 9, no. 6 (May 1, 1997): 4–5; and "U.S. Resolution on Cuban Human Rights Fails at the U.N.," *CubaINFO* 10, no. 6 (April 30, 1998): 3–4.

74. Data and information from "Global Opposition to U.S. Embargo Expressed in U.N. Vote," *CubaINFO* 6, no. 14 (November 3, 1994): 4–5; "UN and Cuba," Reuters news item (November 2, 1995) provided via the Internet by the Cuba-L list; "Open for Business," *Time,* February 20, 1995, 52–53; "UN Votes to Condemn Cuban Embargo," *CubaINFO* 8, no. 15 (November 21, 1996): 3; "In Overwhelming Vote, U.N. Protests Embargo on Cuba," *CubaINFO* 9, no. 15 (November 13, 1997): 1; and "Cuba Wins Another U.N. Victory against U.S. Embargo," *CubaINFO* 10, no. 14 (October 26, 1998): 2.

75. Editorial, "The Hammer That Failed on Cuba," *New York Times,* November 8, 1993 (text provided via the Internet).

76. For example, in January 1995 there was some sentiment in Congress to link approval of a loan guarantee to Mexico to a cessation of its Cuban aid programs (e.g., helping Havana resolve the problem of its debt to Mexico through equity swaps or discount arrangements). Mexico insisted that such provisions not be included in any loan guarantee program, and the Clinton administration agreed. In another instance, the U.S. Treasury Department in June 1995 added four subsidiaries of the Canadian mining firm Sherritt International Incorporated to its list of companies being blacklisted for trading with and/or investing in the island via joint ventures with Cuban state enterprises, thus subjecting them to the same blockade sanctions as are applied to Cuba under U.S. law. Sherritt and the Canadian government insisted that the action was designed not only to punish Sherritt for doing business with Cuba but also to signal Canadians in general that Washington was willing to retaliate if they insisted upon maintaining cooperative relations with Havana.

77. Details concerning these developments can be found in items provided via the Internet Cuba-L list: Martin Crutsinger, "Canada Unhappy," Associated Press wire report, dateline Washington, D.C., March 5, 1996; Gary Abramson, "Allies Criticize U.S. Effort to Squelch Investment in Cuba," Associated Press wire report, dateline Madrid, March 6, 1996; and Bruce Barnard of the *Journal of Commerce,* "European Union Warns U.S. on Cuba Sanctions," March 6, 1996.

78. Quoted from "Eugenia Charles of Dominica on Cuba," *CubaINFO* 5, no. 3 (February 26, 1993): 3.

79. Quoted from "Eugenia Charles on Independence of Caribbean Foreign Policy," *CubaINFO* 5, no. 5 (April 12, 1993): 4.

80. For an overview and analysis of recent developments in Havana's relations

with the CARICOM countries, see Erisman, "Evolving Cuban-CARICOM Relations," 45–66.

81. "Chile, Cuba Restore Relations; U.S. Protests," *CubaINFO* 7, no. 6 (April 27, 1995): 7–8.

82. The CDA—the two main provisions of which prohibited subsidiaries of U.S. companies located in third countries (e.g., Canada or England) from trading with Cuba and imposed a six-month exclusion from U.S. ports on any ship that visited the island—cleared Congress shortly thereafter and was signed into law by President Bush in late October 1992 (just before the presidential balloting).

83. This information was taken from Wayne S. Smith, "Our Cuba Diplomacy: A Critical Examination," *International Policy Report* (Washington, D.C.: Center for International Policy, October 1994), 2–5, where more details concerning the Clinton/CANF connection can be found.

84. These reactions are discussed in "Cuban-American Nixed in Clinton Cabinet," *NY News Transfer Update*, no. 156, January 24, 1993 (text provided via the Internet by the Cuba-L list), and Jorge I. Domínguez, "U.S. Policy toward Cuba in the 1980s and 1990s," *Annals of the American Academy of Political and Social Science* 533 (May 1994): 173–74.

85. Yvette Collymore, "Cuba-U.S.: Clinton Plays to Moderate Cuban-Americans," InterPress Agency, October 6, 1995 (news item provided via the Internet).

7. Conclusion

1. This information comes from "Cuba Sees Economy Growing at Least Four Percent in 1999," a Reuters news report, dateline Havana, September 1, 1999 (downloaded from the CubaNet website on the Internet).

2. These data were found in "Cuban Economy to Recover," a XINHUA news report, dateline Havana, August 31, 1999 (downloaded from CNN's Internet website).

3. This summary was provided in "Cuba Approves Tough Anti-Crime, Anti-Dissent Laws," *CUBAInfo* 11, no. 3 (February 22, 1999): 8–9. As its title indicates, there also was a second law passed that cracked down on more conventional crime concerns such as drug trafficking, prostitution, and violent robberies.

4. The royal visit ultimately did take place in conjunction with the Ibero-American Summit meeting in Havana on November 15–16, 1999.

5. These data were taken from "Victory in Geneva: Castro Loses, Cuban People Win as United Nations Votes to Condemn Regime's Human Rights Abuses," a PSNewswire report, dateline Miami, April 23, 1999 (downloaded from CNN's Internet website).

6. Quoted in Serge Kovaleski, "Cuba Replaces Foreign Minister with Top Aide to Castro," a Washington Post Foreign Service news report, dateline Miami, May 29, 1999 (downloaded from the *Washington Post*'s Internet website).

7. It would appear that the model for this arrangement is the 1980 San José Accords, whereby Venezuela and Mexico pledged to provide various Caribbean

258 | Notes to Pages 212–16

Basin countries a total of 160,000 barrels of oil per day on terms favorable to the recipients. Indeed this initiative in certain respects represented a joint foreign aid program by the two countries, which is still in operation today. Chávez first wanted to bring Cuba into the San José pact, but Mexico balked at the idea (probably fearing that such a move would unduly complicate its relations with Washington). With this avenue closed off, Caracas then proceeded to explore the possibilities for a separate deal with Havana.

8. During a December 1998 research trip to Havana, I discussed the proposed review commission with numerous Cuban academics and governmental officials who specialize in foreign affairs. The exchanges were interesting, for it was I who was highly skeptical about the commission's prospects, while the Cubans were more inclined to give the Clinton administration the benefit of some doubt and thereby envision that it would respond positively. Indeed, they often gently chided me for being too cynical.

9. Quoted in "U.S. Eases Restrictions but Rejects Bipartisan Policy Review," *CUBAInfo* 11, no. 1 (January 11, 1999): 2.

10. For details, see *CUBAInfo* 11, no. 1 (January 11, 1999): 1–3, and "U.S. Eases Travel Restrictions, Allows Limited Sales to Cuba," *CUBAInfo* 11, no. 7 (May 25, 1999): 1–3.

11. Continuing his practice of protecting foreign nationals from lawsuits under the Helms-Burton law, Clinton in July 1999 once again suspended implementation of the relevant provisions of the Title III section of the legislation for six months. As already noted, the White House, responding to criticism of Title III from Canada, Mexico, and various EU governments, had routinely taken such action ever since Helms-Burton had gone into effect.

12. For two interesting news analyses of these developments written by reporters generally not sympathetic to the Castro government, see Serge F. Kovaleski, "Warming Up a Cold War, Castro Cracks Down on Cubans Sympathetic to U.S. Policies," *Washington Post,* February 23, 1999, A13, and Juan O. Tamayo, "Cuba Wary of Clinton Campaign for People-to-People Contacts," *Miami Herald,* March 22, 1999 (downloaded from the *Herald*'s Internet webpage dealing with Cuban news).

13. More information about the Bush and Gore positions can be found in Christopher Marquis, "Candidate Takes Hard Line on Castro," *Miami Herald,* August 21, 1999 (downloaded from the *Herald*'s Internet webpage dealing with Cuban news).

14. See John McLaughlin, *One on One,* with guests Cuban dissident Omar Lopez Montenegro and Cuba experts Pamala Falk and Philip Brenner, taped January 8, 1993 (transcript provided via the Internet by the Cuba-L list).

15. Rich Kaplowitz, "U.S. Subsidiary Trade with Cuba," 245.

16. The *New York Times* reported in August 1995 that pressure from the business community to lift the blockade was growing. Not only had various corporate

executives begun to call publicly for normalization of relations, but (perhaps more important) they had also been increasingly assertive in making their case via private meetings with the Clinton administration. For more information, see "Businesses Press to End Cuba Embargo," August 27. A key element in this story reads as follows: "'Pressure is growing,' a Clinton administration official said, speaking on condition of anonymity. 'Businessmen are expressing interest in a transition in Cuba and complaining that all the deals down there are being cut by foreign competitors. There's a very high degree of business interest in Cuba.' [But] so far, Clinton administration officials have responded only by restating long-held positions." The *Times* commented favorably on this development in an early September 1995 editorial, stating that "if the executives are serious about changing Cuba policy, they need to help the administration find the courage to take on the conservative exile lobby, and make their wishes known to Congress. They are on the right track." See "Helpful Corporate Pressure on Cuba," *New York Times,* September 4, 1995 (news item provided via the Internet by the Cuba-L list).

17. These figures are reported in "News Report Says Careful Investors Can Profit in Cuba," *CUBAInfo* 9, no. 12 (September 11, 1997): 7.

18. See "US Survey Considers Cuba a Safe Place for International Investments," April 10, 1995 (transcript of CubaNews from Radio Havana Cuba provided via the Internet). Cuba is reported as being ranked approximately 26th to 28th in the survey. The rankings of some other countries were PRC 48, Vietnam 75, Brazil and Venezuela both 88, and Russia 98.

19. A good survey of this emerging business interest can be found in Juan O. Tamayo, "U.S. Firms Rush to Explore Cuban Market," *Miami Herald,* February 1, 1999 (downloaded from the *Herald*'s Internet website).

20. Quoted from "Pushed by Farmers, Liberals, Conservatives Push to Ease Cuba Sanctions," an Associated Press wire report, dateline Washington, D.C., August 5, 1999 (downloaded from CNN's Internet website).

21. Tamayo, "U.S. Firms Rush," reported that Archer Daniels Midland, which is headquartered in Peoria, Illinois, and is one of the largest agro-corporations in the United States, had announced in January 1999 that it had on hand a substantial sales order from Cuba and that it intended to be aggressive in seeking Washington's authorization to close the deal. Archer Daniels Midland did not identify the buyer, although existing legislation prohibited doing business directly with the Cuban government or any of its agencies. Given this preexisting interest in trading with the island, observers were not surprised that the corporation strongly supported and enthusiastically participated in the Ryan visit to Havana.

22. This information and more about the business community's growing interest in trading with Cuba can be found in Karen DeYoung, "U.S. Businesses Encouraged to Explore Trade with Cuba," *Washington Post,* July 28, 1999, A1.

23. On November 3–5, 1999, I participated in an international academic conference held at the Universidade Estadual Paulista in Araraquara, Brazil, dealing

260 | Note to Page 222

with the topic "Inter-American Relations: Continuities and Change on the Verge of a New Millennium." Various members of the Cuban delegation that had been invited indicated, both privately and within the public context of the conference, that Havana supported the Neo-Bolivarian concept in general and specifically was hopeful that a much higher level of ACS-MERCOSUR collaboration would be forthcoming in the near future.

Index

ACP (Africa/Caribbean/Pacific) Group,
130–31
ACS (Association of Caribbean States), 47,
159–60, 212, 221
Cuba as a charter member of, 164
and Cuban foreign policy interests, 165–
66, 166–67, 222–23
founding of, 163–64
Mexican role in, 165
and NAFTA, as a response to, 164
pessimistic views of, 165
Afghanistan crisis, 116
and Cuba's Third World leadership aspi-
rations, undermining of, 103–4
AFL-CIO, 218
ALADI (Latin American Integration Asso-
ciation), 160
Alarcón, Ricardo, 33, 211–12
Albright, Madeleine, 213
Algeria, Cuban involvement in its dispute
with Morocco, 66, 93
Allende, Salvador, 83, 218
Alliance for Progress, 98
Andean Group, 159, 160, 166
Angola, 67, 81, 116, 169
Cuban military involvement in, 94–96
Antigua and Barbuda, 124
Arawak Indians, 11
Argentina, 84, 92, 120
Ashcroft, John, 218
Association of Caribbean States. See ACS
Auténtico Party, 15

Baeza, Mario, 201–2, 203
Bardach, Ann, 177
Barbados, 84
Bargaining power, 46, 93–94, 157, 162.
See also Counterdependency politics
Batista, Fulgencio, 39, 40, 55

1952 coup by, 16–17
political career of, 14–18
as a Yankee puppet, 24
Bay of Pigs, 60–62
Ben Bella, Ahmed, 66
Betancourt, Rómulo, 63
Biotechnology industry (Cuban), 126–27,
219
and Brazil, 133–34
Bishop, Maurice, 87, 88, 90. See also
Grenada
Bolívar, Simón, 222
Bolivia, 91, 170
Bonsal, Philip, 56
Brazil, 91, 92, 122
Brezhnev Doctrine, Cuban endorsement of,
76
Brothers to the Rescue (BTTR) crisis, 182,
190
Brundenius, Claes, 7
Burton, Dan, 179
Bush, George, 175, 202, 203
Bush, George W., 214–15, 220
Bush, Jeb, 215

Cabrisas, Ricardo, 163
Canada, 123–24, 139, 159
and Cuba, foreign aid to, 135
and Cuba, private investment in, 135–36
and Cuba, refusal to break relations
with, 124, 134
and Cuba, relations with, 134–36
and the Cuban human rights record,
reaction to, 209–10
and the Helms-Burton law, opposition
to, 199
and the Torricelli law, opposition to,
135, 198
tourism to Cuba, 135

262 | Index

CANF (Cuban American National Foundation), 50, 180, 201–2, 203, 215, 216, 218, 225. *See also* Mas Canosa, Jorge
Caporaso, James, 46
Cardenas, José, 218
Caribbean Committee of Development and Cooperation (CCDC), 84
Caribbean Forum (CariForum). *See* CARICOM
Caribbean Legion, 63
Caribbean Multinational Shipping Company (NAMACUR), 85
Caribbean Tourism Organization (CTO), 129, 161
CARICOM (Caribbean Community and Common Market), 124, 159, 221
and the Caribbean Forum, Cuban membership in, 163
Cuba and observer status in, 162–63
and Cuban foreign policy interests, 130–31, 166–67
Cuban relations with, 127–31, 160–63, 166–67
and the Lomé process, 130–31
and U.S. policy toward Cuba, opposition to, 199–200
CARIFTA (Caribbean Free Trade Association), 159
Carter, James (Jimmy), 176, 204
Castro, Raúl, 33, 173
Castro Ruz, Fidel
assumes power in Cuba, 18
biographical sketch of, 16
charismatic qualities of, 30
declares himself a Marxist (1961), 62
and drug trafficking accusations, 191
guerrilla war against the Batista government, 17–19
inexperience with economic policy, 50
nationalist credentials of, 24, 52–53
potential successors of, 33, 211–12
and the socialist nature of the Cuban Revolution, declaration of (1961), 62
state visit to Moscow by (1963), 72
trail of, 17

CBI (Caribbean Basin Initiative), 123
Central American Common Market (CACM), 165
Chamorro, Violetta, 89, 119, 125
Charles, Eugenia, 199
Chávez, Hugo, 212–13
Chilcote, Ronald, 41
Chile, 83, 133, 200, 218
China. *See* PRC
Chrétien, Jean, 210
CIA (Central Intelligence Agency), 95
and Fidel Castro, attempts to assassinate, 60
and Guatemala, overthrow of Arbenz government in, 61
Ciboney Indians, 11–12
Cienfuegos naval revolt, 18
Cienfuegos oil refinery, 212
Civic Resistance, 18
Clinton administration, relations with Cuba
amateurism, propensity toward, 202–4
and conventional diplomatic considerations, 195–200
Cuban migration, policies regarding, 177, 178, 180
Cuban policies, key components of, 174–75
Cuban policies, reactive versus proactive, 204
economic blockade, actions regarding, 177–78, 181–82, 183–84, 190, 202, 213–14
and electoral politics, 175, 184
and the Helms-Burton law, initial opposition to, 179–80
perspectives upon, 195–205
policy review commission, rejection of, 193–94, 213
and political/electoral expediency, 200–202, 204–5
See also Normalization of U.S./Cuban relations
Clinton, William (Bill), 180
and foreign affairs, inexperience and disinterest in, 203

CMEA (Council for Mutual Economic Assistance), 9, 91, 143, 155, 157
Cuba gains membership in, 77
and Cuban dual-tracking, 79–80
disbands (1991), 105, 111
Coard, Bernard, 90
Collective bargaining, 47, 162, 166. *See also* Counterdependency politics
Collymore, Yvette, 202
Colombia, 73, 84, 104, 122, 124, 166
Columbus, Christopher, 11
COMECON. *See* CMEA
Commonwealth of Independent States (CIS), 111
Congo-Brazzaville, 67, 93
Contadora Group, 91
Containment Doctrine, 52, 98, 207. *See also* U.S. foreign policy
Costa Rica, 84, 85, 127
Counterdependency politics, 20, 143–44, 145, 157–58, 206–7, 213, 220–23, 224–25
and assertive bargaining, 45–47
and bargaining power, 46, 93–94
and collective bargaining, 47, 144, 162
concept explained, 42–47
and developmental coalition-building, 79
and diversification, 43–45, 79
and diversification strategy, criticisms of, 44
and effective sovereignty, 45, 46
and the Lomé process, 162
and revolutionary internationalism, 67, 71
and selective delinkage, 43–44
See also Cuban foreign policy: and developmental coalition-building; and diversification; and dual-tracking
Cuba
armed forces, reduction of, 172, 190–91
demographic profile of, 3
economic crisis in, 9–10, 106–7, 113–14, 146–47, 196
economic profile of, 3–11, 107–8, 113–14, 142–43, 146–47, 148–49, 208–9

economic recovery in, 10, 146–47, 196
economic reforms in, 11, 137–38, 146–47, 171
foreign investment in, 132–33
foreign investment laws of, 137–38, 146–47, 171
geographic profile of, 2–3
historical profile of, 11–19
natural resources of, 3
population of, 3
as a potential U.S. trading partner, 216–17
as a security threat to the U.S., 190–91
social development profile of, 3–4, 8–9, 10
Spanish colonization of, 11
and Third World development, as a model for, 2–3
U.S. occupation of, 13
Cuban Communist Party (PCC), 74
Cuban Constitution
of 1902, 13, 21, 40
of 1940, 15
Cuban Democracy Act (CDA). *See* Torricelli law
Cuban developmental aid
basic elements of, 99–100
compared to U.S. and Soviet efforts, 98–99
data on, 99–100
to Grenada, 87–88
to Sandinista Nicaragua, 88
Cuban exile community, 50, 215–16
and Bay of Pigs invasion, 61
Cuban foreign debt
barter payment plans, 122
debt-for-equity swaps, 122–23
renegotiation of, 6
repayment suspended, 137
with Socialist bloc, 6
with USSR, 6, 77, 108
with Western Europe, 137
with Western nations, 6
Cuban foreign policy
and Brothers to the Rescue (BTTR) crisis, 182

264 | Index

Cuban foreign policy—*continued*
 and developmental coalition-building,
  79, 143–44, 146, 158–67, 221–23
 and diversification of political/economic
  relations, 79, 82–85, 91–92, 143,
  146, 148–58, 225
 and dual-tracking, 79–82, 82–83, 93–
  94, 98–100, 103, 148, 156–57, 223
 and Fidelista personalismo, 30–33
 and guerrilla warfare (*see* Revolutionary
  internationalism)
 nationalistic dimensions, 52–53
 and Neo-Bolivarianism, 222–23
 and Neo-PanAmericanism, 221–22
 and the Nonaligned Movement, 100–104
 and normalization of U.S. relations,
  attitudes toward, 168–69, 213,
  223–24
 pragmatic security considerations,
  impact of, 25–26
 and the Realist scenario, 23–26
 and revolutionary messianics, 26–30
 security interests, conceptualizations of,
  24–25, 106, 147–48, 157–58, 208
 and South-South relations, 80–82, 100–
  104, 115–16, 143–44, 148, 157
 and the surrogate/superclient theses,
  33–36
 and the Third World debt crisis, 115–16
 and Third World leadership aspirations,
  100–104
 and the USSR, disputes with, 68, 70–73,
  74–75
 and the USSR, reconciliation with,
  76–78
 See also Normalization of U.S./Cuban
  relations
Cuban foreign trade, 117–23, 148–56
 with Argentina, 134
 with Asian countries, 138–41, 151–55,
  161
 with Brazil, 133–34
 with Canada, 120, 134–36, 155
 with CARICOM countries, 129, 130,
  161–62
 with Central American countries,
  125–27

 with CMEA, 108–9, 111–12
 with Colombia, 131–32
 with Eastern European countries, 149–
  51, 152, 155–56, 161
 with France, 157
 with Japan, 139–41, 154–55
 with Mexico, 92, 131–33
 with the PRC, 139, 140–41, 155
 with Russia, 155–56
 with the USSR, 68–69, 76–77, 108–9,
  111–12
 with Venezuela, 131–32
 with Western European countries, 136–
  38, 149–51, 152, 155
 with Western Hemisphere countries,
  119–20, 124–36, 149–51, 152
Cuban Missile Crisis, 25
 Cuban anger over Soviet handling of,
  68–70
Cuban Revolution
 institutionalization of, 32
 messianic reputation, reasons for, 27–28
Cuban security aid, 93–94
 to Angola, 94–96
 to Ethiopia, 96–97
 to Grenada, 88
 to Sandinista Nicaragua, 88–90, 170
Czechoslovakia, 76
Czech Republic, 210

Debray, Regis, 73
de Céspedes, Carlos Manuel, 12, 14,
 20
Demas, William, 43
Dependency theory, 36–42
 and the comprador class, 39
 and Cuba, 37, 39, 40
 dependency defined, 41
 and effective sovereignty, 41
 and import substitution, 37
 and a penetrated political system, 38–
  39, 41, 42
 radical conception of, 37–39
 and U.S. foreign policy, 40, 42
Developmental coalition-building. *See*
 Counterdependency politics; Cuban foreign policy

Index | 265

Developmental coalitions
types of, 158–59
in the Western Hemisphere, 159–60
Diaz-Balart, Lincoln, 215
Distributive justice, 4, 7–9
Diversification of political/economic relations. *See* Counterdependency politics;
Cuban foreign policy
Domínguez, Jorge, 33, 59, 81, 92, 107–8,
109, 223
Dominican Republic, 211, 212
Dual-tracking. *See* Cuban foreign policy
Dulles, Allen, 60
Duncan, Raymond, 71

ECLA (Economic Commission for Latin
America), 5, 36
Ecuador, 84
Effective sovereignty, 207. *See also*
Counterdependency politics; Dependency theory
Eisenhower, Dwight, 55, 56, 203
eliminates Cuba's sugar quota, 58–59
Eizenstat, Stuart, 186, 191, 192, 203–4
El Salvador, 87, 89, 91
Eritrea, 96, 97
Escalante, Aníbal, 74–75
Ethiopia, 81
Cuban military involvement in, 96–97
EU (European Union), 159
and the Helms-Burton law, compromise
over, 192–93
and the Helms-Burton law, opposition
to, 186–88, 191–93, 198–99
and the Lomé process, 130–31, 162–63
and the Torricelli law, opposition to,
198

Figueres, José, 63
FMLN (Farabundo Martí Front for National Liberation), 87
Cuban aid to, 170
FNLA (National Front for the Liberation
of Angola), 94, 95
France, 136
Free Trade Area of the Americas, 222
Frei, Eduardo, 83
Frost, Robert, 1, 206

GATT (General Agreement on Tariffs and
Trade), 180
GDP (Gross Domestic Product), Cuban
growth rates of, 9, 113, 147, 208
General Strike in Cuba (1958), 18
German Democratic Republic (East Germany), 110, 136
Germany, 136
Gini coefficient, 7
GNP (Gross National Product), Cuban
growth rates of, 5, 113
Gómez, Gen. Máximo, 12
González, Edward, 35, 77
Gorbachev, Mikhail, 105, 111
Gore, Al, 214, 215, 220
Grabendorff, Wolf, 93–94
Grau San Martín, Ramón, 14, 15, 17
Great Man theory of politics, 30–31
Greene, Graham, 1
Grenada
relations with Cuba, 87–88, 124,
128–29
U.S. invasion of, 90, 128
Group of 77 (G-77), 47
Guantanamo Bay (naval base), 2, 168,
173, 177, 178, 180
Guatemala, 87, 90, 127, 211
Guerrilla warfare. *See* Revolutionary internationalism
Guevara, Ernesto "Che," 18, 50, 63, 67
biographical sketch of, 19
guerrilla activities in Africa, 93
murdered in Bolivia, 73
and revolutionary internationalism, 26
Guinea, 67, 93
Guyana, 84

Hagel, Charles, 218
Haig, Alexander, 89
Haile Mariam, Mengistu, 96, 97
Haile Selassi (Emperor of Ethiopia), 96
Helms-Burton law (1996), 50, 145,
179–84
as an abuse of Cuban human rights,
195–96
compromise on, by Clinton administration and Congress, 183

266 | Index

Helms-Burton law —*continued*
and Cuban elections, demands concerning, 173, 195
destroying the Cuban Revolution, goal of, 182, 224
international opposition to, 184, 185, 186–88, 191–93, 198–99
main provisions of, 179
Title III, suspension of, 184–85, 186–87
U.S. business community, opposition to, 180–81
and U.S. economic blockade, transfers control of to Congress, 183–84, 215
U.S. House of Representatives, action on, 180, 184
U.S.Senate, action on, 181, 184
See also U.S. trade embargo (blockade) against Cuba
Helms, Jesse, 178, 218
Hemingway, Ernest, 1
Herter, Christian, 55–56
Hispaniola, 2
Human rights
Cuban conception of, 172, 173
Cuban policy on, as a reaction to U.S. hostility, 209
Cuban record on, 172–73, 196–97, 209–11
U.S. conception of, 172, 173

Ibero-American summit conference (1999), 212
International Bauxite Association (IBA), 47
International behavior, motivations of, 19–20, 22
Israel, 197

Jamaica, 84, 90, 124, 165
Johnson, Lyndon, 72
Joint ventures, 137–138. *See also* Cuba (foreign investment laws)

Kennedy, John F., 61
Kissinger, Henry, 81, 193
Kosygin, Aleksei, 72

LAFTA (Latin American Free Trade Association), 160

Lage, Carlos, 33, 194, 211
Latin American and Caribbean Sugar Group (GEPLACEA), 84
Latin American Energy Organization (OLADE), 84
LeoGrande, William, 69, 76, 102
Levesque, Jacques, 72
Lewinsky (Monica) scandal, 188–89, 190, 194, 204
Lomé process, 130–31, 144
and the Caribbean Forum, 163
and Cuban foreign policy interests, 131, 162–63
Lost Revolution. *See* Revolution of 1933

Machado, Geraldo, 13–14
Manifest Destiny, 51
Mariel boatlift, 176–77, 204
Marquis, Christopher, 191
Marshall Plan, 98
Martí, José, 12–13, 20, 65
Mas Canosa, Jorge, 175, 216
Clinton administration, influence on, 177–78, 201–2
MERCOSUR (Southern Cone Common Market), 159, 160, 166, 221
Cuban foreign policy interests in, 222–23
Mexican Revolution, 27
Mexico, 92, 104, 120
and the Helms-Burton law, opposition to, 199
and NAFTA, 132, 199
private investment in Cuba, 132–33
refusal to break relations with Cuba, 124
Minh, Ho Chi, 138
Moncada Barracks, 17
Montaner, Carlos, 31
Movement of Nonaligned Nations (NAM), 47
Cuba as a charter member of, 100
Cuba's leadership of and the Afghan crisis, 103–4
Cuba's leadership of, impact on Cuban-Soviet relations, 102–3
Cuba's nonaligned credentials, 100–102
Moynihan, Daniel, 35
Mozambique, 67

MPLA (Popular Movement for the Liberation of Angola), 94, 95

NAFTA (North American Free Trade Agreement), 123, 132, 159, 164, 165, 180
Namibia, 94, 95, 96, 116, 169
Nathan, Peter, 219
National Revolutionary Union (Guatemala), 87
Nationalization disputes (U.S./Cuba), 53–54, 58, 59, 168
Neo-Bolivarianism, 221, 222
Neo-PanAmericanism, 221–22
Neto, Agostinho, 95, 139
New Jewel Movement (Grenada), 87–88
Nicaragua, 87, 88–90, 91, 125
Nickel industry (Cuba), 10, 108, 114, 136
Nixon, Richard, 203, 218
Nonaligned Movement (NAM). See Movement of Nonaligned Nations
Normalization of U.S./Cuban relations
  conservative U.S. support for, 216
  Cuban attitudes toward, 168–69, 213, 223–24
  Cuban exile community support for, 215–16
  and the Cuban Revolution, destruction of, 169, 214
  new U.S. groups supporting, 215–19, 225
  no-rapprochement scenario, 223–24
  pessimism about, 204–5, 219–20
  prospects for, on Cuban terms, 224–25
  U.S. attitudes toward, 144–45, 167–68, 169–74, 213–20
  U.S. business community, support for, 194, 216–17, 219
  U.S. farming community, support for, 217–18
  U.S. hard-line school toward, 144–45, 191, 193, 214–15
  U.S. labor unions, support for, 218
  U.S. moderate school toward, 145
  U.S. pharmaceutical companies, support for, 219
  U.S. preconditions for, 169–73, 195–96
  U.S. public opinion concerning, 189

U.S. state governments, support for, 218–19
  See also Clinton administration; Cuban foreign policy; U.S. foreign policy
North Vietnam, Cuban relations with, 138

OAS (Organization of American States), 81
  Cuban government expelled from (1962), 64
  1960 Foreign Ministers' Meeting (San José, Costa Rica), 60–61
  1962 Foreign Ministers' Meeting (Puenta del Este, Uruguay), 64
  sanctions against Cuba rescinded (1975), 85
Oil. See Cuban foreign trade; Petroleum industry
OLAS (Organization of Latin American Solidarity), 73
OPEC (Organization of Petroleum-Exporting Countries), 47
Ortega, Daniel, 88–89
Ortodoxo Party, 16

Panama, 84, 92
Payne, Anthony, 35
Peaceful coexistence, Cuban/Soviet dispute over, 69–70
Pérez Roque, Felipe, 211
Peru, 83, 85, 122
Petroleum industry (Cuba), 113, 114, 161
  Cuba as a oil exporter, 5, 109
  triangular oil trade among Cuba, USSR, and Venezuela, 131–32
  U.S/Cuban confrontation over (1960), 59
Philippines, 13
Platt Amendment, 13, 20, 40, 51, 195
Poland, 210
Political gangsterism, 15–16
Pope John Paul II, visit to Cuba, 188–90
Popular Socialist Party (PSP), 74
Power politics, 23
PQLI (Physical Quality of Life Index), 8–9
PRC (People's Republic of China), 147
  and Cuba, 138–39
Prebisch, Raul, 37
Prio Socarrás, Carlos, 15, 16

268 | Index

Proletarian internationalism, 82–83, 85, 170
de-emphasized by Cuba, 75–76
defined, 28
See also Revolutionary internationalism
Puerto Rico, 13
Public opinion polls. See U.S. foreign policy

Radio Martí, 175
Rafter crisis (1994), 176–78
Ramphal, Sir Shridath, 163
Ravenhill, James, 46
Reagan, Ronald, 86, 90, 193
Reagan Doctrine, 86, 89, 128
Redistributive policies (Cuban), 7–8, 49–50, 53, 58. See also Distributive justice
Revolution of 1933, 14, 15
Revolutionary Directorate, 18
Revolutionary internationalism (Cuban), 62–73
and Africa, 66–67
Cuban/Soviet dispute over, 68, 70–73, 74
defined, 62
early Fidelista forays into, 62
and Latin America, 65, 67, 73–74, 85–90, 90–91, 170
as a response to U.S. hostility, 67
and the Second Declaration of Havana (1962), 65–66
and the Tricontinental, 72
Rich Kaplowitz, Donna, 127, 216
Robaina, Roberto, replaced as foreign minister, 211
Robinson, William, 174
Ronfelt, David, 33
Roosevelt Corollary (1904), 51
Rosenau, James, 38
Rourke, John, 110
Russia, opposition to Helms-Burton law, 199
Ryan, George, 218–19

St. Lucia, 84
St. Vincent and the Grenadines, 124, 128
Sánchez Parody, Ramón, 128

Sandinistas (Sandinista Front for National Liberation–FSLN), 91
Cuban security aid to, 88–90, 170
Santa Clara, 18
Schultz, George, 214
Seaga, Edward, 90
Second Declaration of Havana (1962), 65–66. See also Revolutionary internationalism
SELA (Latin American Economic System), 84, 85, 160
Serbín, Andrés, 164
Seven Years' War (1756–63), 11
Sherritt Incorporated, 135–36, 185
Sierra Maestra, 3, 18
Smith, Earl, 56
Smith, Wayne, 169, 173–74
Social Darwinism, 23
Somalia, 96, 97
South Africa, 94, 95, 116, 139
Soviet economic aid to Cuba, 108–9
1960 aid package, 57
via subsidized sugar prices, 108
Soviet foreign policy
Angolan conflict, involvement in, 95
Ethiopian conflict, involvement in, 96–97
and the Fidelistas' socialist credentials, doubts about, 57, 68
Soviet military/security aid to Cuba, 60, 77–78
Spain
and Cuba, relations with, 137
Cuban human rights record, reaction to, 210
Spanish-American War (1898), 12, 20
Sphere of influence politics, 24
Starr, Kenneth, 194
START (Strategic Arms Reduction Treaty), 180
Stevenson, Adlai, 64
Student Directorate (Havana University), 14
Sugar Act (1960), 59
Sugar industry (Cuba), 108, 114, 208
10 million ton harvest (1970), 4, 50
Sundelius, Bengt, 44

Suriname, 84, 90–91
SWAPO (Southwest African People's Organization–Namibia), 96
Szulc, Tad, 61

Ten Years' War (1868–78), 12
Torricelli, Robert, 179, 201
Torricelli law (1992), 50, 123–24, 127, 135, 145, 216
  European opposition to, 198
  and extraterritoriality, 198
  provisions of, 124
  See also U.S. trade embargo against Cuba
Tourism industry (Cuba), 117–118, 129, 135, 138
Tricontinental (Organization for the Solidarity of the Peoples of Asia, Africa, and Latin America), 72
Trinidad and Tobago, 84, 165, 166
Trudeau, Pierre, 134
Truman, Harry, 32
Tshombe, Moise, 93
TV Martí, 175
26th of July Movement, 17, 74
Tyndell, Andrew, 189–90

Unemployment rates (Cuba), 6–7
UNITA (National Union for the Total Independence of Angola), 94, 95, 96
United Nations
  Afghan crisis, vote on, 103–4
  Cuban human rights record, votes on, 196–97, 210–11
  Security Council, Cuba's seat on, 104, 116
  U.S. economic blockade of Cuba, votes on, 197
U.S. foreign policy
  Angolan conflict, involvement in, 96
  and the Batista government, relations with, 55–56
  and bipolarity, 52
  and Central America, 86
  Cold War worldview of, 52, 167
  and containment, 52
  and Cuba, abusing Cuban human rights, 195–96

  and Cuba, hegemonic aspirations toward, 51, 195–96, 220
  and Cuba, international opposition to, 196–200
  and Cuba, pre-Castro interventions in, 13, 40
  and Cuba, public opinion polls, 188–89
  and Cuba, success potential of, 196, 224–25
  and the Cuban Revolution, ideological hostility toward, 53–54
  and the Cuban sugar quota, 58–59
  invasion of Grenada, 90, 128
  and macrolinkage, 52
  and Pope John Paul II's visit to Cuba, 188
  and Sandinista Nicaragua, 89–90
  See also Normalization of U.S./Cuban relations; U.S. trade embargo against Cuba
U.S. trade embargo (blockade) against Cuba, 168–69, 173
  Ashcroft-Hagel amendment to modify, 218, 220
  attempts to get other countries to participate in, 65, 123–24
  and the Cuban Revolution, goal of destabilizing and destroying, 65, 107, 114–15, 123–24, 145, 182, 224
  first announced (1962), 64–65
  international opposition to, 197–200
  Pope John Paul II criticizes, 188
  UN votes on, 197
  See also Clinton administration; Helms-Burton law; Torricelli law
Uruguay, 91
USSR
  and the Cuban Surrogate Thesis, 34–35
  Soviet system, demise of, 110–13
  and the superclient concept, 34
  See also Soviet entries

Valdés, Nelson, 26
Vasconcelos, Luiz, 133
Venezuela, 84, 122
  and Cuba, economic cooperation projects, 212–13

270 | Index

Venezuela—*continued*
  and Cuba, oil agreements with, 212
  triangular oil trade with USSR and
    Cuba, 131–32
Vietnam, 147, 167. *See also* North Vietnam
Vogel, Hans, 143

Warsaw Pact, 80
  Cuba never a member of, 102
  dissolved (1991), 110

Watson, Alexander, 181
Welles, Sumner, 14
West Indian Commission, 163–64
Wilhelm, Gen. Charles, 190–91
WTO (World Trade Organization), 186,
  191, 192, 199

Yeltsin, Boris, 105, 111

Zimbalist, Andrew, 114, 123

H. Michael Erisman is a professor of political science at Indiana State University. His main fields of interest are U.S. policies toward Latin America, transnationalism/political economy in the Caribbean Basin, and Cuban foreign affairs. He has been elected to the executive committee of the Section for Scholarly Relations with Cuba (which operates under the aegis of the Latin American Studies Association) and is a member of the editorial board of the *Journal of Interamerican Studies and World Affairs*.

He has written *Cuba's International Relations* (1985) and *Pursuing Post-dependency Politics* (1992), has edited *The Caribbean Challenge* (1984), and has coedited, with John Martz, *Colossus Challenged* (1982) and, with John Kirk, *Cuban Foreign Policy Confronts a New International Order* (1991).